QUALITY ASSURANCE AND ACCREDITATION IN DISTANCE EDUCATION AND E-LEARNING

D0162435

Quality assurance (QA) in open and distance learning (ODL) can be a contentious issue. Some argue that it should be judged by the same criteria and methods as face-to-face education, while others claim that it is so different in its organization, enrolments and operations that conventional QA mechanisms cannot apply. Some advocate the use of specific guidelines and standards for e-learning; others believe that, regardless of the technology, the basic principles of quality teaching and learning should apply. Providers who have enjoyed freedom from external scrutiny may resist attempts at external regulation and auditing and look upon QA as yet another imposition of corporatization and bureaucracy on education. Others see it as a means of establishing a culture of quality, self-reflection and self-improvement.

There is little research-based literature to guide policymakers, managers and practitioners in applying QA in education and training to ensure the right balance is found between accountability and autonomy, as well as assuring quality for the time and costs involved. In this respect, *Quality Assurance and Accreditation in Distance Education and e-Learning* is a book that is long overdue. It explains what is involved in QA and accreditation in education. It describes and analyzes applications of these practices in open, distance, dual-mode and conventional universities throughout Europe, North America, Africa and the Asia-Pacific, looking at open schooling, e-learning in conventional schools, non-formal adult and community education, and corporate and small-to-medium enterprises.

Quality Assurance and Accreditation in Distance Education and e-Learning is edited and authored by experts with extensive international experience in ODL, e-learning and QA who give careful consideration to the possibilities and challenges involved. The book will be an invaluable guide for all policymakers, managers, practitioners and researchers in the field.

Insung Jung is Professor of Education, Media and Society at the International Christian University in Tokyo.

Colin Latchem is an Australian researcher, writer and consultant in open and distance learning.

Open & Flexible Learning Series

Series Editors: Fred Lockwood, A.W. (Tony) Bates and Som Naidu

QUALITY ASSURANCE AND ACCREDITATION IN DISTANCE EDUCATION AND E-LEARNING

Models, Policies and Research

Edited by Insung Jung and Colin Latchem

Foreword by Sir John Daniel

Routledge
Taylor & Francis Group

NEW YORK AND LONDON

First published 2012
by Routledge
711 Third Avenue, New York, NY 10017

Simultaneously published in the United Kingdom
by Routledge
2 Park Square, Milton Park, Abingdon, Oxon, OX14 4RN

Routledge is an imprint of the Taylor & Francis Group, an informa business

© 2012 Taylor & Francis

Library of Congress Cataloging in Publication Data
Quality assurance and accreditation in distance education and e-learning: models,
policies and research / [edited by] Insung Jung and Colin Latchem.
Includes bibliographical references and index.
1. Distance education—Standards. 2. Accreditation (Education) 3. Quality assurance.
I. Jung, Insung, 1959– II. Latchem, C. R. (Colin R.) III. Herrington, Jan.
LC5803.A33Q35 2011
379.1'58—dc22
2011012492

ISBN13: 978-0-415-88734-2 (hbk)
ISBN13: 978-0-415-88735-9 (pbk)
ISBN13: 978-0-203-83449-7 (ebk)

Typeset in Bembo
by Book Now Ltd, London

Printed and bound in the United States of America on acid-free paper
by IBT Global

CONTENTS

TABLES AND FIGURES

Tables

Figures

FOREWORD

For most people involved in higher education, either as students or staff, quality assurance (QA) and accreditation are not the most engaging subjects. Yet, by examining these topics as they apply to open and distance education through a broad but penetrating lens, the editors and contributors to this volume have given us invaluable insights into the contemporary challenges facing higher education generally.

QA processes oblige academics to reflect on their core purposes and how well they are achieving them, while the development of open, distance and e-learning poses crucial strategic challenges to institutional leaders. This fascinating collection not only reveals the wide diversity of approaches to QA and accreditation but also indicates that these different streams are gradually coalescing into a shared philosophy. It also shows that because distance learning is expanding in an unstoppable manner in almost all institutions it has become, unjustly, a symbol for the commercialization of higher education that is a parallel phenomenon not caused by e-learning.

Distance education has always had an image problem. Active QA is a necessary, if not a sufficient condition for improving its reputation, and those institutions that have engaged most intensely with QA processes, such as Open University Malaysia and the UK Open University, have derived clear benefit from doing so. An inspiring chapter on Indonesia's Universitas Terbuka shows how a decade-long institution-wide campaign to embed QA has transformed the reputation of an institution that, in its early days, was seen merely as a leaky safety valve to relieve the pressure on 'real' universities.

My own most intense period of involvement with QA and assessment began when I joined the UK Open University as vice chancellor in 1990. The government was beginning a process of reform that would end the UKOU's separate status and integrate it into a wider system with the old universities and newly promoted polytechnics. Nevertheless, because the UKOU was unique in scale and methods, policymakers had to decide whether to place it within the same funding and QA frameworks as the rest of the system or make special arrangements. We campaigned hard and successfully for the same treatment. I believe that having to cope with the special features of the UKOU pushed the UK Quality Assurance Agency for Higher Education to focus more quickly on outputs and quality enhancement and helped it emerge as a reference point for the world as Chapter 7 shows.

I continue to believe that QA for distance education should be seen as a subset of QA for education generally, but reading this book has convinced me of the case for paying special attention to modern developments such as e-learning, as Chapter 8 argues. This is because e-learning has become, as the riveting account of developments in Australia and New Zealand in Chapter 9 reveals, the primary target for those opposed to the 'enterprise university' they see emerging. As Chapter 4 recalls, these traditionalists can legitimately point to failures like Universitas 21 and Fathom as proof that institutional heads are too easily seduced by the siren song of extra money. To counter the accusation that they represent a Trojan horse that could destroy the academy, it is helpful for providers offering solid e-learning programmes to be able to point to external validation of their educational worth in the online mode.

Against this background, Chapter 6 highlights the double whammy faced by loose federal states like Canada and the United States, where the absence of central QA authorities allows suspicions to hang over the integrity of many institutions. This is leading the provinces and states to attempt to regulate e-learning in their own jurisdictions, creating a nightmare of complex requirements for providers who would like the boundaries of their campuses to be the boundaries of the Internet.

The reviews of developments in Asia and Africa in Chapters 4 and 5 are fundamentally encouraging. While it is true that QA in these regions is only moving slowly towards emphases on outputs and enhancement that are the preferred destinations of most of the contributors, the good news is that more and more countries are paying attention to QA. For the last 3 years, I have served on the steering committee of the UNESCO/World Bank Global Initiative for Quality Assurance Capacity and have seen huge strides made in that time. Furthermore, many institutions in these continents are working hard to instil a culture of quality, as shown in the nice example of the open schools in Botswana and Namibia that help each other by providing neighbourly external verification.

These are two relatively small institutions – very large ones, like many of the open universities, face special challenges. Chapter 10 addresses those issues and resonated well with my experience. Its plea for greater consistency among countries, not least in rules governing the amount of face-to-face contact required in distance education, echoed the conclusions of UNESCO's 2009 World Conference on Higher Education where, perhaps surprisingly, the Indian Minister of Human Resource Development led the argument for the internationalization of QA.

The book also explores QA in more complex arrangements than unitary universities. Open Universities Australia brings public universities together into a consortium that is registered as a private company. Chapter 12 suggests that such an arrangement, which puts the reputation of several universities on the line together, puts those running the consortium on their mettle and yields QA arrangements that may well be more rigorous that those in the member institutions.

The experience of the two multi-country network universities, the University of the South Pacific (USP) and the University of the West Indies (UWI), highlights two issues. First, there is the issue of leadership. It is a truism that the development of a quality culture in any institution is greatly facilitated by the commitment of senior management. The same applies to the successful offering of distance learning programmes. I am frequently amazed when I meet university heads who take little interest in their distance learners, even when they constitute the large majority of their student body. Where institutional leadership is weak, distance learning will have difficulty sustaining its quality. The second issue is whether to place distance learning programmes in a distinct unit, as at UWI, or to decentralise them to academic units as USP currently does. My own bias is in favour of a distinct unit.

The editors have extended their remit beyond higher education. The expansion of open and distance education at the secondary level, through the development of open schooling, will be a vital task in the coming decade given that hundreds of millions of children between the ages of 12 and 17 years are not receiving secondary education. Chapter 16 reports how two large open schools are developing QA processes. It is complemented by the subsequent chapter on school digital ecosystems. Both contributions remind us that QA in such complex multi-stakeholder arrangements must take a holistic approach.

This principle applies even more strongly to the operation of multi-purpose telecentres that are vehicles for promoting informal learning in thousands of communities across the world. Chapter 18 describes this phenomenon and the author notes, wryly, that while many telecentre projects report diligently on lessons learned, those lessons are rarely reflected in subsequent initiatives.

At the other end of the spectrum from informal telecentres is the formal use of e-learning in industry. This is explored in the cases of small-to-medium enterprises in Europe and of larger corporations in Korea in Chapters 19 and 20. Despite the differences of context, the authors reach similar conclusions. Perhaps because the skills and knowledge that these programmes are meant to impart are clearly laid down, QA tends to be too mechanistic and misses some of the important wishes of the trainees, such as certification and human contact alongside their learning.

In three final and important chapters, the editors weave together the threads of the various contributions and emphasise some key issues. They first provide a comprehensive and useful list of the competencies that must be developed across institutions if all are to contribute to the assurance of quality. Next the role of students in QA is examined. Not surprisingly, students' preoccupations vary from one region to another. The stereotype that Asian students feel reassured by face-to-face teaching seems to have some validity, whereas elsewhere students put greater value on flexible study opportunities. However, all students are more interested in the outcomes of their programmes, through the certification and recognition of their achievements, than in the mechanics of programme delivery.

The final chapter recalls how the trend in QA is to give greater attention to performance and outcomes, expressed through the deepening of a quality culture that stresses accountability. After reporting on the OECD's attempt to compare learning outcomes through the AHELO project, the writers recall that straitened financial times require educational programmes to operate economically while retaining full legitimacy.

This book could not come at a better time. We face the paradox that while open and distance education is growing rapidly in popularity with students and institutions, thanks in part to online technologies, hostility to it is also growing. Solid QA systems are an important weapon in parrying that hostility. I congratulate the contributors and editors for providing us with excellent insights about how to assure quality in diverse circumstances.

Sir John Daniel
President
Commonwealth of Learning

PREFACE

Insung Jung and Colin Latchem

Open and distance learning (ODL) is being embraced by developed and developing countries alike. The open and flexible admission procedures, innovatory and cost-efficient methods, economies of scale and uses of technology are enabling countless millions of school-age children, school leavers and mature-aged learners to access formal and non-formal education to an extent unparalleled in human history. The applications of instructional design and new technology are helping to bring about consistency in the standards of content, teaching and learning and enabling knowledge and expertise to be captured, used and shared by many providers and learners. The flexible delivery methods allow learners to study at the time and pace that suit them best, learning times to be reduced or expanded to suit quick and slow learners and remedial, refresher and reference materials and support to be available as needed. And the learner-centred pedagogy, applications of technology and episodic opportunities for networked lifelong learning pioneered by distance educators are also helping to transform conventional education.

However, not everyone looks upon ODL in such a positive light. As Daniel (2010) observes, there has always been hostility to the methods of distance education. Education is a conservative area of human activity and many people do not regard education as legitimate unless a live teacher faces a live class. At the time of writing, The International Council for Open and Distance Education had commissioned a study on regulatory frameworks in open and distance education.[1] Drawing on their initial findings, Daniel cites some instances of the rising tide of restrictive legislation and practices by governments which are hindering applications of distance education. The Ethiopian Ministry of Education had recently announced that all distance education provided by private and public institutions would cease, claiming that it was no longer necessary. This was despite the fact that the Prime Minister and most of his cabinet are graduates of The Open University's MBA. In India, growing concerns over the quality of distance education had led the Minister for Human Resource Development to propose that no new university should be permitted to offer off-campus programmes for 5 years. The Chinese government was only permitting the Open University of China (http://en.crtvu.edu.cn/) to offer 2- or 3-year junior college degree programmes rather than the 4-year bachelor degree programmes offered by the conventional universities, condemning many hundreds of thousands of students to low status qualifications, regardless of their abilities and potential. Other governments were legislating for the percentage of degree courses that must be provided face-to-face; Brazil was stipulating 80%, Malaysia, 20%. And some governments and professional associations were insisting that degrees and diplomas should state the modality in which they were taken and refusing employment to graduates of distance education programmes.

In the United States, the federal regulators and media organizations including Marketplace (2009), National Public Radio (2010) and American Broadcasting Company (2010) are looking closely at the for-profit colleges and universities that cater to non-traditional students, often confer degrees over the Internet and successfully capture billions of federal financial aid dollars. PBS (2010) reveals that more than 80% of the for-profits' revenue comes from these (most commonly under the Title IV Financial Aid Program). These providers enrol 10% of all post-secondary students, but receive almost a quarter of federal financial aid. They claim to be enabling an underserved student population to obtain a quality education and marketable job skills. But some spend more on marketing than on teaching and learning and develop new courses in a weekend. They boost their profits by maximizing online student enrolments and staff–studio ratios, their students' dropout and default rates are much higher than those of the public and non-profit institutions, and some offer worthless degrees that leave students with mountainous debts (PBS).

There are also growing concerns about the quality of e-learning in the US public institutions. The Chronicle of Higher Education (2010) reports that 48% of US faculty who have taught online courses conclude that they are inferior to face-to-face instruction, and only 15% rate online learning as superior to face-to-face instruction. Shrock (2010) reports that 'We do not accept online coursework' statements are appearing on more and more websites of such prestigious institutions as the University of California, University of Southern California, University of Colorado and University of Wisconsin. Schools of pharmacy, medicine, nursing and the visual and performing arts have been the first to exclude transfer credit for online laboratory courses. However, many universities fail to reveal to their students that their online courses will not be accepted for those applying to transfer to other universities or to further their studies. Shrock (2009) also reports that not only is the value of the online degree being questioned by more and more employers, some universities are also rejecting job applications from academics with online degrees – even degrees they themselves offer.

Such distrust of, and antagonism towards, e-learning derives from the fact that all too often, it is adopted for commercial reasons or because it appears to offer a cheaper solution. Some critics of e-learning claim that it is no more than digital page turning, denying the all-important teacher–student relationship and trivializing learning. Bagaric (2011, p. 14) writes:

> But what about positive educational outcomes? On balance, there are probably none. The research shows us the internet is probably making us dumber. It allows us to access millions of facts but does nothing to improve our problem-solving and cognitive capabilities. While screen-based learning can enhance visual–spatial intelligence, it weakens our higher-level intellectual functions.

Such observations are reminiscent of Socrates' denigration of the then relatively new technology of writing in Plato's *Phaedrus*. Steeped in his belief in inquiry and debate as a means of stimulating critical thinking and illuminating ideas, Socrates characterized writing as disrupting traditional social relationships, providing the appearance rather than the reality of wisdom, and leading those who used it to imagine they understood a great deal when in fact they knew nothing of value.

Supporters of the new methods and technologies will claim that such criticisms are unfounded and that all forms of teaching and learning can be subject to poor practice. They can point to the fact that in many countries, concerns are being expressed over the quality of education in general, that there are perceptions that curricula are being dumbed down and the standards of teaching, learning and awards are falling. There are also calls for better regulation of online offshore education and entry standards for transnational providers. As the Australian University Quality Agency observes, once an institution has been accredited, it can be extremely difficult for regulators to withdraw this at a later date, and the closure of an institution can impact adversely on the staff and students and the sector as a whole through media exposure (Lane, 2010).

Given all of these concerns, learners, teachers, decision-makers and the public at large must be confident that quality is assured in these newer forms of teaching and learning. As Daniel (2010) urges, it is important to establish sound QA and regulatory systems to counter hostility towards the values and methods of ODL and remove any bad apples from the barrel. However, not all governments or institutions have yet established systems to assure quality in ODL, not all ODL providers meet or even aspire to meet the highest standards, not all providers are *bona fide* and not all countries, cultures or institutions are ready to embrace the openness, transparency and accountability called for in QA.

There is also disagreement on how QA should be managed. Some support the idea of consumer protection for the learners. Others complain that QA audit cycles involve too much bureaucracy, incur too high costs and constrain academic freedom. Some hold that the same measures should apply to the on-campus and ODL modes of learning. Others believe that the differences in enrolment, intakes, organization, logistics and scale and nature of operations in ODL call for different criteria. There are differences of opinion over assessing the learning outcomes. Some say the focus should be the knowledge and skills graduates need to do their jobs, and others say that it should be on the generic attributes that will enable the learners to operate in tomorrow's ever-changing and challenging world. Some critics of ODL seize on the fact that the sheer scale of some systems leads to the use of multiple-choice assessment, which may show that students can recognize and recall facts or procedures but not demonstrate the ability to apply or question what has been learned.

There is relatively little in the literature about QA and accreditation in distance and online schooling, college or university education, non-formal adult and community education or workplace training. Drawing on international theory, research and the experience and expertise of the contributors, this book shows why and how these are applied across the globe, considers the lessons learned, and suggests frameworks and guidelines for their implementation. Chapters 1 and 2 examine policies and procedures for QA and accreditation in conventional, face-to-face education and distance education. Chapters 3 to 9 describe international, regional and national QA and accreditation organizations and frameworks around the globe. Chapters 10 to 20 provide case studies of QA and accreditation in various ODL settings. Chapters 21 to 23 address emerging issues in QA and accreditation and contain recommendations for future policy-making, practice and research.

Note

1 http://www.icde.org/?module=Articles;action=Article.publicShow;ID=1765

References

American Broadcasting Company. (2010, August 19). *For-profit colleges under investigation (Broadcast)*. Retrieved from http://blogs.abcnews.com/nightlinedailyline/2010/08/for-profit-colleges-receive-f-in-ethics.html

Bagaric, M. (2011, January 31). Flood of bad decisions from Gillard. *The Australian* (p. 14). Retrieved from http://www.theaustralian.com.au/national-affairs/

Daniel, J. (2010, October). *Distance education under threat: an opportunity?* Keynote address at the IDOL & ICEM 2010 Joint Conference and Media Days in Eskisehir, Turkey. Retrieved from http://www.col.org/resources/speeches/2010presentation/Pages/2010-10-06.aspx

Lane, B. (2010). Raise bar for new colleges. *The Australian: Higher Education* (p. 23). Retrieved from http://www.theaustralian.com.au/higher-education/raise-bar-for-new-colleges-report/story-e6frgcjx-1225967197125

Marketplace. (2009, November 3). *Allegations against U of Phoenix persist (Broadcast)*. Los Angeles, CA: Marketplace Productions. Retrieved from http://marketplace.publicradio.org/display/web/2009/11/03/pm-phoenix-one

National Public Radio. (2010, March 13). *The allure of for-profit universities grows (Broadcast)*. Retrieved from http://www.npr.org/player/v2/mediaPlayer.html?action=1&t=1&islist=false&id=124655777&m=124655768

PBS. (2010). *College Inc. US: Public Broadcasting Service*. Video retrieved from http://www.pbs.org/wgbh/pages/frontline/collegeinc/view/. Transcript retrieved from http://www.pbs.org/wgbh/pages/frontline/collegeinc/etc/script.html

Shrock, J. R. (2009). US: No job if you only have an online degree. *University World News*, Issue: 0075. Retrieved from http://www.universityworldnews.com/article.php?story=20090508115810625

Shrock, J. R. (2010). US: marks from online courses being rejected. *University World News*, Issue: 142. Retrieved from http://www.universityworldnews.com/article.php?story=20101002100346835

The Chronicle of Higher Education. (2010, October 31). *Faculty views about online learning*. Retrieved from http://chronicle.com/article/Faculty-Views-About-Online/125200//

ACKNOWLEDGEMENTS

We thank Sir John Daniel for writing the Foreword, all of the authors for their hard work and insights from around the globe, Tan Sri Dato Emeritus Professor Gajaraj (Raj) Dhanarajan of Wawasan Open University, Penang, Malaysia, for his advice on QA in Asia, and Professor David Woodhouse of the Australian Universities Quality Agency for his advice regarding regional and international QA. We also acknowledge the encouragement and support of Alex Masulis, Editor at Routledge/Taylor & Francis and Marion Latchem for their help in bringing this book to fruition.

1

QUALITY ASSURANCE AND ACCREDITATION IN HIGHER EDUCATION

Denise Chalmers and Shannon Johnston

Introduction

Quality assurance (QA) has long been applied in the corporate sector to ensure stakeholder satisfaction, compare standards with those of other organizations and raise standards in the face of competition. Applying rigorous QA and accreditation to educational processes and outcomes, particularly in higher education, is a more recent phenomenon. This chapter examines these issues in regard to conventional university education.

Defining Quality

The meaning of 'quality' has long been contested in higher education. Harvey and Green's (1993) five discrete but interrelated ways of thinking about quality are frequently cited as capturing the meanings of quality in the context of education:

1. Excellence. Quality as something exceptional, distinctive and elitist.
2. Consistency. Quality as a perfect, consistent or flawless outcome.
3. Fitness for purpose. Quality as fulfilling pre-determined requirements, needs or desires.
4. Value for money. Quality as return on investment.
5. Transformation (e.g., the enhancement and empowerment of students or the development of new knowledge).

QA in higher education is most typically judged in terms of fitness for purpose or value for money (judged by governments and, with the introduction of fees, students). But it may involve some or all of these meanings. For example, in judging online learning resources for a particular group of students, if quality of learning is the defining criterion, these may be evaluated in terms of the purposes for which they are intended, their content and instructional design, the quality of the learning outcomes they aim to elicit and their capacity to challenge and transform the students' understanding. If consistency is the main criterion, they may be judged against the equivalent face-to-face offerings and, if value for money is the main criterion, they may be judged in terms of the costs and cost benefits and how these compare with the face-to-face alternatives.

These different emphases or definitions of quality can contribute to a misalignment of focus and purpose in quality reviews and processes. While governments may be primarily interested in efficiency, cost-effectiveness, community satisfaction and accountability, institutions may be more concerned with assuring or improving the quality of their courses, learning processes and outcomes, management and staffing, while students may be more concerned with the costs, convenience and career opportunities. These different 'stakeholders may also disagree on the criteria and standards by which institutions should be assessed. Institutions may claim that they operate to a high academic standard, while employers complain that their courses do not meet labour market needs, and the students believe that the teaching and support do not meet their needs. QA requires that all of these different viewpoints be reconciled. So agreement must be reached on the key performance indicators (PIs) in regard to:

- Student outcomes.
- Curriculum, courses and courseware.
- Teaching and learning.
- Student and staff support.
- Assessment, evaluation and internal QA systems.
- Management.
- Staff.
- Resourcing.
- Returns on investment and benefits to the national economy and society.

In reality, agreement is not always achieved and the determination of the PIs and measures to be used is often contentious. The more powerful stakeholder's perspective is usually the one that prevails. Gallagher (2010) provides a detailed review of QA in higher education, which highlights the ways in which the agendas of powerful stakeholders dominate.

Judging Quality

Performance Indicators and Performance Models

The rationale behind the use of PIs and performance models by governments and QA agencies is to ensure that the education equips students for employment and provides the nation with a highly skilled workforce that supports economic growth. PIs identify the achievement of what is deemed to be important. They are categorized into four types: input, output, process and outcome, each of which has different characteristics and objectives which are operationally related and may be judged qualitatively or quantitatively (Borden & Bottrill, 1994). Qualitative indicators are based on non-numerical assessments, typified by process and outcome indicators, while quantitative indicators are based on numerical assessments of performance, typified by input and output indicators. Each type of indicator yields valuable information regarding quality. At the same time, each type is subject to limitations and criticisms. No single indicator or single type of indicator can objectively capture all of the aspects of quality. Therefore, a range of indicators from each of the four types must be used in order to adequately assess the quality of the institutions and ensure that no one type of indicator is privileged over another.

There are five performance models: accreditation, quality audits, performance-based funding, performance reporting, and surveys and tests of learning (Fisher, Rubenson, Rockwell, Grosjean, & Atkinson-Grosjean, 2000). Each of these employs a variety of PIs, all of which require contextualization and interpretation and need to be situated in the assumptions inherent in their adoption (Chalmers, 2008).

Accreditation

Accreditation is a process of assessment and review by an accreditation or certification body which enables an institution, programme or course of study to be recognized or certified as meeting certain required standards. The endowment of accreditation is binary: an institution, a course or a programme either receives or does not receive accreditation. However, minimum standards usually apply and the pass/fail nature of accreditation is often softened by the provision of probationary periods and opportunities to reapply for accreditation. While accreditation methods and purposes are similar to audit and other forms of external review, they require applicants to prove their suitability by fulfilling the accreditation criteria, while auditing presumes the institution is functioning appropriately, and the external review is responsible for proving otherwise.

Accreditation is an increasingly popular form of performance model, particularly in European higher education. It is used in countries such as the United Kingdom and Sweden as a mechanism to upgrade providers such as colleges and polytechnics to university status. Government accreditation agencies also become more prevalent in countries with a burgeoning private higher education sector, for example in Eastern Europe and some Asian countries. In the United States, accreditation agencies are self-regulated and independent of the Federal and State Governments. The various agencies have established their own QA regulations and performance funding requirements but these are found to be generally ineffective in strengthening institutional processes for academic quality (Dill, 2003). Charged with recommending a national strategy for reforming post-secondary education, the Report of the Commission appointed by Secretary of Education Margaret Spellings – the Spellings Commission (US Department of Education, 2006) – signalled the US Federal Government's intention to use institutional accreditation as an aggressive QA tool, but this has been strongly resisted, despite persistent attempts from the current administration (Gallagher, 2010) (see also Chapter 6).

Quality Audits

Quality audits are typically conducted by QA agencies established by government ministries or departments. Some countries have several QA agencies which themselves are reviewed and accredited against national protocols. The audits require institutions to conduct self-reviews which are verified by external review teams which then make recommendations for improvement and monitor progress. Audits can be administered at institutional or subject/programme level and typically involve drilling down through the different levels of operation to check consistency, due diligence and quality in all policymaking, management and practice. Audits tend to use predominantly qualitative process PIs that are developed and collected at the institutional level, although some countries have standardized national PIs against which institutions are audited.

Audits can lead to positive outcomes, but critics of this approach suggest that the focus on 'fitness-for-purpose', which is defined by the institutions themselves, is not rigorous and can allow the setting of low expectations. Consequently, there has been a trend for audits to review both for 'fitness-for-purpose' and 'fitness-of-purpose'. Over 70 countries currently have QA agencies, but audits may not be compulsory for all of the higher education institutions in all of these countries.

Until recently, the Australian Universities Quality Agency monitored, audited and reported on QA in Australian higher education. The Australian Federal Government has now established a new body, the Tertiary Education Quality and Standards Agency, a super authority with responsibility for accreditation, auditing and establishing and monitoring standards for all tertiary education institutions, including universities and private providers of tertiary education. While the purposes of accreditation and auditing remain distinct, bringing these functions together under a single, responsible entity is an uncommon response that will be watched closely by other nations.

Performance Funding and Performance Budgeting

Performance funding typically involves national or state governments rewarding performance, using indicators that reflect national or state priorities. For example, the UK government has adopted this approach to provide incentives for universities to increase their enrolment of students from low socio-economic backgrounds. Australia has also recently established performance funding on the basis of mission-based compacts, 3-year agreements that show how each university's mission contributes to the Government's goals for higher education and include details of major higher education and research funding and performance targets. Universities are allocated performance funding on the basis of meeting university targets agreed as part of these compacts and set against a framework of PIs related to the quality of teaching and learning, the student experience, participation and attainment. Performance funding can be the most contentious of the performance models as it employs a limited set of indicators that do not necessarily account for the variety in institutional missions, contexts or resources and tends to favour the well-established, better-resourced institutions.

Performance budgeting also ties funding to institutional performance, requires the key PIs to be defined at the outset and is concerned with final outcomes and the strategies and activities employed in achieving these outcomes. Generally speaking, this involves a larger set of indicators but each indicator is only one factor in determining the total allocation of funds. This approach is usually used for budget preparation rather than as a reward for performance.

Governments, educational authorities and institutions often prefer performance budgeting over performance funding because the looser association allows for more discretion and flexibility in determining funding allocation and this approach can take account of individual institutional circumstances. However, the boundaries between performance budgeting and performance funding can be blurred and initiatives often borrow elements from both approaches.

The advantages of performance budgeting over performance funding are that the larger set of indicators allows a broader scope of performance to be evaluated. It is thus more valid and reliable as a result of having multiple measures, allows greater consideration of an institution's circumstances and is more flexible. The disadvantage is that there is less direct incentive for institutions to perform well on particular indicators. In both cases, choice and weighting of input and output indicators will depend upon political agendas and the priorities of the funding agencies.

Performance Reporting

Performance reporting refers to the reporting of institutional performance to national and/or state authorities. Performance is reported on a selected set of indicators pertinent to national and/or state goals. The reports provide valuable information for policymakers and other stakeholders and they reflect the customer-centred, market-driven focus of today's education systems. They may range from such issues as the participation of equity groups and graduation rates of students to the appropriateness, extent and quality of the programmes and courses on offer. No financial incentives are involved, so this method is less costly and less controversial than performance funding. It has been found to be a powerful model and highly effective in improving performance because the institutions are required to submit performance reports which are then published in some form for the stakeholders and general public and this provides an incentive for institutions to perform well. This is the most ubiquitous performance model.

Performance reporting is also employed by international agencies such as UNESCO, OECD and the World Bank. For example, UNESCO provides benchmarks, guidelines and indicators for member states to gauge their success in achieving higher education priority actions both nationally and regionally. UNESCO and OECD also develop and publish indicators and analyses of the operation, evolution and impact of education from early childhood through formal education to lifelong learning. OECD produces annual reports such as *Education at a Glance*[1] and *Education Policy Analysis.*[2]

Surveys and Tests of Learning

Surveys that gather information on the experiences and perceptions of students, teachers and employers are used as proxy measures of quality in teaching and learning. Different surveys are designed to assess different goals: students' perceptions of the quality of the teaching; students' engagement with their institutions; students' perceptions of the courses or awards; graduates' perceptions of their courses, degrees and career prospects; staff satisfaction with the institution or perceptions of their own or peers' teaching; employers' perception of graduates, degree programmes and their relevance to industry, and so on. The results of these surveys are often used in other performance models, such as performance funding, performance reporting, audits and accreditation.

A major strength of using surveys is that they allow the various stakeholders to contribute to the QA process. The use of student evaluations to assess the quality of teaching and learning is particularly valued by governments, student bodies and parents. Nevertheless, a number of concerns remain over the widespread use of national level student surveys which were intended to be used by teachers and institutions for diagnostic and enhancement purposes, but which are more frequently used for primarily QA purposes (Anderson, 2006).

National- or sector-wide student perception or student experience surveys are now part of the QA models used in Australia, North America and the United Kingdom. There is also growing interest in surveying employers and staff on their perceptions of students and the institutions in which they study. However, this can be difficult as employers may appoint students from a number of different institutions over a period of time and find it difficult to identify what is attributable to the courses they studied, the students' individual qualities and their workplace experience.

Identifying standard ways of measuring the quality of student learning and, by extension, the value added by the school, college or university, has been a goal of governments, researchers and testing houses for a considerable time. Tests of learning are controversial and generally viewed with suspicion by schools and universities alike for failing to take into account the range and depth of learning that is actually occurring, as well as the contexts, student population, institutional goals and course focuses. Despite strong empirical research over 40 years that questions the feasibility, methodology and assumptions of national and international standardized tests of learning (see, for example, Banta & Pike, 2007; Koretz, 2008), they continue to be pursued by governments and testing houses as measures of quality.

Australia and the United Kingdom are two of the few countries that utilize all five types of performance models outlined above as part of their quality management frameworks. Most countries utilize some of the models and all countries utilize the performance reporting model. For a detailed review of the ways in which several countries have applied the models, see Chalmers, Lee, and Walker (2008).

Cross-border Accreditation and QA

Many countries, particularly in the developed world, are competing to attract foreign students or establishing a presence in another country through partnerships with other providers, off-shore campuses and/or distance and online learning. Whether real or virtual, staff and student mobility and the articulation and sharing of courses and programmes can help to improve the quality of higher education. The most advanced example of this is the Bologna Process[3] which aims to create a European Higher Education Area based on international cooperation and academic exchange that is attractive to European students and staff as well as to students and staff from other parts of the world (see also Chapter 8).

Capacity-building through cross-border higher education can bridge the gap between supply and demand in developed and developing countries and help the latter to develop domestic capacity to provide quality higher education. However, as shown elsewhere in this book, both conventional and distance cross-border higher education initiatives may also be undertaken for less altruistic purposes and in some cases, quality may be compromised by the pursuit of profit or larger market share. To address this issue, UNESCO and OECD have jointly developed the *Guidelines for Quality Provision in Cross-border Higher Education* (2005).[4] While these guidelines are voluntary and non-binding, access to funding for educational development from bodies such as the World Bank is generally contingent upon their adoption and implementation. These guidelines are valued as a means by which standards measured by QA agents can be developed to a similar maturity, quality and depth, and issues in low-quality provision of cross-border higher education can be identified and addressed (Stella, 2006). However, there is concern that they do not acknowledge the associated cost and responsibility, the tension between the perspectives of the international bodies on 'good' and 'proper' educational practices, and the sociocultural and political realities of the recipients of the cross-border education (Blackmur, 2007).

The means of evaluating and accrediting overseas providers are also being addressed by national governments, regional associations and international bodies such as the International Network for Quality Assurance Agencies in Higher Education (Rawazik, Carroll, Fox, & Harvey, 2009; Woodhouse, 2010). Despite these laudable initiatives, the evaluation and quality control of overseas higher education providers is still very much at the formative stage.

University Rankings

In recent years, university ranking systems have gained renewed interest among institutions, the public, governments and other stakeholders keen for easily interpretable information on institutional standing. Shrinking resource allocations, competition among universities, higher tuition fees and intensified calls for educational quality and efficiency are among the current claims in support of university rankings. It is also often argued that these rankings – sometimes known as 'league tables' and 'score cards' – are important for ensuring more transparency and accountability and for helping universities with their benchmarking and strategic planning.

National rankings include those provided in the *US News and World Report*,[5] *Australian Good Universities Guide*[6] and *German CHE University Ranking*.[7] World university rankings are published by the *Times Higher Education*[8] and the Shanghai Jiao Tong University.[9]

Such high-profile rankings invariably attract controversy and debate about methodology, objectivity, impact and validity. For example, the ranking tables are strongly biased towards research performance and reputation rather than the teaching and learning experience. There is evidence that rankings do not encourage improvement in teaching quality and may actually discourage improvement (Dill & Soo, 2005; Vaughn, 2002). In response to these criticisms, the most recent *Times Higher Education (THE) World University Rankings* (2010–2011) have included indicators and weighting on teaching quality, teaching qualifications, staff–student ratios, international staff and international student numbers as well as the traditional research indicators.

Serious concerns also exist over the use of single, numerical and comparative indicators in these league tables. These may appear to offer easy-to-refer-to information about educational quality, but it is questionable whether quality can be expressed in such simplistic terms or whether the various stakeholders can make sense of the rankings without understanding how the particular scores have been arrived at or what they actually signify. For example, the rankings do not necessarily represent meaningful differences between the various institutions. This may mislead prospective students when they would be much better advised to ask whether a particular institution would suit their particular learning and career aspirations.

Another criticism of rankings is that they discourage diversity because, in order to improve their position in the tables, universities may be more selective in terms of whom they enrol or even restrict student intake from particular backgrounds (Clarke, 2007; Tight, 2000). This is disadvantageous in terms of structural diversity, which has been empirically shown to improve quality learning (Terenzini, Cabrera, Colbeck, Bjorklund, & Parente, 2001; Umbach & Kuh, 2006). Even more concerning in terms of equity and open access to higher education is that low-income and minority students could be disadvantaged amidst the competition for high-achieving students (Clarke, 2007).

It is also observable that the countries rating highly in the league tables are those that are investing heavily in higher education – currently the United States, Canada, China and South Korea. Since rankings and associated funding usually reward the 'elite' institutions, it is much harder for lower-ranking institutions to enhance their teaching and learning circumstances (Stella & Woodhouse, 2006). Despite these well-founded concerns about rankings and their impact, we are likely to have more, not less, specialized and fine-grained ranking tables (Marginson, 2010).

As rankings seem likely to stay, there is need to rethink the methodologies currently in use. The International Rankings Expert Group,[10] a joint initiative of the UNESCO European Centre for Higher Education and a group of international ranking experts concerned with the quality of academic ranking, has developed the *Berlin Principles on Ranking of Higher Education Institutions*,[11] which acknowledge diversity among institutions, cultures and educational systems. They place strong emphasis on methodology and weighting and the design of appropriate indicators, and take into account the consumers' needs as well as facilitating their understanding of ranking results.

In an attempt to enact these principles, a feasibility study to develop a multi-dimensional global university ranking (U-Multirank)[12] system and process is currently under-way with the support of the European Commission. The interim report (CHERPA-Network, 2010) provides an overview of the issues and challenges facing the development of ranking tools that account for factors such as institutional mission, student body and disciplines offered. This work builds on a number of European initiatives including the U-Map project,[13] which has defined a core set of indicators under six dimensions: teaching and learning profile, student profile, research involvement, regional engagement, involvement in knowledge exchange, and international orientation. Similarly, the European Observatory for Assessment of University-based Research[14] is developing indicators and databases of research quality. These and other initiatives create rich databases which may lead to more informative ranking systems for others to follow. An additional QA mechanism will be provided when the International Rankings Expert Group begins auditing the rankings tables for their application and adherence to the Berlin Principles.

Conclusion

Ironically, governments in many countries are exerting increasing pressure on universities to be more accountable for the results they achieve with the resources available to them, intruding into areas which have long been regarded as the prerogatives of the universities themselves and driving increased student participation in QA while at the same time cutting back on government funding. Universities have long demonstrated a commitment to quality and monitoring their own performance. So there can be tensions if governments and agencies attempt to prescribe standards, require compliance and apply sanctions such as loss of registration or eligibility for funding (Gallagher, 2010). It has been repeatedly demonstrated that external QA processes are most effective when they encourage and support institutions in devising and monitoring compliance with their own self-regulatory standards and in creating a culture of quality rather than imposing heavily regulated compliance and control (Chalmers et al., 2008).

Questions about what constitutes quality, for which stakeholders quality needs to be assured, and the most appropriate models and indicators for examining the multiple dimensions of quality for a variety of stakeholders also need to be addressed. What is uncontested in the QA agenda is that students and society should be confident that the students' learning experiences and outcomes should be of the highest standard, regardless of location or mode of provision.

Notes

1 http://www.oecd.org/edu/eag2010
2 http://www.oecd.org/document/34/0,3343,en_2649_39263231_34989090_1_1_1_1,00.html
3 http://www.coe.int/t/dg4/highereducation/ehea2010/bolognapedestrians_en.asp
4 http://www.oecd.org/dataoecd/27/51/35779480.pdf
5 http://www.usnews.com/sections/rankings
6 http://www.gooduniguide.com.au
7 http://www.daad.de/deutschland/hochschulen/hochschulranking/06543.en.html?module=Show&tmpl=ha2
8 http://www.timeshighereducation.co.uk/
9 http://www.topuniversities.com/university/559/shanghai-jiao-tong-university

10 http://www.ireg-observatory.org/index.php?option=com_content&task=view&id=3&
    Itemid=3
11 http://www.che.de/downloads/Berlin_Principles_IREG_534.pdf
12 http://www.u-multirank.eu/
13 http://www.u-map.eu/
14 http://ec.europa.eu/research/science-society/document_library/pdf_06/assessing-
    europe-university-based-research_en.pdf

References

Anderson, G. (2006). Assuring quality/resisting quality assurance: Academics' responses to 'quality' in some Australian universities. *Quality in Higher Education, 12*(2), 161–173.

Banta, T. W., & Pike, G. R. (2007). Revisiting the blind ally of value added. *Assessment Update, 19*(1), 14–15.

Blackmur, D. (2007). A critical analysis of the UNESCO/OECD guidelines for quality provision of cross-border higher education. *Quality in Higher Education, 13*(2), 117–130.

Borden, V., & Bottrill, K. (1994). Performance indicators: Histories, definitions and method. *New Directions for Institutional Research, 82*, 5–21.

Chalmers, D. (2008). *Indicators of university teaching and learning quality.* Australian Learning & Teaching Council. Retrieved from http://www.altc.edu.au/system/files/International%20and%20national%20indicators%20and%20outcomes%20of%20quality%20teaching%20and%20learning%20currently%20in%20use.pdf

Chalmers, D., Lee, K., & Walker, B. (2008). *International and national indicators and outcomes of quality teaching and learning currently in use.* Australian Learning & Teaching Council. Retrieved from http://www.altc.edu.au/teaching-quality-indicators

CHERPA-Network. (2010). *U-Multirank interim progress report: Preparation of the pilot phase.* Retrieved from http://www.u-multirank.eu/project/U-Multirank%20Interim%20Report%202.pdf

Clarke, M. (2007). The impact of higher education rankings on student access, choice, and opportunity. In Institute for Higher Education Policy (Ed.), *College and university ranking systems: Global perspectives and American challenges* (pp. 35–48). Washington DC: IHEO.

Dill, D. (2003). *The regulation of academic quality: An assessment of university evaluation systems with emphasis on the United States: Background paper.* Chapel Hill, NC: Department of Public Policy, The University of North Carolina at Chapel Hill. Retrieved from http://www.unc.edu/ppaq/docs/Tokyo2_new.pdf

Dill, D., & Soo, M. (2005). Academic quality, league tables, and public policy: A cross-national analysis of university ranking systems. *Higher Education, 49*, 495–533.

Fisher, D., Rubenson, K., Rockwell, K., Grosjean, G., & Atkinson-Grosjean, J. (2000). *Performance indicators: A summary.* Vancouver: Centre for Policy Studies in Higher Education and Training (CHET), University of British Columbia. Retrieved from http://www.fedcan.ca/content/fr/365/performance-indicators-a-summary.html

Gallagher, M. (2010). *The accountability for quality agenda in higher education.* Canberra, ACT: Group of Eight Australia. Retrieved from http://www.go8.edu.au/government-a-business/go8-policy-a-analysis/2010/238-the-accountability-for-quality-agenda-in-higher-education

Harvey, L., & Green, D. (1993). Defining quality. *Assessment and Evaluation in Higher Education, 18*(1), 9–34.

Koretz, D. (2008). *Measuring up: What education testing really tells us.* Cambridge, MA: Harvard University Press.

Marginson, S. (2010). Global comparisons and the university knowledge economy. In L. M. Portnoi, V. D. Rust, & S. S. Bagley (Eds.), *Higher education, policy, and the global competition phenomenon* (pp. 29–42). New York: Palgrave Macmillan.

Rawazik, W., Carroll, M., Fox, W., & Harvey, L. (2009, March–April). *A new way of evaluating overseas providers*. Paper presented at *INQAAHE 2009 Conference*, UAE.

Stella, A. (2006). Quality assurance of cross-border higher education. *Quality in Higher Education, 12*(3), 257–276.

Stella, A., & Woodhouse, D. (2006). *Ranking of higher education institutions*. Melbourne, VIC: AUQA Occasional Publications.

Terenzini, P. T., Cabrera, A. F., Colbeck, C. L., Bjorklund, S. A., & Parente, J. M. (2001). Racial and ethnic diversity in the classroom: Does it promote student learning? *Journal of Higher Education, 72*(5), 509–531.

Tight, M. (2000). Do league tables contribute to the development of a quality culture? Football and higher education compared. *Higher Education Quarterly, 54*(1), 22–42.

Times Higher Education (THE) World University Rankings. (2010–2011). *Behind the numbers: Reputation ranking methodology explained*. Retrieved from http://www.timeshighereducation.co.uk/world-university-rankings/2010-2011/reputation-methodology.html

Umbach, P. D., & Kuh, G. D. (2006). Student experiences with diversity at liberal arts colleges: Another claim for distinctiveness. *Journal of Higher Education, 77*(1), 169–192.

US Department of Education. (2006). *A test of leadership: Charting the future of US higher education*. Washington, DC: Department of Education. Retrieved from http://www2.ed.gov/about/bdscomm/list/hiedfuture/reports/final-report.pdf

Vaughn, J. (2002). Accreditation, commercial rankings, and new approaches to assessing the quality of university research and education programmes in the United States. *Higher Education in Europe, 27*(4), 433–441.

Woodhouse, D. (2010, May). *The pursuit of international standards*. International Leadership Colloquium, Madrid. Retrieved from http://www.auqa.edu.au/files/presentations/the_pursuit_of_international_standards.pdf

2

QUALITY ASSURANCE AND ACCREDITATION IN OPEN AND DISTANCE LEARNING

Colin Latchem and Insung Jung

Introduction

Applying QA and accreditation processes to open and distance learning (ODL) is a relatively new phenomenon. This agenda is driven by the growing demand for accountability and cost–effectiveness in education generally, the need to show that the quality of ODL institutions, programmes and learning outcomes compares well with more traditional systems and concerns over the entry of private for-profit providers into the 'market'. QA and accreditation in ODL can give rise to some contentious issues. Distinctive factors and features need to be taken into account and different approaches may be called for in the various international, national, cultural and institutional contexts.

Differences and Challenges in QA and Accreditation in ODL

Some argue that distance and face-to-face education should be judged by the same criteria and methods. Others uphold that ODL is so different in its aims, organization, enrolments and operations that the QA criteria and mechanisms used in judging conventional education cannot apply. Some argue that specific guidelines and standards are needed for e-learning. Others claim that, regardless of the technology, the fundamentals of quality in teaching and learning are unchanged. Some hold that QA in ODL should be mandatory, externally managed and concerned with accountability. Others counter that QA should be voluntary, conducted internally and concerned with developing an institutional culture of quality. Some argue that the onus is on ODL providers to prove that their processes and outcomes are at least as good as those of conventional institutions. Others argue that traditional teaching and learning methods are outmoded and that by applying more learner-centred, constructivist and connectivist methods and finding the best fit between technology-enhanced, face-to-face and hands-on learning, ODL is spearheading the way to improve pedagogical paradigms.

Traditional education institutions typically operate a 'quality in' model. They are highly selective and apply conventional assessment of learning achievement and capability in determining which, and how many, students they will admit. Those who already enjoy some educational or social advantages are the most likely to gain further privileges and opportunities, while those with latent or less-conventional abilities are likely to be excluded from realizing their potential. Sometimes the perceptions of quality in these traditional institutions derive from their age, exclusivity, wealth, limited enrolments and class sizes, rather than objective evidence of their actual quality. This may be seen in the Japanese higher education system. What is known as the 'examination hell' imposes very high standards for entry into the small number of 'top-tier' or 'brand-name' universities. But the graduates are then almost automatically guaranteed prestigious jobs and upward social mobility. McVeigh (2002) indicts the university system as a de facto system of employment agencies or a waiting room before students hit the working world. Japanese universities have been criticized for their poor quality and most of them rank low internationally. Yakushiji (2002) tells of the President of one of Japan's oldest and most prestigious universities refusing to respond to a questionnaire from an Asian higher education accreditation agency because, wishing to preserve the prestige of his university, he was fearful of its being ranked lower than other Japanese universities as had happened previously.

By contrast, ODL providers operate a 'quality out' model. Believing that it is never too late to succeed, they accept entrants with no or lesser formal qualifications whose strengths and talents may not be easy to identify and then work to help them achieve the national standards required in the secondary or tertiary education systems. This places enormous demands upon staff and resources. It also implies that different performance indicators (PIs) may be required to assess the value-adding dimensions of the educational provision, the extent to which learners improve on their earlier performance or exceed what they might reasonably have been expected to achieve, and the long-term benefits of their education in terms of employment and contribution to society. Many ODL students are based in rural, remote or otherwise disadvantaged communities. They may lack any tradition of formal education or access to knowledge through libraries and the other resources taken for granted in more privileged settings. They may be trapped in societies without role models to show them how to learn or positive examples of the benefits of learning, where there are conflicts between non-school and school cultures or where gender or other forms of discrimination are deeply entrenched and widely tolerated. The curricula, teaching styles, assessment methods and support mechanisms needed to help such learners develop the necessary values, attitudes, knowledge and skills to find pathways out of their disadvantaged social and economic circumstances again call for special effort and special PIs.

Many ODL providers must perforce serve mass markets. The Open University of China (formerly China Radio and Television University), with over 2.5 million students, India's Indira Gandhi National Open University with over 2.8 million students and Turkey's Anadolu University with over 1 million Turkish citizens studying at a distance in Turkey, the Turkish Republic of Northern Cyprus and Western European countries, may truly be termed 'mega-universities' (Daniel, 1996). Mass-produced education is not necessarily the best education. Providing quality print, broadcast, online and face-to-face teaching, learning and support for large numbers of off-campus learners can be costly and challenging. Many institutions are forced to provide for enormous groups of learners with minimal instructional support. Such stripped-down methods and learning schedules may be attractive for many learners who are eager to obtain qualifications in the shortest possible time, and the low-overhead approaches may appeal to governments and private providers. But they can be impersonal, lead to soft marking, result in high non-completion and failure rates and destroy the credibility of ODL.

America's largest private for-profit university, the University of Phoenix (UoP), designed to provide bachelor and graduate degree programmes for part-time students through evening, weekend and online classes, has recently come in for considerable criticism. UoP's student profile shows that the university is providing an alternative means to higher education for more disadvantaged students than public conventional universities in the United States (Bates, 2011). However, students have called into question UoP's claims of caring for working adults and providing quality instruction. Their time with instructors is limited to 20–24 hours per course, compared with 40 hours in the conventional US universities. Ninety-five percent of the instructors teaching the 420,700 undergraduate and 78,000 graduate students on 'campuses' in office blocks and online are 'come-and-go' part-timers. UoP's graduation rates are among the lowest in the United States and, while the university is regionally accredited (see Chapter 6), it lacks approval from the prestigious Association to Advance Collegiate Schools of Business, which accredits bachelor's, master's and doctoral degree programmes in business administration and accounting, partly because of the high turnover in its faculty. And Intel has excluded it from its tuition reimbursement programme, saying that it lacks major accreditation. UoP has also been the subject of costly lawsuits and disputes with the US Department of Education and its profits have tumbled (Dillon, 2007; Lewis, 2007).

Many ODL providers are challenged, not only by the tyranny of distance, but by the requirement to operate across political boundaries. The University of the South Pacific and The University of the West Indies (see Chapter 13) must serve learners in various island nations and meet the expectations of the governments of their member countries. The scale and complexity of some ODL operations necessitates partnerships and networks. The Spanish National University of Distance Education provides distance education for more than 180,000 students by means of 60 study centres in Spain and 20 international centres in Bata, Berlin, Berne, Brussels, Buenos Aires, Caracas, Lima, London, Malabo, Mexico City, Paris and Sao Paulo. The Virtual University for Small States of the Commonwealth involves 30 small nations in creating courses in tourism, entrepreneurship, professional development, disaster management and technical and vocational subjects provided within a Transnational Qualifications Framework which can be readily adapted to specific national contexts and delivered online by recognized institutions to provide credit-bearing qualifications. India's National Institute of Open Schooling serves a cumulative student enrolment of 1.9 million and, with only 251 full-time staff, relies upon thousands of managers, teachers, facilitators and other personnel in a network of regional centres, study centres, schools, vocational institutions and non-governmental organizations across the subcontinent (see Chapter 16). The Open University (OU) operates from its base at Walton Hall in Milton Keynes in England and 13 regional centres throughout the United Kingdom, one centre in the Republic of Ireland and another in continental Europe. The Open Education Faculty of Turkey's Anadolu University serves its well over 1 million distance students through 88 centres in Turkey and offices and centres in Northern Cyprus, Cologne, Stuttgart, Hamburg, Frankfurt, Munich, Berlin, Paris, Vienna, Berne, Brussels and The Hague. Its operations require 600 locally recruited part-time tutors and the management of one of the world's largest university examination systems involving 245,000 personnel and 92,000 examination rooms in 5,700 separate buildings (Latchem, Özkul, Aydin, & Mutlu, 2006). How effectively and efficiently such partnerships and networks are coordinated and managed clearly affects the quality of educational services.

The circumstances and motivations of ODL students vary. While many students in Western countries opt for distance study for reasons of convenience and flexibility, many ODL students in other parts of the world have no choice. They would far prefer to study on campus in conventional institutions where they could feel like 'real students' and be sure that their qualifications were fully recognized. Not all jurisdictions, professional bodies or employers look favourably upon degrees conferred by dual-mode or open universities.

Learning at a distance, often without anyone to immediately turn to, places a heavier reliance upon the students' motivation and capacity to take responsibility for their learning than in on-campus study. Non-completion rates are typically far higher in ODL than in campus-based courses. Even well-established ODL institutions experience drop-out rates of over 50% (Simpson, 2004). A significant factor in this, particularly in the critical first year, is a lack of ready to hand administrative, academic, technical and social support. The use of information and communications technology can certainly help in these regards, but many providers have yet to establish the means of bridging the digital divide to achieve this sense of belonging across space and time. The logistics of serving large groups of dispersed students, some of whom may be of different cultures and speak different languages, can severely limit or even prevent the all-important interaction between the teachers and students and students and students, especially where there are problems of access and reliability in Internet connection. Kristoffersen and Woodhouse (2005) observe that the lack of interaction with other students and staff and lack of a campus culture account for the negative views of distance education. Against this, it could be argued that with funding per student in free fall in some countries, on-campus class sizes growing, and students often attending only for the minimum time because of competing demands, the conventional universities are also finding it difficult to assure academic standards, quality of provision and duty of care.

Quality education requires quality teachers. As evidenced by Bernard et al. (2004), distance education learning outcomes depend on the instructional strategies employed, feedback provided, and degree of learner engagement rather than the media or technology. Thus, teachers engaged in ODL need very special pedagogic competencies. Staff appointed to dedicated open institutions are more likely to comprehend and accept the commitment, knowledge and special skills required of them. For example, Brennan, Holloway and Shah (n.d.) observe that the innovative nature and ideology of The Open University has attracted academic staff who are committed as much to teaching as to research. Appointees to conventional or dual-mode institutions, in which hiring, tenure and promotion depend more upon research than on teaching ability, may have less commitment to distance teaching as an additional duty. Few of them are likely to have educational or teaching qualifications, let alone qualifications or experience in instructional design or pedagogy exploiting the new technologies. Tutoring online, at local centres or on campuses is typically undertaken by short-contract, hourly-paid, part-time staff. They experience all the disadvantages of casualization – low pay, lack of training and lack of access to the on-campus facilities and benefits enjoyed by their full-time counterparts. Very few of these tutors engage in research or have any involvement in developing the courses or programmes. So they are likely to have only limited understanding of the content and values and aims of the courses and pedagogy. Not surprisingly, in many countries and institutions, it can be difficult to find, fund and retain qualified, dedicated teachers capable of distance teaching and tutoring. Brennan, Holloway and Shah (op. cit.) observe that in the OU system, the regional centres are responsible for selecting and training the tutors who have the status of 'associate lecturers'. They stress that assuring quality in this large army of part-time personnel who also undertake most of the continuous assessment 'remote' from the central operations requires significant investment in staff development and human resource management.

Governments, policymakers and planners and institutions' senior managers often fail to recognize that developing and delivering quality distance and online courses and providing appropriate support for the learners require significant funding. Such is the scale of the mega-universities' operations that while their fees may be low, some can generate significant revenues. But it does not always follow that they are allowed to retain such income. For example, in Turkey, the government draws down some of Anadolu University's profits to fund the establishment of new universities in some of the poorest regions of that country. In the developing countries, ODL providers must often work with severely limited resources to achieve economies of scale and may find it difficult to achieve quality and change or update their offerings. They may also be driven to import learning packages from developed countries whose educational philosophies, methods and content may be inappropriate to the local cultures, needs and learners. This is why, for example, UNESCO (2003) expressed concern over the heavy dependency of the Arab Open University on The Open University for its courses and teaching materials, observing that these might be educationally and culturally inappropriate and develop a culture of dependency rather than local expertise in course and instructional design.

Recognition is not normally a problem for dual-mode universities with long-standing reputations which offer the same awards for on- and off-campus study. An example is the University of London, once described by Charles Dickens as the 'People's University', which in 1858, became the world's first provider of distance learning degrees. It has many notable alumni, including Nobel Prize winner Nelson Mandela who studied law while incarcerated on Robben Island, and five other Nobel Laureates. Twelve of the 19 University Colleges, including Birkbeck, Goldsmiths, King's College, London School of Economics and University College of London, offer distance programmes. With the UK Quality Assurance Agency confirming the high quality of its management, programmes and awards and rating it as one of the best universities in the country, students and employers need harbour no doubts about the standards of its courses and awards. Another institution that is able to evidence its highly credible awards and accessible, affordable and flexible provision is the University of South Africa (Unisa). With 200,000 students, it qualifies as one of the world's mega-universities. It is the country's oldest university and in its early years was an examining agency for the Oxford and Cambridge universities. In 1946, it introduced correspondence education through what was then called the Division of External Studies, now the Institute for Open and Distance Learning. The university's Quality Assurance and Promotion Directorate ensures that Unisa fulfils its QA obligations vis-à-vis the Higher Education Quality Committee of the Council for Higher Education and South African Qualifications Authority. Market research shows that Unisa is rated as one of the top universities in South Africa and yet its courses are offered at one-quarter to one-third the price of the residential universities and it allows students who do not qualify for direct admission to register for special access courses after which, if successful, they can study further for a degree.

Some ODL providers evidence their standing by obtaining International Organization for Standardization (ISO) certification – for example, Universitas Terbuka (see Chapter 11) and the University of Southern Queensland. The University of the Philippines Open University can vouch for its standing by being the fifth constituent university of the University of the Philippines, the nation's premier university, and by being declared the National Centre of Excellence in Open Learning and Distance Education by the Philippines Commission on Higher Education. Indira Gandhi National Open University's degrees, diplomas and certificates are recognized by all the members of the Association of Indian Universities and are equivalent to those of all other Indian universities. And in 1993, IGNOU was designated by the Commonwealth of Learning as its first Centre of Excellence for Distance Education.

The OU, which has gained an enviable international reputation in its four decades of operation, provides an interesting case of a radically different kind of institution seeking and assuring quality. In the 1960s, the then British Prime Minister, Harold Wilson, envisaged providing higher education for lower income groups by means of radio and television. On winning the election, he charged his Minister for the Arts, Jennie Lee, to bring his vision to fruition. She later recalled:

> Harold Wilson asked me to go to Chicago and Moscow. Neither was any-thing like what I wanted to do. The Chicago lads were lovely but they were only short-circuiting the first year or two of the degree. In Moscow all they were doing was routine long-term broadcasting and some corre-spondence courses . . . I had a different vision from that. And I hated the term 'University of the Air' because of all the nonsense in the Press about sitting in front of the telly to get a degree. I knew it had to be a university with no concessions, right from the very beginning. After all, I have gone through the mill myself, taking my own degree, even though it was a long time ago. I knew the conservatism and vested interests of the academic world. I didn't believe we could get it through if we lowered our standards.
>
> *(The Open University, 2010)*

She was right – the new university attracted hostility and criticism. Conservative MP Iain Macleod described it as 'blithering nonsense'. But the inaugural Vice-Chancellor, Walter Perry, had other ideas:

> I came to The Open University from a wholly traditional background . . . I had no experience of any of the new universities, nor had I ever been involved in adult education. I had heard about the University of the Air, but I regarded it as a political gimmick unlikely ever to be put into practice.

It wasn't until my son read out the advertisement for the post of Vice-Chancellor that I began to think seriously about the proposal and the challenge it presented. It wasn't that I had any deep-seated urge to mitigate the miseries of the depressed adult; it was that I was persuaded that the standard of teaching in conventional universities was pretty deplorable. It suddenly struck me that if you could use the media and devise course materials that would work for students all by themselves, then inevitably you were bound to affect – for good – the standard of teaching in conventional universities. I believed that to be so important that it overrode almost everything else. And that is what I said in my application.

(The Open University, 2010, p. 2)

Today, the OU has little difficulty in convincing even the most hardened sceptics of its academic excellence. It ranks among the top UK universities for teaching quality, rates highly in its organization, management and research and has topped the national student surveys which form part of the revised QA framework for higher education for overall satisfaction, assessment and feedback. The Higher Education Funding Council for England (HEFCE, 2011, p. 3) says that 'the UK set a world standard for distance learning by establishing, some 40 years ago, The Open University'. At some stage of their lives, a large percentage of the OU's 2 million alumni were judged incapable of higher study, but taking advantage of the open entry policy, they engaged in highly regarded undergraduate and postgraduate study and now contribute at many levels of society. In accord with Walter Perry's vision, the OU does not merely seek to equal, but to surpass, the standards of the conventional institutions.

Setting higher benchmarks should be the aim of all ODL providers. Many conventional providers now acknowledge that ODL's methods and uses of technology can improve learning processes and outcomes. Unfortunately, there are still far too many politicians, policymakers, institutions and teaching departments that place too much faith in the technology. Setting their eyes on achieving more at lower cost, they fail to recognize that what assures quality is investment in people.

Unfortunately too, there are still ODL institutions that are deemed inferior to conventional institutions and there is still some prejudice against degrees taken through open or distance study. For example, the Indian Bar Council will not recognize law degrees studied through distance mode (The Hindu, 2010). However, as Daniel (2010) observes of such hostility to ODL, 'There are many forces at work. Partly it is the old empire fighting back. But I think it is bolting the stable door after the horse has gone. All universities are so involved in bits of ODL that they will have great difficulty unscrambling it.'

Conclusion

In this chapter, we have laid the foundations for the proposition that QA should be central to all policymaking, management, pedagogy, instructional design, technology provision and learner support in ODL. Providers who were previously free from external scrutiny may complain about the additional regulations and workload in external and internal assessment of quality and question whether the extra costs and effort are justified. In some settings, there may be a great deal of lip-service to QA but little non-compliance. But if ODL is to be highly regarded in academic and political circles and by the public at large, it is essential to evidence the quality of the providers, teaching and learning and outcomes, demonstrate the benefits and advantages of the new approaches to those committed to traditional means of education, and work for continuous improvement. At the same time, the distinctive factors and features of ODL and different international, national, institutional and cultural contexts need to be accommodated in applying QA. These issues are examined further in the remainder of the book.

References

Bates, T. (2011, January 2). *How does the University of Phoenix measure up?* e-Learning and Distant Education Resources. Retrieved from http://www.tonybates.ca/2011/01/02/how-does-the-university-of-phoenix-measure-up/

Bernard, R. M., Abrami, P. C., Lou, Y., Borokhovski, E., Wade, A., Wozney, L., et al. (2004). How does distance education compare to classroom instruction? A meta-analysis of the empirical literature. *Review of Educational Research, 74,* 379–439. Retrieved from http://rer.sagepub.com/content/74/3/379.full.pdf

Brennan, J., Holloway, J., & Shah, T. (n.d.). *Open University The United Kingdom.* OECD/IMHE. Retrieved from http://www.oecd.org/dataoecd/49/23/1871706.pdf

Daniel, J. (2010). (in interview). Q&A with on-line pioneer John Daniel, 26 September 2010. *University World News,* Issue: 141, Retrieved from http://www.universityworld-news.com/article.php?story=2010092516094755

Daniel, J. S. (1996). *Mega-universities and knowledge media: Technology strategies for higher education.* London: Kogan Page.

Dillon, S. (2007, February 11). Troubles grow for a university built on profits. *The New York Times.* Retrieved from http://www.nytimes.com/2007/02/11/education/11phoenix.html?_r=1&th&emc=th

HEFCE. (2011). *Collaborate to compete: seizing the opportunity of online learning for UK higher education.* Report to HEFCE by the Online Learning Task Force, January 2011. Bristol: Higher Education Funding Council of England. Retrieved from http://www.hefce.ac.uk/pubs/hefce/2011/11_01/11_01.pdf

Kristoffersen, D., & Woodhouse, D. (2005). *An overview of world issues in quality assurance for higher education.* Australia: Australian Universities Quality Agency.

Latchem, C., Özkul, A. E., Aydin, C., & Mutlu, M. (2006). The open education system, Anadolu University, Turkey: e-Transformation in a mega-university. *Open Learning, 21*(3), 221–235.

Lewis, T. (2007, February 11). *University of Phoenix staggers under growing criticism.* Retrieved from http://www.consumeraffairs.com/news04/2007/02/univ_phoenix.html#ixzz0mw3Qf9Pm

McVeigh, B. J. (2002). *Japanese higher education as myth*. New York: M.E. Sharpe, Inc.

Simpson, O. (2004). The impact on retention of interventions to support distance learning students. *Open Learning, 19*(1), 79–95.

The Hindu. (2010, February 15). *Bar Council of India does not recognise distance mode degrees*. Retrieved from http://www.hindu.com/edu/2010/02/15/stories/2010021550300300.htm

The Open University. (2010). *History of the Open University*. Retrieved from http://www.mcs.open.ac.uk/80256EE9006B7FB0/(httpAssets)/F4D49088F191D0BF80256F870042AB9D/$file/History+of+the+Open+University.pdf

UNESCO. (2003, June). *Higher education in the Arab Region 1998-2003*. Document prepared by the UNESCO Regional Bureau for Education in the Arab States, UNESCO, Paris.

Yakushiji, T. (2002, May 30). *Changes in Japan's higher education system*. Global Communications Platform, Japanese Institute of Global Communications. Retrieved from http://www.glocom.org/opinions/essays/200205_yakushiji_changes/index.html

3

INTERNATIONAL AND REGIONAL QUALITY ASSURANCE AND ACCREDITATION

Colin Latchem and Anuwar Ali

Introduction

Olcott (2009) observes that most cross-border higher education is delivered face-to-face through branch campuses or partnerships with universities in the host countries. However, a political and economic environment that favours global trade in products and services and the opportunities provided by the Internet are leading to a growth in cross-border higher education delivered wholly or partly online. A 2002 Observatory on Borderless Higher Education survey in Commonwealth countries revealed that 11% of all international students were studying online at a distance (OBHE, 2002). However, it was noted that these figures were skewed by a few major providers. For example, about 30,000 or 14% of Open University students were outside the United Kingdom, while another 10,000 were studying through partnerships with other UK or overseas institutions. At the majority of institutions, the proportion of international students studying at a distance online was 3–4%. A year later, Pohl (2003) reported that 60,000 of the University of Phoenix's (UoP) 140,000 students were studying online but only 4000 or again just over 3% of these were overseas, mostly US military personnel or other American citizens.

This was certainly not the massive worldwide market envisaged at the start of the new millennium by private for-profit providers such as UoP or Universitas 21 Global. When UoP went public in 2000, it was regarded as one of the best Internet companies this side of eBay, raising over US$73.8 million on Wall Street. U21 Global, a joint venture between Australian, New Zealand, US, Canadian, UK, Swedish, German, Chinese, and Singaporean universities with Thomson Learning, envisaged its business growing to 500,000 students throughout Asia, Oceania,

Europe and North America by 2011. In the event, both providers failed to attract large numbers of students. They had placed too much faith in the technology and their attitudes and approaches were essentially those of business, not academe. They failed to recognize that global 'brand recognition' accrues over many years and derives from the quality of institutions' faculty, programmes, student support services and commitment to research and service – all of which come at a cost.

Today, cross-border education through distance and online learning is essentially the preserve of institutions with well-established reputations within their own jurisdictions: United Kingdom, United States, Canadian, Australian, German, French and other Western providers and institutions such as India's Indira Gandhi National Open University, Turkey's Anadolu University and the Korea National Open University. In another form of transnational distance education, the Commonwealth Executive Master of Business Administration and Public Administration Programme involves collaborative development and delivery by the Commonwealth of Learning, Pakistan's Allama Iqbal Open University, Bangladesh Open University, Indira Gandhi National Open University, Open University of Sri Lanka and other Asian, South Pacific, African and South American universities.

This last initiative is an example of what Dhanarajan (2001) calls the 'internationalization of education which does not endorse the over-commercialization of what is essentially a social good'. However, in the main, as Perraton (1997) observes, the rhetoric concerns international cooperation and exchange, but the agenda is driven by financial ambitions. Duke (2002) concludes that the over-riding concern is not with curriculum and content but with commercialization and commodification. Carr-Chellman (2005) observes that it is rare to see online courses other than those that are nakedly economic or utilitarian in purpose. Cain and Hewitt (2004) suggest that selling online education to the world represents a regrettable transition of the university from public institution to corporation.

Cross-border distance education can have great benefits, but not if it is regarded as a commodity to be traded in competitive markets and disreputable providers see it as an opportunity to offer low-quality courses and worthless qualifications. As Aboul-Ela (2009) observes, if education is to be seen as a market opportunity and offered as a Free Trade, as set out in the 1995 General Agreement on Trade in Services (GATS), it must be subject to quality checks for consumer protection. Sauvé (2002) suggests that since the internationalization of education involves collective actions on the part of governments, these may be the best agencies for regulating cross-border provision, rather than within GATS. However these agendas are pursued, as Marginson and McBurnie (2004) observe, QA guidelines are essential to ensure that the public duty of universities to undertake teaching and research is not endangered, that their prestige as public institutions is upheld, that students do not become victims of entrepreneurial activities and that entrepreneurial risks are not shifted onto the taxpayers. Martin (2007) observes that the provision of what she terms 'transnational commercial higher education', particularly by 'diploma mills' that are not subject to national quality checks, challenges quality standards and consumer rights in countries where administrative capacity is weak and there are no effective QA systems. These issues are explored further in this chapter.

National QA and Accreditation of Cross-border Education

The OECD (2005) reports on the impressive increase in national QA and accreditation agencies for higher education. But it also observes that because countries attach great importance to their sovereignty over their higher education systems, the resultant diversity and unevenness in these systems stand in the way of comprehensive QA frameworks for cross-border higher education. Cross-border education can play an important complementary role to public higher education in developing countries where there is pressure to increase participation rates but public funds are increasingly scarce and private provision may be opportune to improve higher education access. But few of these countries have yet established comprehensive or rigorous policies and regulatory frameworks to stimulate and support the growth of cross-border provision and partnerships of quality (Martin, 2007). Where countries do have systems in place to protect students against substandard overseas distance education providers, their practices vary. The Australian Department of Education, Employment and Workplace Relations' National Protocols for Higher Education Approval Processes[1] and national guidelines for the registration of overseas higher education institutions seeking to operate in Australia, define the criteria and procedures by which these providers may use the title 'university'. They must be accredited in their countries of origin, their courses, academic oversight and QA arrangements for delivery within Australia must be comparable to their Australian equivalents, their local partners must have appropriate standing, and their financial and other arrangements should permit the successful delivery of their courses in Australia. The Hong Kong Council for Accreditation of Academic and Vocational Qualification requires overseas providers applying for registration in Hong Kong to be registered in their countries of origin and offer programmes and services comparable to those in their home countries. However, the registration requirement does not apply to distance education courses delivered solely by correspondence or online without institutions, professional bodies or other agents in Hong Kong providing the lectures, tutorials or examinations. Some receiving countries, for example, Israel, Malaysia and South Africa, have tough regulations covering nonnational providers of education seeking accreditation. In Europe, the most common approach is not to regulate non-national providers unless they seek to become officially recognized institutions within national systems and to regard these more favourably if they are recognized in their countries of origin (Adam, 2001). The exception is Greece. Despite being a member of the EU, which is spearheading the promotion of transnational education among member states, the country's constitution explicitly prohibits recognition of private and/or foreign higher education institutions (Corlett, 2003).

In most countries, setting and appraising distance education standards is in the hands of the national agencies responsible for QA in the conventional universities. In a few countries, there are distinct QA and accreditation bodies for distance education. In the United States, for example, the Distance Education and Training Council Accrediting Commission defines, maintains and promotes quality in distance education institutions. However, it is not responsible for cross-border accreditation. Responsibility for this lies with the individual states and territories plus a whole range of accrediting organizations recognized by the US Department of Education (see Chapter 6). Thus, when the Open University and Canada's Athabasca University sought accreditation in the United States, they did so through the Middle States Commission on Higher Education, which accredits degree-granting colleges and universities in Delaware, the District of Columbia, Maryland, New Jersey, New York, Pennsylvania, Puerto Rico, US Virgin Islands and several overseas locations. In India, the Distance Education Council (DEC), which was established under the Indira Gandhi National Open University Act of 1985 to assure the standards of distance education in India, applies its own criteria for accrediting overseas distance providers. However, Daniel (2010) opines that while the DEC was intended to assure the quality of open and distance learning (ODL) offerings in all Indian institutions, its placing within IGNOU, which was also supposed to do this but has not really done so, gives rise to a conflict of interest, which prevents any serious QA of ODL in either the private or the public sectors.

International and Regional QA and Accreditation of Cross-border Education

The OECD's (2005) *Guidelines for Quality Provision in Cross-border Higher Education* were jointly elaborated with UNESCO and developed in consultation with 30 member countries and expert bodies to encourage and support international cooperation in QA in cross-border higher education. They argue that multilateral commitment to good practice and socially, culturally and linguistically relevant higher education is essential for the good standing of cross-border education. They set out how governments, higher education institutions and other providers, student bodies, QA and accreditation agencies, and academic and professional recognition bodies in the sending and receiving countries can share responsibilities. These *Guidelines* are not legally binding and, mindful of the diversity of national higher education systems, they leave the member countries to assume responsibility for their own QA frameworks. However, they have been endorsed by the American Council of Education, International Association of Universities and Association of Colleges and Universities of Canada and they form the basis for the QA and accreditation systems of:

- African and Malagasy Council for Higher Education (CAMES)
- Arab Network for Quality Assurance in Higher Education (ANQAHE)
- ASEAN Quality Assurance Network (AQAN)
- Asia–Pacific Quality Network (APQN)
- Association of Quality Assurance Agencies of the Islamic World (AQAAIW)
- Caribbean Area Network for Quality Assurance in Tertiary Education (CANQATE)
- Central and Eastern European Network of Quality Assurance in Higher Education (CEENQA)
- Central Asian Network for Quality Assurance and Accreditation (CANQA)
- Eurasian Quality Assurance Network (EAQAN)
- European Association for Quality Assurance in Higher Education (ENQA)
- European Consortium for Accreditation (ECA)
- European Network for Accreditation of Engineering Education (ENAEE)
- Ibero-American Network for Quality Assurance in Higher Education (RIACES)
- Quality Assurance Network for African Higher Education (AfriQAN).

All of these networks have signed memorandums of understanding with the International Network for Quality Assurance Agencies in Higher Education (INQAAHE), the worldwide association of 200 or so organizations involved in QA in higher education. INQAAHE collects and disseminates information on QA theory, research and practice and assists in establishing new QA agencies and systems. Its *Guidelines of Good Practice in Quality Assurance*[2] assists QA agencies in their operations and INQAAHE encourages these agencies to subject themselves to external review. With support from the World Bank and UNESCO, INQAAHE has also developed the freely available online *QAP Graduate Programme Materials*.[3] These deal with: higher education in a global world: the context of QA; external QA: what is quality and how has it been implemented in different countries; operating an external quality agency: the structure and management of QA agencies around the world; and maintaining quality within the institution: assessing learning, conducting a self-study and using data.

The Global Initiative for Quality Assurance Capacity,[4] a partnership between the World Bank, UNESCO, APQN, RIACES, AfriQAN, ANQAHE and INQAAHE has been established to:

- Improve the efforts of regional networks to build QA capacity of accreditation agencies, tertiary education institutions and government staff with QA functions.
- Serve as a worldwide focal point for knowledge sharing among regional networks.

- Help support regional networks in the development of their work programmes and identification of additional resources to ensure their long-term sustainability.

Lemaitre (2001) observes that QA is often regarded as something which can be dealt with in terms of handbooks and procedures, the principles and standards of which apply in all countries with little or no modification. She observes that the tendency is for developing nations to import developed nations' definitions of quality and means of promoting, measuring and guaranteeing this when in fact they still have to develop the conditions that make quality possible. Klaasen (2009) reports that the challenges facing regional collaboration in QA and accreditation lie in the different legal frameworks, interpretations of terminology and cultural attitudes towards such issues as transparency and accountability, handling criticism and involving students in QA assessment. How governments adapt or adopt the concepts and practices of QA also depends on their political agendas and attitudes towards cross-border education and the free market economy. Their willingness to collaborate in these matters may also depend upon whether or not they already have QA systems in place and how resistant they are to external interventions. The nature of cross-border provision – whether face-to-face, blended, distance or online – and the stage of development, scale of operations and resource issues must also be taken into account.

The strongest political basis for mutual accreditation is the 1999 Bologna Declaration.[5] This proposed a European Higher Education Area (EHEA) in which students and graduates could move freely between countries, using prior qualifications in one country as acceptable entry requirements for further study in another, and led to the establishment of the European Credit Transfer and Accumulation System. In 2003, the Ministers of the signatory states charged the European Network for Quality Assurance in Higher Education (ENQA) with developing an agreed set of standards, procedures and guidelines on QA for higher education. ENQA's 2009 *Standards and Guidelines for Quality Assurance in the European Higher Education Area*[6] contains three sets of standards and guidelines: one for internal QA, one for external QA and one for the external QA agencies themselves. ENQA observed that if these standards and guidelines for reviewing and reporting on higher education institutions, programmes, awards, students, staffing, learning resources, support and information services were implemented, the consistency of QA within the EHEA would be improved and institutions and QA agencies would have common reference points. However, ENQA also stressed that the main responsibility for QA must remain with the universities themselves and that this requires the creation of an institutional quality culture.

Other useful guidelines and examples of good practice for QA in overseas provision and collaboration include:

- The UNESCO/APQN Toolkit: *Regulating the Quality of Cross-Border Education.*[7]
- The UNESCO/Council of Europe *Code of Good Practice in the Provision of Transnational Education.*[8]
- The International Association of Universities, Association of Universities and Colleges of Canada, American Council on Education and Council for Higher Education Accreditations' *Sharing Quality Higher Education Across Borders: A statement on behalf of higher education institutions worldwide.*[9]

QA and Accreditation in Cross-border Distance and Online Education

In order to safeguard their reputations, some cross-border distance education providers establish their own QA procedures. In exporting its distance education programmes, Indira Gandhi National Open University establishes the credibility of its partner institutions with the assistance of the Indian High Commissions and Embassies, scrutinizes the curricula vitae of the local tutors and provides them with the necessary training, but still assesses all examination scripts centrally to ensure consistency in standards. At the Open University, overseas provision and partnerships are included in the *Quality and Standards in the Open University* documentation prepared by the Quality Office and the Curriculum Partnerships Committee is responsible for all regulatory matters relating to these partnerships and their approval by Curriculum and Awards Boards.

The International Council for Open and Distance Education (ICDE) believes that a review of distance education regulatory frameworks is timely to encourage and inform legislative change and policy development at the international level. At the time of writing, ICDE was co-funding DEHub, an Australian research group comprising the University of New England, Charles Sturt University, Central Queensland University, University of Southern Queensland and Massey University, Australian Universities Quality Agency, INQAAHE and Australasian Council on Open, Distance and e-Learning to undertake a pilot review of the regulatory frameworks for distance education in the Southwest Pacific/South East Asia Region. In another recent initiative, the Asian Association of Open Universities has developed the *AAOU Quality Assurance Statements of Best Practice,*[10] an updated version of its earlier QA framework referred to in Chapter 11. e-Learning and Open Educational Resources (OER) are included in these statements. This may serve to provide common reference points for QA in ODL institutions across Asia. More such international and regional efforts are needed to monitor, promote and support QA in cross-border distance education.

As yet, there is no agreement on the standards and accountability measures to be applied to cross-border ODL, and whether these should be the same as for conventional higher education. Kirkpatrick (2005) argues for the organizational differences to be taken into account and Shale and Gomes (1998) the differences in students and circumstances. The US Council for Higher Education Accreditation (CHEA, 2002) holds that the new types of provider and teaching and learning methods present new challenges to accreditation standards, policies and procedures, so accrediting organizations should not only ensure that the standards of the distance courses are commensurate with those of conventional courses, but should subject the unique features of distance education to particular scrutiny. Woodhouse (2006) holds that the criteria for judging inputs and processes and their correlation with quality outcomes is similar in both face-to-face and distance education cross-border programmes but suggests that because teachers, students and resources are dispersed or online, in assessing their quality, different questions may need to be asked and different enquiry methods employed.

There is also ongoing debate about assessing the quality and standardization of e-learning. The European Foundation for Quality in e-learning (see Chapter 8) aims to create a European community of users and experts to share experiences of online learning and certify quality in e-learning through a system called UNIQUe.[11] However, globally, 'e-learning' has different meanings, so what is relevant and rated highly by certain criteria in one culture may be quite different in another. For example, Western e-learning makes use of individual or collaborative constructivism and connectivism, holds students responsible for their own learning and makes use of technologies such as wikis, blogs and discussion boards for collaborative knowledge building. Asian e-learning is often more instructivist and, because the students are more teacher dependent and the cultures are high-context, it makes greater use of pre-corded or live televised lectures and videoconferencing (Latchem & Jung, 2009). So trying to develop and apply one set of standards in judging the quality of cross-border e-learning processes and outcomes may prove tricky indeed.

Conclusion

Cross-border ODL clearly has great potential. Davis (2010) envisages the growth of international networks comprising competing institutions, providers, websites, products and educational philosophies, all seeking to package, share and sometimes profit from, knowledge. UNESCO (2007) observes that the Internet creates a global intellectual commons of learning materials and pedagogy and slashes the costs of education to learners. As this chapter has shown, national, regional and international bodies are seeking to ensure quality in conventional cross-border higher education but there is still need for QA frameworks and guidelines for transnational ODL. There is the ever-present risk of students being exposed to low-quality provision and/or unscrupulous providers. All too often, the onus is on them to verify the quality of the providers, programmes and awards by checking websites such as UNESCO's Portal on Higher Education Institutions[12] or the US Department of Education Database on Accredited Postsecondary Institutions and Programs.[13]

Cultural differences also need careful consideration. UNESCO (2007) observes that different cultural understandings of quality and management can lead to differences in QA between developed and developing countries. Afele (2003) argues that all nations can gain from incorporating the knowledge of other countries and cultures into their thinking and actions and that cross-border ODL can play an important role in this regard. Mason (2003) agrees that such cross-cultural education offers the richness of multiple perspectives but observes that there can be challenges where the students' first language is not English and their schooling has imbued them with a less critical, more deferential and teacher-dependent approach to learning. Goldsmith (1993) warns that countries with a legacy of colonialism, racism or fear of hegemony will reject any approaches they see as paternalistic or culturally imperialistic. It is therefore important that cultural appropriateness, inclusiveness and acknowledging cultural, ethnic, social and linguistic diversity in the teachers and learners should be key performance indicators in assuring quality in cross-border ODL.

Notes

1 http://www.deewr.gov.au/HigherEducation/Programs/StudentSupport/National ProtocolsforHEApprovalProcesses/Pages/default.aspx
2 http://www.inqaahe.org/admin/files/assets/subsites/1/documenten/1231430767_ in qaahe—guidelines-of-good-practice%5B1%5D.pdf
3 http://www.inqaahe.org/main/capacity-building-39/giqac-50/download-the-qap-graduate-programme-materials?VV485ZE=1?ID=166
4 http://web.worldbank.org/WBSITE/EXTERNAL/TOPICS/EXTEDUCATION/ 0,,contentMDK:21723791~isCURL:Y~menuPK:617592~pagePK:148956~piP-K:216618~theSitePK:282386,00.html
5 http://ec.europa.eu/education/policies/educ/bologna/bologna.pdf
6 http://www.enqa.eu/files/ENQA%20Bergen%20Report.pdf
7 http://www2.unescobkk.org/elib/publications/087/APQN_Toolkit.pdf
8 http://portal.unesco.org/education/en/ev.php-URL_ID=22236&URL_DO=DO_TOPIC&URL_SECTION=201.html
9 http://www.chea.org/pdf/StatementFinal0105.pdf
10 http://www.aaou.net/index.php?option=com_content&view=category&layout=blog &id=29&Itemid=30
11 http://www.qualityfoundation.org/unique-certification/
12 http://portal.unesco.org/education/en/ev.php-URL_ID=49864&URL_DO=DO_TOPIC&URL_SECTION=201.html
13 http://www.chea.org/search/default.asp

References

Aboul-Ela, B. (2009). *Quality assurance at a distance* [PowerPoint presentation]. Keynote presentation, *Biennial INQAAHE Conference*, 30 March–2 April 2009. Hosted by the Commission for Academic Accreditation, Ministry of Higher Education in the United Arab Emirates. Retrieved from http://www.inqaahe.org/main/conferences-and-fora/ inqaahe-2009-conference

Adam, S. (2001). *Transnational education project report and recommendations. Confederation of European Union Rectors' Conferences.* Retrieved from http://www.sc.ehu.es/siwebso/Bolonia/textos/AEES_EHEA/Malmoe_transnational_education_project.pdf

Afele, J. S. C. (2003). *Digital bridges: Developing countries in the knowledge economy.* Hershey, PA: Idea Group Publishing.

Cain, J., & Hewitt, J. (2004). *Off course: From public place to marketplace at Melbourne University.* Melbourne: Scribe Publications.

Carr-Chellman, A. A. (Ed.). (2005). *Global perspectives on e-learning: Rhetoric and reality.* Thousand Oaks, CA: Sage.

Corlett, J. (2003). *Trade in educational services: The case of Greece.* TED Case Studies Number 689. Washington, DC: American University. Retrieved from http://www1.american.edu/ted/distance-learning-trade.htm

Council for Higher Education and Accreditation (CHEA). (2002). *Accreditation and assuring quality in distance education.* Washington, DC: CHEA. Retrieved from http://www.chea.org/Research/Accred-Distance-5-9-02.pdf

Daniel, J. (2010, October 6). *Distance education under threat: An opportunity?* Keynote address at the *IDOL & ICEM 2010 Joint Conference and Media Days* in Eskisehir, Turkey. Retrieved from http://www.col.org/resources/speeches/2010presentation/Pages/2010-10-06.aspx

Davis, G. (2010, November 14). The global movement. The first of the 2010 ABC Boyer Lecture Series. *The Republic of Learning.* Broadcast on ABC National Radio.

Dhanarajan, G. (2001). *Internationalisation of education without commercialisation: Resources.* Vancouver: Commonwealth of Learning. Retrieved from http://www.col.org/resources/speeches/2001presentations/Pages/2001-05-DD.aspx

Duke, C. (2002). Cyberbole, commerce and internationalisation: Desperate hope and desperate fear. *Journal of Studies in International Education, 6*(2), 93–114.

Goldsmith, E. (1993). *Development and colonialism.* Ecoscript, 35. Retrieved from http://www.edwardgoldsmith.org/36/development-and-colonialism/#FED

Kirkpatrick, D. (2005). *Accreditation and assuring quality in open and distance learning.* Vancouver: Commonwealth of Learning. Retrieved from http://www.col.org/SiteCollectionDocuments/KS2005_QA.pdf

Klaasen, L. (2009). *Collaboration in quality assurance and accreditation, global and regional.* [PowerPoint presentation]. *INQAAHE.* Retrieved from http://www.ehef-bangkok09.org/web/images/stories/doc/symposium/session1.2_leendert.pdf

Latchem, C., & Jung, I. S. (2009). *Distance and blended learning in Asia.* New York: Routledge.

Lemaitre, M. J. (2001, May 25–26). *Quality as politics.* Keynote address at the *Sixth QHE Seminar,* The End of Quality? Birmingham, UK. Retrieved from http://www.qualityresearchinternational.com/eoq/mariejose.pdf

Marginson, S., & McBurnie, G. (2004). Cross-border post-secondary education in the Asia-Pacific region. *Internationalisation and Trade in Higher Education: Opportunities and challenges* (pp. 137–204). Paris: OECD.

Martin, M. (Ed.). (2007). *Cross-border higher education: Regulation, quality assurance and impact,* 1. Paris: International Institute for Educational Planning. Retrieved from: http://unesdoc.unesco.org/images/0015/001538/153897e.pdf

Mason, R. D. (2003). *Online learning communities for global courses.* Paper presented at the *International Symposium: Networks without borders – Towards cross-cultural learning communities.* National Institute of Multimedia Education, Chiba, Japan.

OBHE. (2002). *Online learning in commonwealth universities,* Observatory on Borderless Higher Education Briefing Note, No. 7 and 8, August and October.

OECD. (2005). *Guidelines for quality provision in cross-border higher education.* Paris: OECD. Retrieved from http://www.oecd.org/dataoecd/33/8/34258720.pdf

Olcott, D. (2009, May). Going global: Trends in cross-border higher education for ODL: Interview with Dr. Don Olcott, Jr. *Journal of Open Education Research, 15*(2), 67–71. Retrieved from http://www.eden-online.org/contents/Olcott_interview.pdf

Perraton, H. (1997). *The virtual wandering scholar: Policy issues for international higher education.* Keynote paper presented at the *Higher Education Research and Development Society of Australia (HERDSA) Conference,* Adelaide, Australia.

Pohl, O. (2003, March 26). Universities exporting M.B.A. programs via the Internet. *The New York Times.* Retrieved from http://w4.stern.nyu.edu/news/news/2003/march/0326nyt.html

Sauvé, P. (2002, May 23–24). *Trade, education and the GATS: What's in, what's out, what's all the fuss about?* Paper presented at the *OECD/US Forum on Trade in Educational Services, OECD Trade Directorate,* Paris. Retrieved from http://www.oecd.org/dataoecd/50/50/2088515.pdf

Shale, D., & Gomes, J. (1998). Performance indicators and university distance education providers. *Journal of Distance Education, 13*(1), 1–20.

UNESCO. (2007, September 14). *Learners and new higher education spaces: Challenges for quality assurance and recognition of qualifications.* Third Global Forum on International Quality Assurance, Accreditation and the Recognition of Qualifications in Higher Education, Dar es Salam, Tanzania. Retrieved from http://unesdoc.unesco.org/images/0015/001559/155919e.pdf

Woodhouse, D. (2006, May). *The quality of transnational education: A provider view.* INQAAHE Workshop. Retrieved from http://www.inqaahe.org/admin/files/assets/subsites/1/documenten/1259589098_quality-assurance-of-transnational-education-a-providers-view.pdf

4

QUALITY ASSURANCE IN ASIAN OPEN AND DISTANCE LEARNING

Insung Jung

Introduction

As the world's largest continent, comprising 50 or so nations, Asia has great diversity in its peoples, traditions, cultures, languages, governmental systems and legislative and regulatory environments. Its educational systems, policy frameworks and practices are correspondingly diverse, as are its QA policies and procedures and applications of ODL in basic, technical and vocational, higher and non-formal education. There is some evidence, however, that globalization and technology are bringing Asian governments and ODL providers closer in regard to administering QA and promoting a culture of quality. This chapter examines QA policies and practices in Asian ODL. It concludes that QA in Asia should acknowledge the uniqueness of ODL, focus more on outcomes and pay greater attention to quality in open schooling and NFE.

QA Policies in Asia

In most Asian countries, the prime focus has been on achieving more equitable and economic provision through ODL rather than inculcating and regulating quality practice. China provides a prime example. The Open University of China (OUC) (formerly China Central Radio and TV University) was established in 1979, and for 20 years, it was the country's sole ODL provider. Then between 1998 and 2003, the Ministry of Education (MOE) licenced 68 online colleges within conventional universities including Tsinghua University and Peking University. These now offer 1,674 majors in 11 disciplines and 300 specialties at junior college and undergraduate levels. By 2008, the number of active distance students in China was 3,560,000, 2,250,000 of whom were studying through the OUC and 1,310,000 through the online colleges. They constituted 12% of all higher education students in China (Chen Li, 2011). However, faced with growing public concern over the quality of these courses and programmes, in 2003, the MOE stopped granting approval for new online colleges and introduced a QA system. This required the OUC and online colleges to adopt nationally standardized syllabi and examinations and follow the Annual Reporting and Censorship procedure which involves annual internal reviews and external audits by the Distance and Continuing Education Office of the MOE's Department of Higher Education.

It was only in the 1990s, with growth in cross-border education, the use of e-learning and the participation of private for-profit ODL providers, that Asian nations began developing QA policies for ODL. In 1991, the Distance Education Council was established by India's Indira Gandhi National Open University (IGNOU) to oversee the quality of ODL (as well as operating as an open university, IGNOU was mandated by the 1985 IGNOU Act to assure quality in the country-wide provision of ODL). In 1994, the Indonesian National Accreditation Board of Higher Education was instituted to accredit all higher education institutions including Universitas Terbuka (see Chapter 11). In 1996, Malaysia established a National Accreditation Board to oversee QA and accreditation of all private higher education institutions, regardless of delivery. In 2007, this board was merged with the Ministry of Education's two QA Divisions, renamed the Malaysian Qualifications Agency and made responsible for applying the Malaysian Qualifications Framework to all higher education institutions and programmes. 2003 saw the establishment of the Sri Lankan Quality Assurance and Accreditation Council of the University Grants Commission, and 2004 the creation of the Higher Education Quality Assurance Section of the Singapore MOE to oversee QA in all higher education institutions including ODL providers. In the Philippines, the Commission on Higher Education set out QA policies for ODL in the CHED Memorandum Order No. 27 Series of 2005.[1] This stipulated that only graduate-level programs with Level III accreditation could be offered in distance mode, the assumption being that undergraduate students needed face-to-face contact for optimal learning. However, CHED has authorized some institutions, including the University of the Philippines Open University, to offer undergraduate programmes at a distance and officially recognizes these (Arinto, 2011).

Most Asian QA guidelines apply to all forms of higher education delivery (Belawati & Baggaley, 2010). However, it would be argued that dedicated QA policy frameworks are now needed for ODL, to assure the quality of ODL to students and the public and to safeguard against unscrupulous providers and practices. Such frameworks would need to address the following issues:

- Access and equity. Overcoming discrimination against girls and women and girls and religious or ethnic minorities, enabling people to fully understand their human and civil rights, and providing people with equitable opportunities for lifelong learning.
- Teaching and learning. The quality, relevance and appropriateness of courses, courseware and methods, sensitivity to learners' needs and circumstances, and attention to the logistics of distance and online study.
- Learner support. Face-to-face and/or online support is particularly critical for Asian students who tend to be more teacher dependent as a consequence of their earlier schooling and high-context cultures.
- Learning outcomes. Evidence of the learners' vocational capacities and generic attributes as a consequence of their learning are important to graduates and employers and the retention and graduation rates are also critical to the reputation of ODL.
- Return-on-investment. Governments, taxpayers, students and teachers alike expect optimum outcomes with the constrained resources, so this too needs to be evidenced.

Unfortunately, sound policymaking and governance, accountability and transparency are not always evident in Asian ODL, which can suffer from:

- A 'Fordist' or mass-production approach to ODL and an inability to customize provision for the different needs of marginalized, remote and otherwise disadvantaged learners.
- Failure to serve the remoter communities due to the lack of technology, infrastructure and study centres.
- Weaknesses in course/programme design, development and delivery, owing to the lack of instructional designers, staff development and incentives.
- Limited provision for off-campus learning such as public libraries, laboratories, local support centres, ICT access and qualified tutors.
- Limited motivation and capacity in staff to engage in quality practice because of poor pay and conditions and lack of training.
- Ineffectual leadership, poor governance, political interference and corruption.
- Inadequate budgets and resources.
- Prejudice against ODL on the part of politicians, policymakers and employers (Dhanarajan, 2010).

QA and Higher Education

Asian higher education systems vary from extremely centralized and regulated by the Ministries of Education/Higher Education to semi-autonomous or autonomous. There can even be a mix of these within the same country. However, growing public pressure and government demand for accountability have led to the establishment of national QA and accreditation agencies. In 2008, the Asia Pacific Quality Network (APQN) identified 38 QA systems in 30 countries or territories across the region. Table 4.1 presents the findings from the 26 QA/ accreditation agencies in 20 Asian countries/territories responding to this APQN survey.

In most countries, QA is managed by Ministries of Education/Higher Education or funding councils. In a few cases, it is entrusted to non-government organizations or the institutions themselves although even here, the governments tend to guide and influence the QA procedures. Some national agencies are concerned only with QA (e.g. Bangladesh, China, Japan and South Korea); others also provide accreditation (e.g. Malaysia and Indonesia). In some countries (e.g. Malaysia), the QA standards apply to private and publicly funded institutions alike. In others (e.g. Singapore), only private institutions are subject to scrutiny. In some countries (e.g. China, India, Japan, Philippines and Singapore), responsibility for QA is divided between different agencies. In India, for example, the National Assessment and Accreditation Council, All India Council for Technical Education and National Accreditation Board of Higher Education function in parallel, applying slightly different QA approaches in assessing face-to-face education, while until recently, the Distance Education Council was wholly responsible for assuring quality in ODL.

In Asian ODL, QA practices vary. Authorities in, for example, Hong Kong, Malaysia, Indonesia, Sri Lanka and Singapore, regard ODL as an integral part of their higher education systems and ensure parity of academic standards by applying same procedures and criteria to ODL and conventional providers and programmes. In Korea, all 4-year universities, including the Korea National Open University must conduct self-evaluations at least every 2 years and submit their findings to Korean Council for University Education. However, in the case of the cyber universities, the Korea Education and Research Information Service is charged with monitoring their quality in accord with a *Cyber University Evaluation Handbook*. Other countries apply specific guidelines in judging distance education quality. Sri Lanka uses the Commonwealth of Learning *Quality Assurance Toolkit for Distance Higher Education Institutions and Programmes* (COL, 2009), and the Malaysian Qualifications Agency uses its own *Guidelines to Good Practices for Open and Distance Learning* (Wong & Liew, in press). Several QA and accreditation agencies apply their procedures both at institutional and programme level. Exceptions to this are, for example, South Korea (institutional level only) and Indonesia (programme level only).

Some QA systems are in a state of flux. All ODL programmes in India used to be assessed and accredited solely by the Distance Education Centre (DEC). Under the 2009 *New Policy on Distance Learning in Higher Education*,[2] all new ODL programmes must now be approved by the DEC and accredited by the

TABLE 4.1 Asian QA and/or accreditation agencies (revised from APQN, 2008)

Country	Name of agency	Nature of agency (Govt., HEI or NGO)	Target institutions (ODL, F2F or both)	Mandatory (M) or voluntary (V)	Specific QA reference for ODL	Assessment outcome	QA outcome report to the public
Bangladesh	University Grants Commission	Govt.	Both	M	None	Recommendations and suggestions for corrective action	Full QA report
Brunei	Brunei Darussalam National Accreditation Council	Govt.	Both	M	None	–	Accreditation status
Cambodia	Accreditation Committee of Cambodia	Govt.	F2F	M	None	Recommendations for improvement	
China	Department of Higher Education Evaluation Centre, Ministry of Education	Govt.	F2F	M	None	Recommendations, commendations and suggestions for corrective action	Accreditation status
China	Evaluation Department of China Academic Degrees and Graduate Education Development Centre	Govt.	F2F	V	None	Recommendations, commendations and suggestions for corrective action	Accreditation status
Hong Kong SAR (China)	Hong Kong Council for Accreditation of Academic and Vocational Qualifications	Govt.	Both	M	None	Varies – normally recommendations, suggestions, observations and accreditation in some cases	Accreditation status

(Continued)

TABLE 4.1 (Continued)

Country	Name of agency	Nature of agency (Govt., HEI or NGO)	Target institutions (ODL, F2F or both)	Mandatory (M) or voluntary (V)	Specific QA reference for ODL	Assessment outcome	QA outcome report to the public
India	National Assessment and Accreditation Council	Govt.	F2F	V	None	Overall analysis, commendations and recommendations	Full QA report and accreditation status
India	Distance Education Council	Govt.	ODL only	V	Handbook on Assessment and Accreditation of Open and Distance Learning Institutions	Overall analysis, commendations and recommendations	Full QA report and accreditation status
India	All India Council for Technical Education	Govt.	Both (For ODL, quality and relevance of contents only	V	None	–	Full QA report and accreditation status
Indonesia	National Accreditation Board of Higher Education	Govt.	Both	V	Accreditation Instrument for Distance Education Study Programmes	Recommendations and suggestions for programme improvement	Accreditation status
Japan	Japan University Accreditation Association	HEI	Both	M	None	Recommendations, commendations and suggestions for corrective action	Full QA report and accreditation status
Japan	Japanese Institute for Higher Education Evaluation	HEI	Both	M	None	Recommendations, commendations and suggestions for corrective action	Accreditation status

(Continued)

TABLE 4.1 (Continued)

Country	Name of agency	Nature of agency (Govt., HEI or NGO)	Target institutions (ODL, F2F or both)	Mandatory (M) or voluntary (V)	Specific QA reference for ODL	Assessment outcome	QA outcome report to the public
Japan	National Institution for Academic Degrees and University Evaluation	Govt.	Both	M	None	Achievement to the standards – comments on areas that are excellent and areas that need improvement	Full QA report and summary
Kuwait	Private Universities Council	Govt.	F2F	M	None	Recommendations and commendations	Accreditation status
Lao PDR	Ministry of Education	Govt.	F2F	M	None	Recommendations	Summary of the QA report
Malaysia	Malaysian Qualifications Agency	Govt.	Both	M	Guidelines to Good Practices for Open and Distance Learning	Recommendations, commendations, suggestions for corrective action, programme accreditation	Accreditation status and summary of the QA report
Nepal	University Grants Commission's QA and Accreditation Committee	Govt.	F2F	V	None	Recommendations and institutional accreditation	
Pakistan	Higher Education Commission	Govt.	Both	M	None	Suggestions, recommendations for suggestions for corrective action	Summary of the QA report

(Continued)

TABLE 4.1 (Continued)

Country	Name of agency	Nature of agency (Govt., HEI or NGO)	Target institutions (ODL, F2F or both)	Mandatory (M) or voluntary (V)	Specific QA reference for ODL	Assessment outcome	QA outcome report to the public
Philippines	Philippines Accrediting Association of Schools, Colleges and Universities	HEI	F2F	M	Commission on Higher Education's QA System for Distance Education	Commendations and recommendations for improvement	Accreditation status
Philippines	Accrediting Agency of Chartered Colleges and Universities in the Philippines	HEI	F2F	M	None	Identifies strengths and area needing improvement and makes recommendations	Accreditation status
S. Korea	Korean Council for University Education	HEI	Both	M	Cyber University Evaluation Handbook (for self-evaluation)	Identifies strengths, and weaknesses and makes suggestions for corrective action	Full QA report, summary and accreditation status
Singapore	Consumers Association of Singapore	NGO	Both (Private education institutions only)	V	None	No longer administering an accreditation scheme for private education	–
Singapore	Higher Education QA Section of Ministry of Education	Govt.	Both (Private education institutions only)	M	None	Commendations and recommendations for improvement	None

(*Continued*)

TABLE 4.1 (Continued)

Country	Name of agency	Nature of agency (Govt., HEI or NGO)	Target institutions (ODL, F2F or both)	Mandatory (M) or voluntary (V)	Specific QA reference for ODL	Assessment outcome	QA outcome report to the public
Sri Lanka	QA and Accreditation Council	Govt.	Both (but utilizing QA guidelines specific to ODL)	M	QA Toolkit for Distance Higher Education Institutions and Programmes	Provides evidence-based judgments and recommendations	Full QA report
Syria	Directorate of Evaluation and Accreditation	Govt.	F2F	M for Private/V for Public	None	Suggestions for corrective action followed by recommendations	–
Thailand	Office of National Educational Standards and Quality Assessment	Govt.	Both	M	Criteria for Asking Permission to Offer and Manage Degree Programs in the Distance Education System	Assessment of standards, commendations, and suggestions for corrective action	Accreditation status and summary of the QA report
Vietnam	General Department of Education Testing and Accreditation of the Ministry of Education and Training	Govt.	Both	M	None	Assessment of standards and makes recommendations for improvement	Accreditation status

National Board of Accreditation. In the Philippines, the Open University of the Philippines (UPOU), which is part of the University of the Philippines system, is not audited by the Philippines Accrediting Association of Schools, Colleges and Universities. However, the lack of jurisdictional clarity is now leading the Commission on Higher Education to develop a separate QA instrument for UPOU and all other ODL providers. China, Japan, Thailand, Vietnam and some other countries are only just beginning to develop specific QA protocols for ODL. While various agencies and institutions in the Arab States are seeking to strengthen QA arrangements and accreditation standards, few of the region's distance education providers have as yet developed systematic procedures for QA (Gani, 2009). The Syria Virtual University has been accredited by the Syrian Ministry of Higher Education. The Arab Open University in Kuwait has acquired both institutional accreditation and validation of its programmes as a partner of the Open University and its Lebanon branch has also received recognition of all its degrees by the Lebanese Ministry of Higher Education. The Palestinian Al-Quds Open University is the only institution in the region to have established internal QA procedures and invited an external QA review (see Chapter 14).

Asian QA systems for ODL tend to follow those in the rest of the world. Most require institutions and programmes to self-evaluate and submit evidence of compliance with required standards to external auditors who then verify this by means of site visits, examining documentation and interviewing stakeholders. Most provide, or are moving towards, wider public disclosure (Jung, 2011), but sometimes only the final outcomes of the QA or accreditation process are published or the reports are only made available to the institutions and authorities concerned.

The use of performance indicators (PIs) is low, but on the increase. As noted above, Sri Lanka uses the PIs in the Commonwealth of Learning *Quality Assurance Toolkit for Distance Higher Education Institutions and Programmes*.[3] Now in use across the globe, this toolkit was developed as part of the Sri Lankan Distance Education Modernization project and resonates with the *Guidelines of Good Practice in Quality Assurance* by the International Network for Quality Assurance Agencies in Higher education (INQAAHE, 2007).[4] It proposes 386 PIs across 10 QA criteria at the institutional level and 276 PIs across six QA criteria at the programme level and shows how these can be applied in assessing and improving quality in ODL. The Malaysian Qualifications Agency has recently developed the *Guidelines to Good Practices for Open and Distance Learning* which includes 177 benchmarked and enhanced PIs across nine QA areas.

A number of Asian regional associations are concerned with QA and some of these are members of the International Network for Quality Assurance Agencies in Higher Education (INQAAHE). The ASEAN Quality Assurance Network (AQAN) is concerned with developing an ASEAN QA framework, promoting harmonization, sharing best practice, collaborating in capacity building in QA, and facilitating the recognition of qualifications and cross-border mobility. The AUN-QA Network is a group of Chief Quality Officers appointed by ASEAN University Network member universities to coordinate activities in harmonizing educational standards and continuous quality improvement in universities in ASEAN. The Asia-Pacific Quality Network serves the needs of QA agencies in higher education in all Pacific island nations and territories, New Zealand, Australia and Papua New Guinea, and all island and mainland nations and territories of Asia, including Russia, Afghanistan, the other central Asian'stans and Iran, but excluding the Gulf states. The Arab Network for Quality Assurance in Higher Education works in collaboration with the Association of Arab Universities. Another regional QA initiative is the Asian Association of Open Universities (AAOU) *QA Statements of Best Practice*. The AAOU's membership covers the Far East, East, South-east, South and West Asian regions, so this framework may also prove valuable in encouraging and supporting external and internal QA in ODL across the continent.

QA and Open Schooling

As Daniel (2010) observes, open schooling is the most cost-effective means of providing basic, elementary and secondary education to many children and young adults in Asia deprived of access to conventional schools. Achieving quality in such provision is enormously challenging, not least because it involves so many learners. Some open schooling systems seek to ensure that their curriculum, learning materials and materials measure up to the standards of conventional schools (Priyadarshini, 2006; UNICEF, 2009). India's National Institute of Open School and Indonesia's Open Junior Secondary ensure that they meet the national examination standards, despite many constraints (see Chapter 16). QA in curriculum development and learner support is also applied in the Open School run by the National Institute of Education in Sri Lanka, and the Secondary, Higher Secondary and School Certificate programmes operated by Allama Iqbal Open University in Pakistan. The Bangladesh Open University Open School has developed guidelines for course and materials development, but Akhter (2008) reports that while the majority of teachers and students agree that the materials are up-to-date and well presented, the tutors still resort to lecturing methods and need training in more appropriate methodologies.

One very useful QA framework and set of standards for open schooling is the *Quality Assurance Toolkit for Open Schools* (COL, 2009). This toolkit comprises: the theoretical aspects of open schooling and QA; quality criteria and their components; and case studies from different countries illustrating how the different quality criteria are applied.

QA in Non-Formal Education

Non-formal education (NFE) plays an important role in Asia, in providing programmes for persons with broken educational and employment careers, in offering programmes in literacy, numeracy and basic employment skills, rural transformation, childcare, healthcare and nutrition. NFE means different things in different contexts, and the dividing line between formal and non-formal education is sometimes definitional rather than actual. As Singh (2009) observes, NFE needs to be considered within national qualifications and QA frameworks because it is important to have systems for recognizing prior informal and non-formal learning and providing pathways for certification and subsequent progression within formal learning systems. Otherwise, NFE can be a low-status dead end. With the exception of India, where NFE is embedded within the National Qualifications Frameworks, Asian countries and NFE providers have no mechanisms to assure quality or articulation in the face-to-face or ODL NFE programmes on offer.

While the formal sector has powers to confer credentials and require QA, NFE providers are mostly non-governmental (albeit sometimes funded by governments) and they generally shy away from bureaucracy. QA requires both fiscal and human resources and again, while the formal sector has access to these, NFE providers may have difficulty in mobilizing the funds and means for quality practice and assurance. In formal education, the lead times for programme and course planning and implementation allow for QA. NFE timeframes are typically much shorter, making it difficult to build QA into the planning and implementation. Despite these difficulties, it is important that governments, donors and other NFE providers develop and apply national qualification frameworks and quality indicators for informal and lifelong learning. Access and equity are important. But so too is quality.

Conclusion

Asia is sometimes referred to as the continent of diversity and contrast and as shown in this chapter this is certainly true of QA in ODL. Nevertheless, common elements may be found: growing awareness of the need for ensuring quality as well as access and cost-effectiveness; the use of pre-determined standards and criteria; the use of internal and external assessment and a recognition of the need for greater accountability and transparency. However, most QA systems for ODL are still not explicit in articulating or assessing learning outcomes and often online education is not included (APQN, 2008). In light of the above observations, it is concluded that:

- Governments, QA agencies and ODL providers should not compromise on standards between ODL and conventional education provision, but should acknowledge the unique features of ODL in developing QA guidelines and auditing systems.

- On- and off-campus applications of e-learning should be included in national quality frameworks.
- There is urgent need for national qualification frameworks to help open schooling and NFE providers monitor, evaluate and improve their performance, evidence the benefits, justify the resource investments and enhance the reputation of these means of provision.
- Applying some of the QA approaches used in formal education may be appropriate in judging quality in open schooling and NFE, but account must be taken of the different principles, modalities and approaches involved, diversity of target groups, contexts and circumstances, and the all-important issues of participation, sustainability and long-term as well as short-term outcomes and impact.
- In implementing QA and accreditation systems, as elsewhere in the world, the methods used in gauging processes, performance and outcomes must be robust, reliable and valid and the data must be interpreted and reported in ways that are transparent and appropriate to, and interpretable by, the various stakeholders.

Notes

1 http://202.57.63.198/chedwww/index.php/eng/Information/CHED-Memorandum-Orders/2005-CHED-Memorandum-Orders
2 http://stusupport.ignou.ac.in/dec/PolicyDraft-DL.pdf
3 http://www.col.org/PublicationDocuments/pub_HE_QA_Toolkit_web.pdf
4 http://www.inqaahe.org/admin/files/assets/subsites/1/documenten/1231430767_inqaahe—guidelines-of-good-practice[1].pdf

References

Akhter, Z. (2008). Quality assurance in secondary education program of Bangladesh Open University: Present status and challenges. *The Turkish Online Journal of Distance Education*, *9*(2), 35–45. Retrieved from http://tojde.anadolu.edu.tr/tojde30/pdf/Volume9Number2.pdf

APQN. (2008). *Quality assurance arrangements in higher education in the broader Asia-Pacific region*. Australia: Asia Pacific Quality Network. Retrieved from http://www.aei.gov.au/AEI/GovernmentActivities/BrisbaneCommunique/Quality_Assurance_pdf.pdf

Arinto, P. (2011). *National quality assurance systems in distance education in Asia: the Philippines*. Report submitted to International Development Research Centre.

Belawati, T., & Baggaley, J. (2010). *Policy and practice in Asian distance education*. Ottawa: International Development Research Centre.

Chen Li. (2011). *National quality assurance systems in distance education in Asia: China*. Report submitted to International Development Research Centre.

COL. (2009). *Quality assurance toolkit: Distance higher education institutions and programmes*. Vancouver: Commonwealth of Learning.

Daniel, J. S. (2010). *Mega-schools, technology and teachers: Achieving education for all*. New York and London: Routledge.

Dhanarajan, G. (2010, October 25–28). *Thoughts on open distance education: Has it outlived its course?* Paper presented at the *Asian Association of Open Universities 24th Annual Conference Hanoi*, Vietnam.

Gani, A. (2009). Quality assurance of the Arab Open University in Saudi Arabia. *Asian Journal of Distance Education*, 7(2). Retrieved from http://www.asianjde.org/2009v7.2. Gani.html

INQAAHE. (2007). *Guidelines of good practice*. Hague: International Networks for Quality Assurance Agencies in Higher Education.

Jung, I. S. (2011). *National quality assurance systems in distance education in Asia: Summary and conclusions*. Report submitted to International Development Research Centre.

Priyadarshini, A. (2006, October 30–November 3). *Basic education through open schooling*. Paper presented at the *Fourth Pan-Commonwealth Forum*, Ocho Rios. Retrieved from http://pcf4.dec.uwi.edu/viewabstract.php?id=274

Singh, M. (2009). *Informal and non-formal learning and frameworks in the development context*. Retrieved from http://www.meda-ete.net/eventsmgmt.nsf/(getAttachment)/FB1391 CC32C7E2E8C125758B00392B61/$File/30%20Jan%2002%20Informal%20and%20non %20fomal%20learning%20(UIL_ETF%20UNESCO).pdf

UNICEF. (2009). *Open and distance learning for basic education in South Asia*. Nepal: United Nations Children's Fund. Retrieved from http://www.unicef.org/rosa/ODL_Report_ (Final_version)___10_Dec_09.pdf

Wong T.M., & Liew, A. (in press). Production of quality graduates through a high quality learning experience: Wawasan Open University. In I.S. Jung, T.M. Wong, & T. Belawati (Eds.), *Quality assurance in distance education and e-learning: Best practices, challenges, solutions, and lessons from Asia*.

5

QUALITY ASSURANCE FOR DISTANCE EDUCATION IN SUB-SAHARAN AFRICA

Sarah Hoosen and Neil Butcher

Introduction

Distance education (DE) has a tremendous potential to meet Africa's educational needs as the demand for all levels and forms of education grows rapidly. Many African countries and institutions have deployed DE to meet the growing need for higher education and, to a lesser extent, secondary and non-formal education. DE is seen as a cost-effective and efficient means of increasing access to education and enabling Africans to improve their qualifications without the high costs of building facilities and learners leaving their communities, jobs or other commitments. But several major challenges are becoming apparent. There is a perception that DE cannot offer the same quality of education as conventional face-to-face education. Many African educational policymakers and planners are sceptical about its legitimacy and standards, and therefore afford only limited political support and/or funding to DE undertakings. Most African countries lack policies to guide the development and implementation of DE programmes at national and institutional levels. There is inadequate information and communications technology (ICT) infrastructure and a shortage of the qualified staff required for influencing and implementing DE policies and practices. There are dangers of increasing enrolments with little regard for the quality of the learning experience or whether the programmes are relevant to the human resource development needs and the adoption of DE by educational institutions driven primarily by a desire for financial gain (Pityana, 2008). Other challenges facing higher education in Africa include gender and regional disparities, a mismatch between the skills acquired by university graduates and those demanded by industry, imbalances in terms of the number of students studying sciences and humanities, rigid admission criteria, lack of modalities for credit transfer between universities and other post-secondary institutions, lack of recognition of prior learning, the brain drain and the threat posed by HIV and AIDS (Hoosen, Butcher, & Njenga, 2009).

Fewer than one-third of African countries have quality assurance (QA) bodies of any kind, and even fewer have QA agencies that have quality frameworks or guidelines regarding DE. Given the paucity of suitable QA policy bodies and frameworks, the possibility of exploitative practices by unregulated private providers and the increasing amount of cross-border higher education, there is a growing sense of the need for continental, regional and national harmonization of QA processes.

Continental and Regional Frameworks for QA

Growing recognition of the importance of QA in conventional higher education in Africa has led to the establishment of various continental initiatives. For example, the UNESCO Arusha Convention on the Recognition of Academic Qualifications in Higher Education in African States[1] was adopted under the auspices of UNESCO at Arusha in December 1981 and revised in Cape Town in June 2002 by the Ministers of Education of African Member States. The Arusha Convention is a legal framework agreement which provides general guidelines intended to facilitate implementation of continental cooperation relative to the recognition of studies and degrees through national, bilateral, regional and continental mechanisms that already exist or are created for that purpose. However, only 20 countries have ratified this agreement, fewer still are implementing it and the poor quality of the existing national QA and accreditation systems has limited the success of this Convention. Consequently, the African Union Commission (AUC), in partnership with UNESCO, is revising this mechanism so that the Conference of Ministers of Education of the African Union can approve a more effective Arusha Convention in the near future. To further advance the QA agenda, UNESCO has hosted annual international conferences on QA in African higher education since 2006.

The AUC identifies QA as a key issue in its Plan of Action for the Second Decade of Education for Africa.[2] It has developed a 'harmonization strategy', which aims to align and streamline existing regional QA processes so that they cohere into a single, common continental framework.[3] The AUC has also developed an African Higher Education Quality Rating Mechanism,[4] which incorporates quality criteria for DE and online delivery.

In another international initiative, the Association of African Universities (AAU), the apex organization and forum for consultation, exchange of information and cooperation among institutions of higher education in Africa, with its headquarters in Accra, Ghana, has developed a Quality Assurance Support Programme for African Higher Education, a programme promoting the establishment of regional, national and institutional QA systems. In association with the Global Initiative for Quality Assurance Capacity,[5] the AAU has also launched the African Quality Assurance Network or AfriQAN to provide assistance to institutions concerned with QA in higher education, harmonize QA systems in Africa and collaborate with similar organizations on other continents.

At the regional level, several bodies have addressed the issue of QA in education. For example, the Southern African Development Community (SADC) has established a Technical Committee on Certification and Accreditation to develop policy guidelines and mechanisms for harmonizing academic programmes and qualifications in the region. This Committee initiated the SADC Qualifications Framework,[6] which focuses on university and school education. However, this work is still at the formative stage and it is unclear whether DE will be specifically covered.

In Francophone Africa, the African and Malagasy Council for Higher Education (CAMES) is responsible for QA, the mutual recognition of qualifications, promoting professional mobility amongst the 16 member states and accrediting new private higher education institutions in the region. However, the Francophone countries appear to be lagging the Anglophone countries in establishing formal QA processes at national level. Twelve of the 17 CAMES member states have no national QA agencies. This may be because some of the governments assume that responsibility for QA has been assigned to CAMES while CAMES itself has limited capacity for monitoring and accrediting conventional and DE provision.

In East Africa, the Inter-University Council for East Africa (IUCEA), a regional intergovernmental organization established by Kenya, Tanzania, and Uganda, recently developed a Regional Quality Assurance Framework for the countries of East Africa. The IUCEA's five-volume *A Road Map to Quality: Handbook for Quality Assurance in Higher Education* (2007) was developed to help implement QA within universities, share understanding of quality issues and QA and harmonize standards. It also includes a diagnostic model for internal QA and external assessment. However, here again, there is no specific reference to QA in DE.

Thus, there have been some continental and regional efforts to promote QA in higher education, but, to date, there are no frameworks that make specific provision for QA in DE. However, they do provide a basis for QA in higher education within which DE providers and programmes can be assessed.

The Role of African DE Associations in QA

African DE associations also play a role in promoting and supporting QA in DE. The African Council for Distance Education (ACDE) is a continental educational organization comprising African higher education institutions which are committed to expanding access to quality education and training through distance and e-learning. It is registered under the laws of Kenya as an international educational non-profit organization, and is headquartered in Nairobi. It has established a Working Group on Quality Assurance and Accreditation in partnership with the AUC with the aim of establishing a continental QA and accreditation agency, the terms of which are to:

- Develop protocols, policies and a repertoire of instruments and tools to inform the code of conduct, criteria and standards for quality DE provisioning in Africa.
- Ensure a phased and systematic implementation of various QA processes, programme audits and reviews, accreditation and credit transfer systems based on voluntary participation.
- Contribute to the further development of national and regional DE QA systems on the continent (Jegede, 2009).

At the regional level, the Distance Education Association of Southern Africa (DEASA), whose mission is to promote quality in DE through policies and frameworks, records in its Strategic Focus Plan for 2010–2015 that its strategies are to:

- Assess current QA practices in the SADC region to develop a standardized framework.
- Develop criteria and standards for DE in line with the SADC QA framework.
- Facilitate capacity building to promote the implementation of QA.
- Promote continuous inter-institutional audits.

Quality promotion was one of the four themes of the 45th DEASA Conference and Annual General Meeting held in Malawi in 2010. While the efforts of the ACDE and DEASA appear promising, they are still at the planning stage, and it is not yet possible to determine how they will operate and with what mandate, how they will be sustained, or what effect they will have in practice.

The work of the National Association of Distance and Open Education Organizations of South Africa (NADEOSA) provides the best example of country-level QA activity by an association. The overarching aim of NADEOSA is to act as a forum for the South African public, private for-profit and non-governmental organizations committed to increasing access to an affordable, cost-effective and quality learning environment in which learners are empowered to become self-sufficient members of society. NADEOSA has coordinated the development of a set of quality criteria for designing and delivering DE (Welch & Reed, 2005). There are 13 criteria, dealing with policy and planning, learners, programme development, course design, course materials, assessment, learner support, human resource strategy, management and administration, collaborative relationships, QA, information dissemination and results. Each criterion is accompanied by an explanation of what it entails. For example, the criterion on course materials reads:

> The content, assessment and teaching and learning approaches in the course materials support the aims and learning outcomes; the materials are accessibly presented; they teach in a coherent way that engages the learners; there is an identified process of development and evaluation of course materials.

The eight elements (performance indicators) for this criterion are organized under the following headings: materials development, planning, quality course materials and QA. For the 13 criteria, there are 212 elements in total.

Welch and Reed (2005) point out that the problems with criteria in general are that they can never be comprehensive enough, that there is always potential to add further criteria and that detailing criteria does not necessarily lead to shared understanding of how they are intended to guide practice. Consequently, the NADEOSA booklet also includes 14 case studies derived from evaluation and research in DE carried out over the previous 10 years by the South African Institute of Distance Education. In introducing these case studies, the authors observe that while there has been growth in the understanding and practice of DE in South Africa, much of it is still of a poor standard. They suggest that the financial gains from large-scale provision and the complexity of providing adequate support to large numbers of students combine to make providers resistant to change. So the purpose of the case studies was to illustrate good practice and give readers insights that would prevent them from interpreting the criteria in a reductionist fashion. These quality criteria are not binding, but the association is able to report on successful outcomes from their application. A number of South African institutions have engaged in internal self-evaluation using NADEOSA's criteria and they are also in use in other countries. For example, Namibia now bases its approach to QA in DE upon these criteria. The Higher Education Quality Committee (HEQC), the one permanent committee of the South African Council on Higher Education (CHE), has endorsed these criteria, and NADEOSA has collaborated with the HEQC in providing institutional capacity development and a guide for good practice in QA.

QA at the National Level

As noted above, more than two-thirds of all African countries have no agencies or other bodies that deal with QA, and, even where such organizations exist, they are unlikely to have developed any QA frameworks or guidelines for DE. In

Nigeria, the National University Commission (NUC) is responsible for accreditation, quality control and assessment of conventional universities, but there is no framework for QA for DE, nor is there any specific regulatory body for assessing DE programmes. Olojede (n.d.) argues the need for such a body, suggesting that this should not be the NUC, but an independent body focused solely on DE provision.

In South Africa, the CHE and the HEQC take the view that the QA mechanisms for contact and DE programmes should be the same. Thus, there is only one set of institutional audit criteria and one set of programme accreditation criteria for all modes of delivery. However, they do take account of the different modes of delivery by noting particular concerns within the criteria and providing training for the evaluators in regard to specific DE issues. Also in South Africa, the Council for Quality Assurance in General and Further Education and Training and the recently established Quality Council for Trades and Occupations are responsible for the quality of instruction and training in schools, further education and training colleges and adult learning centres. In reviewing the design and development of courses and programmes, materials and support and the standards of assessment, their QA systems are designed to take account of the different modes of delivery employed in skills development and training, including DE.

Namibia is developing its own DE policies and frameworks. The country's four DE providers (the Centre for External Studies at the University of Namibia, the Centre for Open and Lifelong Learning at the Polytechnic of Namibia, the Namibian College of Open Learning and the National Institute for Educational Development) work with the Ministry of Education to coordinate their activities through the Namibian Open Learning Network Trust (NOLNet). NOLNet and the individual providers are working with the country's National Council for Higher Education to develop appropriate QA mechanisms for tertiary and non-tertiary level DE.

QA at the Institutional Level

Regardless of a lack of national DE policies and QA frameworks, some African institutions are developing their own QA systems. For example, the Institute of Adult Education in Tanzania, which is implementing five DE programmes for primary school leavers, secondary education dropouts and adult learners, places great emphasis on QA as it faces the challenge of dealing with negative stereotyping of DE (Lugakingira, 2008). The Open University of Tanzania has also adopted and adapted various processes to enhance QA, such as building regular formative and summative evaluation into its programmes. The National Open University of Nigeria (NOUN) has embedded QA into the activities of its Course Materials Development Unit which is responsible for identifying course and resource materials available to the various academic units of the university, organizing course writing workshops within and outside NOUN and ensuring quality in all course materials. NOUN participates in external QA through the national accreditation process of the Nigerian regulatory agency for higher education, the NUC. In Uganda, there are no national standards for QA in DE, but the Department of Distance Education at Kyambogo University has established its own policies and procedures (Binns & Otto, 2006). The University of South Africa (Unisa) is another university which has established its own QA framework for DE. Like all South African higher education institutions, Unisa follows the external national QA guidelines and criteria of the CHE, is accredited by the CHE, and all of its qualifications are registered with the South African Qualifications Authority. It has also obtained accreditation from the US Distance Education and Training Council. Unisa has a Department of Strategy, Planning and Quality Assurance, which is located in the Portfolio of the Vice-Principal and is the custodian for academic and institutional quality matters. The university conducts its own internal QA reviews of governance, planning, resource allocation, capacity building and the quality management system itself. It also has support unit and college-level quality committees focusing on such issues as scholarly publication, quality teaching and learning and community engagement. In regard to DE, the university has put in place a DE Policy, a Tuition Policy and a Framework for the Implementation of a Team Approach to Curriculum and Learning Development, all of which make reference to QA processes.

The Botswana College of Distance and Open Learning (BOCODOL) was established to improve access to learning opportunities on a nationwide scale for the out–of-school young adults. BOCODOL offers school equivalency programmes, certificate level vocational management and professional programmes and through collaboration with other regional open and distance learning institutions, has ventured into higher education, starting with diploma level programmes. The college plans to increase and diversify its higher education programmes. BOCODOL's senior management was only too aware of the stigma that could be attached to DE and alert to the negative forces of apathy, scepticism and resistance to change. To counter these, it established legislation and related strategies for QA and embedded these and DE policies in the college operations in such a way that they enhanced the activities but did not face staff resistance. To help build appreciation of the need for QA in DE operations, the managers adopt a consultative approach, regard the sensitization of staff as a continuous process and annually allocate funding for quality improvement activities such as staff training (Tau & Thutoetsile, 2006).

Transnational QA

The need for a 'home-grown' but collaborative approach to developing transnational QA and quality control mechanisms and sharing and scaling up programmes where universities have excess demand and limited supply has led to the formation of the Pan-African initiative, the African Virtual University (AVU). The AVU operates in a number of African countries, including Zambia, Ethiopia, Kenya, Madagascar, Mozambique, Senegal, Somalia, Tanzania, Uganda and Zimbabwe. It has phased out its earlier certificate, diploma and degree programmes brokered from foreign universities and is now collaborating with governments, universities, development agencies and private providers to offer academic and non-academic programmes and courses relevant to African contexts and the needs of local employers. In such a virtual network, establishing a QA system among different institutions with no or limited localized QA frameworks is very challenging. Dzvimbo and Kariuki (2006) observe that the AVU experience has shown that African institutions without mature QA systems tend to be more willing and likely to adopt other countries' QA systems, while universities with more established QA systems are likely to resist the imposition of external QA mechanisms.

One example of successful transnational collaboration in QA for DE is BOCODOL and the Namibian College of Open Learning. These two institutions signed a Memorandum of Understanding in 2002, which has resulted in the institutions jointly developing an inter-institutional quality framework, collaborating on QA issues and appointing quality audit teams to identify areas requiring improvement in the two institutions.

Conclusion

The exponential expansion of higher education enrolments throughout sub-Saharan Africa has led to the establishment of many new public and private universities offering face-to-face, blended and DE programmes. The growing realization of the need for QA and QA frameworks is reflected in the reported 40% growth in national QA agencies in the last 5 years (Okebukola, 2009) and the growing interest in QA at the institutional level. However, clearly there is still a great deal of work to be done here. There are significant variations in policies and procedures for QA and little has yet been done in regard to monitoring and assessing the quality of DE provision. Most of the work at national and at regional levels is concerned with QA in university-level DE. This is not surprising, because this is where the growth in DE and enrolment in cross-border programmes has been greatest. As interest grows in the use of DE in other sectors, the focus may need to broaden, particularly in regard to open schooling systems which are increasingly required in countries where entry into mainstream secondary schooling is constrained (Butcher, 2010).

Cross-border DE offers learners increased access to learning opportunities and higher quality education. It also builds international cooperation and enables virtual staff mobility. However, there is currently a lack of transnational QA frameworks and national regulatory mechanisms for cross-border higher education in

Africa. This calls for a code-of-good-practice in national, regional and continent-wide regulatory frameworks and, as Magagula (2005) observes, such a code would also need to provide assessment criteria for cross-border higher education programmes by foreign and private providers. There are great opportunities for the AUC, ACDE, AfriQAN and others to engage in such work, strengthen existing regional QA bodies and initiatives, become models for good practice and draw on their expertise and experience to help other countries and regions in Africa to establish similar systems. These agencies can also help to promote and maintain comparability and harmonization in African higher education quality standards. It is not yet possible to determine how these different agencies would operate and with what mandate, how they would be sustained, or what overall impact they might have. Nevertheless, the move towards continental and regional agencies providing QA for DE will be worth tracking in the future.

Where there is concern for the revitalization of higher education and improvement and assurance of quality, with a few exceptions, the quality guidelines and processes are concerned with higher education provision as a whole, rather than with the specific requirements of DE. Given that there are relatively few national QA guidelines in use in Africa, there would appear to be merit in incorporating QA of DE into broader educational QA guidelines and policies. This would mean that where countries and institutions do not have, or are developing, their QA frameworks, it would be possible to include DE and e-learning elements early in the formation of such frameworks, thus making it easier to ensure that innovation and QA go hand in hand. Further, if regional, national and institutional QA systems employ the same QA frameworks for conventional, distance and online learning, this may help to dispel any negative stereotyping of DE and e-learning. However, it could also be argued that dedicated DE QA policies can ensure that issues such as the quality of distance course and materials development, student and technology support receive the necessary degree of attention. Regardless of which approach is adopted, it is clear that additional QA focus on DE is required within continental, regional, national and institutional frameworks.

Notes

1 http://www.accesstosuccess-africa.eu/web/images/literature/mindafviii_arushacon
   v1.pdf
2 http://www.africa-union.org/root/ar/index/INDICATORS%20AND%20DATA%20
   FOR%20MONITORING%20-REPORT.pdf
3 http://www.africa-union.org/root/UA/Newsletter/EA/Vol3%20No1/Hoosen_Butcher_
   Njenga.pdf
4 http://www.africa-union.org/root/UA/Conferences/2007/aout/HRST/06-10%20
   aout/African%20HE%20Quality%20Rating%20Mechanism-%20E.doc
5 http://unesdoc.unesco.org/images/0015/001591/159197e.pdf
6 http://www.nqf.org.za/

References

Binns, F., & Otto, A. (2006). Quality assurance in open distance education – Towards a culture of quality: A case study from the Kyambogo University, Uganda. In B. N. Koul, & A. Kanwar (Eds.), *Perspectives on distance education: Towards a culture of quality* (pp. 31–34). Vancouver: Commonwealth of Learning.

Butcher, N. (2010, March). *Quality assurance of distance education: Lessons emerging from regional initiatives* [PowerPoint presentation]. Paper presented at the *Joint Seminar on Quality Assurance in e-Learning and Open Education Resources* (Africa, Arab States, Asia and the Pacific and Latin America), UNESCO, Paris. Retrieved from http://www.eadtu.nl/files/UNESCO%20March%202009/Presentations/day1_2009.03.12.UNESCO%20QA%20on%20DE%20presentation.ppt

Dzvimbo, K. P., & Kariuki, C.W. (2006). Quality assurance in the African Virtual University: A case study. In B. N. Koul, & A. Kanwar (Eds.), *Perspectives on distance education: Towards a culture of quality* (pp. 59–72). Vancouver: Commonwealth of Learning.

Hoosen, S., Butcher, N., & Njenga, B. K. (2009). Harmonization of higher education programmes: A strategy for the African Union. *African Integration Review, 3*(1), 1–36. Retrieved from http://www.africa-union.org/root/UA/Newsletter/EA/Vol3%20No1/Hoosen_Butcher_Njenga.pdf

Jegede, O. (2009, August). ACDE continental quality assurance initiative. *Proceedings of the First Vice-Chancellor's Workshop Organized by the African Council for Distance Education – Technical Committee on Collaboration (ACDE-TCC),* (pp. 37–45). Nairobi, Kenya: African Council for Distance Education.

Lugakingira, E. R. (2008). Quality assurance practices: The experience of the Institute of Adult Education in the provision of open schooling and distance learning in Tanzania. *COL Quality Assurance Workshop Report.* Vancouver: Commonwealth of Learning. Retrieved from http://www.col.org/SiteCollectionDocuments/Quality-Assurance-Wrkshp-Report.pdf

Magagula, C. M. (2005). *The benefits and challenges of cross-border higher education in developing countries.* Boston College & Council for the Development of Social Science Research in Africa. *JHEA/RESA, 3*(1), 29–49. Retrieved from http://unpan1.un.org/intradoc/groups/public/documents/IDEP/UNPAN022975.pdf

Okebukola, P. (2009, January). *African higher education and quality assurance.* Paper presentation at the *CHEA 2009 Annual Conference and National Accreditation Forum,* Washington, DC. Retrieved from http://www.chea.org/pdf/2009_IS_African_Higher_Education_and_Quality_Assurance_Okebukola.pdf

Olojede, A.A. (n.d.). *Issues and challenges in enhancing quality assurance in open and distance learning in Nigeria.* Retrieved from http://www.wikieducator.org/images/3/35/PID_628.pdf

Pityana, N. B. (2008, April). *A decade of development and education in Africa: The promise of open and distance learning.* Keynote address presented at the *5th Pan Commonwealth Forum on Open Learning,* London, UK. Retrieved from http://uir.unisa.ac.za/bitstream/handle/10500/33/PCF_5Speech_NBP_editedFinal.pdf?sequence=1

Tau, D., & Thutoetsile, T. (2006). Quality assurance in distance education: Towards a culture of quality in Botswana College of Distance and Open Learning. In B. N. Koul, & A. Kanwar (Eds.), *Perspectives on distance education: Towards a culture of quality* (pp. 19–30). Vancouver: Commonwealth of Learning.

Welch, T., & Reed, Y. (2005). *Designing and delivering distance education: Quality criteria and case studies from South Africa.* Johannesburg: NADEOSA.

6

QUALITY ASSURANCE AND ACCREDITATION IN THE UNITED STATES AND CANADA

Nancy K. Parker

Introduction

The past two decades have witnessed expansion, diversification and the wide adoption of various forms of distance and online learning in higher education in North America. In the United States, between 1988–2008 the total number of degree-granting institutions grew by more than 1,000, the for-profit sector evidenced some of the strongest growth and the expansion of distance and online enrolments outstripped the growth in campus-based operations. The same period also witnessed growing concerns over the quality of higher education in the United States and the effectiveness of the self-regulating accreditation agencies.

In Canada, public institutions still largely define the post-secondary system but the increased number of degree-granting institutions is also generating new demands for accountability. The net of common understanding which prized input measures (entering class averages, seat time, faculty qualifications, the number of volumes in the library and so on) to rank a narrow group of more elite institutions no longer applies.

Canada and the United States both lack central regulatory bodies to oversee higher education and, as federations, both countries exhibit tensions between local and national systems. A complicated patchwork of licensing requirements and accreditation standards confronts providers wishing to extend their reach beyond a single state or province. Rogue operators take advantage of the regulatory gaps, and their operations have a negative impact on the reputation of online learning as a whole. Various initiatives aimed at consumer protection also create tensions as the universities strive to maintain their traditional autonomy and competitive market positions.

US QA and Accreditation Systems

As Gallagher (2010) observes, many countries have established comprehensive arrangements for quality assurance (QA) in higher education that feature direct oversight by government organizations. The United States has no central regulatory body to oversee QA or accreditation in the higher education sector. The licensing of institutions and authority to grant degrees is within the jurisdiction of individual states and there is no national qualifications framework. The US Department of Education recognizes institutions, including those which provide open and distance learning (ODL) programmes, that are licensed to operate and meet the minimum standards set by accrediting organizations recognized by the Department as 'reliable authorities'. These include six large regional accrediting associations such as the Middle States Commission on Higher Education and the Northwest Commission on Colleges and Universities, four faith-based accrediting associations such as the Association for Biblical Higher Education Commission and the Accreditation Commission of the Association of Advanced Rabbinical and Talmudic Schools, 22 specialized and hybrid associations largely for single-purpose institutions (including such bodies as the Accreditation Commission for Midwifery Education and American Board of Funeral Service Education), five sector- or career-based national associations (for example, the Accrediting Council for Continuing Education and Training and the Distance Education and Training Council or DETC) and one state system (New York State Board of Regents and the Commissioner of Education). In addition to accrediting organizations which review standards at the institutional level, there are more than 60 programme-based organizations engaged in discipline-specific accreditation reviews. This range of accrediting organizations reflects the diversity in the higher education system and the autonomy of institutions in setting and implementing their distinct missions.

Self-assessment and peer review are the hallmarks of US accreditation processes. These seek to address both minimum standard requirements and encourage continuous quality improvement. They are not transparent auditing systems, they do not allow for direct comparisons of institutions and only the final decisions of the accreditation agency are required to be made public. The strongest federal lever on the system is through student financial aid. This is most commonly administered through the federally-funded Title IV programme which encompasses a number of grant and loan programmes to support qualified students in post-secondary and higher education. To be eligible for these, students must be attending an institution which is held to be in good standing by a recognized accreditation agency.

The lack of national standards which would allow for consistency and reciprocity between state regulators is problematic for institutions operating in more than one state. Some states may recognize regional accreditation as a proxy for regulatory oversight, but the possibility of circular requirements is real. If, in order to be accredited by a regional association, an institution must be licensed to operate in all of the states where it has students, and if, in order to be licensed, an institution must be accredited, then gaining accreditation can be problematic (Kelderman, 2010a). Also, depending on the definition of 'physical presence', online institutions could be in violation of federal student loan regulations if their students maintain their enrolments and loans while moving between states. Obtaining multiple licenses is possible for large operators, but places a disproportionate regulatory burden on the smaller operators. However, the notion of federal departments dictating how the states should regulate public and commercial enterprises within their borders raises constitutional and political questions.

The gaps between state jurisdictions and variability in enforcement of licensing requirements provide room for rogue operators (Ezell & Bear, 2005; Pina, 2010). The need for additional quality standards and recognition processes becomes more pressing for institutions when state regulatory bodies are not sufficiently rigorous in protecting students and the reputation of higher education. The opportunities for online providers to offer degrees to students everywhere but in the state from which they actually operate, is a recipe for the operation of 'degree mills', and regulatory improvements in one state have prompted less reputable operators to move to another state (Gruver, 2007).

The complexity of the US accreditation system, the operations of degree mills and the rising public and private expenditures have led to increased demands for accountability and transparency. In 2005, under the Bush administration, Secretary of Education Margaret Spellings sponsored the formation of the Commission on the Future of Higher Education (also known as the Spellings Commission).[1] In its 2006 report, the Commission focused on four key areas: access, affordability, quality in instruction and the accountability of institutions to their constituencies. The President of the Council for Higher Education Accreditation openly acknowledged the criticism of the accreditation system, saying, 'It is charged with neglect of the rigor of undergraduate education and an inability to provide comparable data about the quality of institutions and programs (and) failing to meet current transparency expectations' (Eaton, 2008). The change of administration may have changed the tone, but not the need for reforms. Addressing the Council of Higher Education Accreditation Meeting in 2010, Under Secretary of Education Martha J. Kantar urged higher education to 'work toward a modern culture of accountability' (Lederman, 2010).

Canadian QA and Accreditation Systems

Unlike the United States, with its 50 states, Canada comprises ten provinces and three territories. However, while notably smaller, the Canadian post-secondary system has even less cohesion than the US system. There is no national or even regional accreditation. There is only voluntary membership of the Association of Universities and Colleges of Canada (AUCC), a non-governmental, not-for-profit organization representing 95 Canadian public and private not-for-profit universities and university-degree level colleges. Membership of the AUCC along with a provincial charter to grant degrees is used as *de facto* accreditation in Canada. The federal government in Ottawa operates the Canada Student Loan Programme, but eligibility is determined on a programme-by-programme basis by the provincial regulators. A degree qualification framework was developed nationally by the Council of Ministers of Education in Canada (CMEC) and has been adopted by individual provinces, but degree-granting authority within one province does not necessarily permit operations in another.

Determining how to approach ODL and its cross-border implications has been a topic for discussion by the Quality Assurance Working Group of the CMEC. The regulation of e-learning within each province partly depends upon the definition of 'physical presence'. Institutions from different provinces actively recruit students from across the country but may be barred from offering onsite services such as academic advising or examination invigilation, if they have not had each of their programmes reviewed by the provincial authority. The provincial QA bodies that do exist generally require review of the appropriateness of the delivery method, faculties' qualifications, students' characteristics, admissions, student support services, library resources, resources to support the mode of delivery and policies on student protection. The national degree qualifications framework and review processes do not distinguish between the different modes of delivery, but the assessment boards in British Columbia, Ontario, and Alberta do have additional benchmark statements for distance delivery.

In the past two decades, Alberta, British Columbia, New Brunswick and Ontario have introduced legislation to permit new private degree-granting institutions and to establish arms-length quality assessment agencies to review providers and their programmes. For the most part, pre-existing programmes in public institutions are exempt from the new regulatory regimes. However, relaxing the regulations for private providers and allowing new for-profit institutions in Canada has proved to be a perilous course of action, as shown below.

Issues of QA and Accreditation in North American ODL

The variability in accreditation and licensing standards between jurisdictions continues to raise issues in Canada. In 2006, student complaints sparked an investigation into the activities of the private, for-profit Kingston College in Burnaby, British Columbia, which had brought Indian students to Canada to study for a 2-year master's degree to be awarded from the unaccredited American University in London (which had already been fined in the UK for misleading prospective students by representing itself as an accredited institution) or Armstrong University, a small private company incorporated in California (now closed). The former Private Post-Secondary Education Commission of British Columbia had attempted to close down this institution in 2000, 2001 and 2004, and its successor, the Private Career Training Agency of British Columbia (PICTIA) finally achieved this in 2006. Because the Kingston Education Group also had campuses in Toronto and Niagara Falls, PICTIA then alerted its Ontario counterpart to the results of its investigation (Steffenhagen, 2006). The students who originally sparked the investigation into Kingston College said they felt betrayed by a country they once viewed as a bastion of education. A wider consequence of these incidents in British Columbia and Ontario was that the Chinese government warned students not to enrol with any Canadian private colleges (Schmidt, 2007). Rogue operators cast a much wider shadow than in a single regulatory area.

Lansbridge University in Vancouver was also part of the Kingston Education Group. In June 2005, it won approval to operate as a private, for-profit university offering bachelor and master's programmes in business administration, online or at its West 12th Avenue campus. Its previous application, in 2001, had been rejected. In February 2007, the British Columbia government also ordered this institution to close for non-compliance after an independent inspector found serious violations of provincial law similar to those uncovered at Kingston College (Steffenhagen, 2007). It can still be found on directories of non-accredited institutions. In 2004, Lansbridge University had also been granted authority to offer degrees in New Brunswick. Lansbridge University New Brunswick (LUNB) was accredited by the US DETC in 2005 and described itself as Canada's premier online business university, offering MBA and Executive MBA programmes. Degree subject specialists' reports from the DETC posted on LUNB's website[2] noted that these programmes only partially met the required standards for curriculum currency and failed to meet the standards for student assessment. However, this had no immediate effect on the institution's status. LUNB was then reviewed by the Maritime Provinces Higher Education Council, the body responsible for the review of private, degree-granting institutions. On August 20, 2010 LUNB was notified that, as a consequence of the shortcomings found during two separate council reviews and a subsequent onsite inspection, under the Degree Granting Act of the Province of New Brunswick, the Minister of Post-Secondary Training and Labour revoked permission for the institution to operate within that province. The Minister, Donald Arseneault, observed:

> We have an obligation to ensure that our online universities offer high-quality programs. We have a number of other online universities operating in the province that offer quality programming, and, as such, we must ensure standards are upheld across the board
>
> *(Government of New Brunswick, Post-Secondary Education,*
> *Training and Labour, 2010)*

Whether these regulatory actions will actually protect the reputation of the sector as a whole is still open to question.

Online education carries the dual burdens of rapid growth and deepening suspicion about its quality, especially as for-profit providers attract larger proportions of student financial assistance. The growth in the for-profit sector, wherein the number of institutions in the United States increased by more than 200% between 1998–2008 and enrolments by more than 500%, has been phenomenal. Another significant increase has been in the use of distance and online education. In the 2006–2007 academic year, 66% of the 4,160 2-year and 4-year public and private for-profit degree-granting post-secondary institutions in the United States offered distance education courses. Of the estimated 12.2 million enrolments in distance education, 77% were in online courses, 12% in hybrid or blended online courses and 10% in other types of distance education provision (IES, 2008).

The rapid growth of the for-profit institutions and their dominance in online education is having an impact on perceptions of the sector and the effectiveness of regional accreditation. In the early 1990s in the United States, in an attempt to curb the rise of the degree mills, there was a ban on student aid funding for programmes in which more than 50% was taken at a distance. The easing of the 50% rule in 2006 was seen as both a harbinger of change for higher education and a testament to the successful lobbying of the for-profits (Dillon, 2006). However, the more recent amendments to the Higher Education Opportunities Act (Public Law 110–315)[3] requiring online post-secondary institutions to verify and validate that the students who are awarded college degrees actually complete the coursework arose from persistent concerns about fraud. With total federal aid to students now running in excess of $150 billion (US Department of Education, 2010a) attention is being given to the higher education system as a whole and for-profit institutions in particular.

In a testimony to a Senate subcommittee in 2010, the US Government Accountability Office reported on its undercover investigation of 15 for-profit colleges in six states and Washington DC (Government Accountability Office, 2010). It had found aggressive, misleading and sometimes fraudulent recruitment tactics and far higher student loan default rates in the for-profit sector than in the private non-profit and public sectors. In releasing these findings, US Secretary of Education Arne Duncan observed:

> While for-profit schools have profited and prospered thanks to federal dollars, some of their students have not. Far too many for-profit schools are saddling students with debt they cannot afford in exchange for degrees and certificates they cannot use. This is a disservice to students and taxpayers, and undermines the valuable work being done by the for-profit education industry as a whole
>
> *(US Department of Education, 2010b)*

For-profit providers are not new to the US higher education system but their degree-granting status and the prevalence of a few very large players are certainly having an impact. Jones International University, founded in 1993, claims to be the first completely virtual university in the United States to be accredited by one of the six regional commissions – the Higher Learning Commission of the North Central Association of Colleges and Schools. The 19-state territory of this regional accreditor also includes such well-known for-profit institutions as University of Phoenix (UoP), DeVry University, Walden University, Kaplan University, Capella University and most recently, the American Intercontinental University – about which questions have already been raised by the Department of Education in regard to the validity of its application of credit hours and the effectiveness of its peer review processes (Kelderman, 2010b).

Concerns about the quality of the institutions accredited by the Higher Learning Commission of the North Central Association of Colleges and Schools were heightened by an investigation into student recruitment practices. In 1992, Congress banned all post-secondary institutions, including private for-profit, public and private non-profit providers participating in federal student aid programmes, from paying commissions, bonuses or other financial incentives to individuals, based on their success in enrolling students or securing their financial aid. Fines levied against institutions, including $9.8 million dollars paid by UoP in 2004, do not appear to have stopped these questionable practices. In 2010, the US Government Accountability Office found evidence of deceptive or fraudulent recruitment practices in certain institutions which had misrepresented programmes or encouraged students to falsify their financial aid applications to obtain federal student aid. Shortly after the release of this report, the Higher Learning Commission (2010) announced that it would enquire further into the integrity of the criteria of these for-profit providers. The Apollo Group, which owns UoP and several other for-profit educational institutions, immediately posted a notice that it was required to provide evidence of compliance with all state and federal laws in its accreditation standards and recruitment practices (Apollo Group, 2010a). For better or for worse, UoP attracts far more attention than the other for-profit institutions, partly due to its size, scope and rapid growth. It has been estimated that a quarter of the total enrolment increase in the for-profit sector between 1999–2003 was directly attributable to its online division. Currently, UoP has nearly 400,000 students, more than some state systems.

In response to growing criticisms about recruitment practices and student aid, and presumably to falling stock prices, the Apollo Group issued a position paper in August 2010 stressing the proprietary colleges' and universities' role in meeting the needs for US labour force development (Apollo Group, 2010b). It underscored the organization's commitment to 'delivering quality education to those *who are willing to work hard enough* [emphasis added] to realize its benefits', and accused critics of the proprietary sector's reliance on student financial aid funds of 'questioning whether non-traditional and socio-economically disadvantaged individuals deserve the right to [have]…access to education'. Thus, the high withdrawal and subsequent loan default rates were attributed to the students' lack of diligence and totally unconnected to institutional practices. The document positioned profit interests as aligning with a nationalist aim of increasing the global competitiveness of the US workforce. The Apollo Group acknowledged the importance of regulatory compliance, noting their authorization to operate in 43 states, accreditation by the Higher Learning Commission and their own internal QA mechanisms. At the same time, they also announced a new evaluation and compensation plan for instructors and councillors and that their payments would not be linked to the number of students they enroled or taught. It remains to be seen whether these moves will be sufficient to ease the concerns of the regulators and accreditors.

The success of the large for-profit multi-campus and online providers rests on different operating assumptions from the other degree-awarding institutions. Their curricula are specifically designed to appeal to employers and adult learners desirous of flexible scheduling, lesser prior learning requirements and speedier degree completion. Institutionally, lower overheads are achieved by economies of scale, lighter campus footprints and the use of part-time instructors. Since the input measures for such operations do not fit the traditional quality markers, greater emphasis is placed on accessibility and learning outcomes.

Tools for Greater Transparency

So what can be done about rogue operators and degree mills? Clearly greater vigilance and transparency are needed. However, in the US, as Gallagher (2010) observes, there appears to be little appetite for a centralized model of government regulation.

The state of Oregon is known for its rigorous approach with its Office of Degree Authorization maintaining a website of unaccredited institutions,[4] and its provisions to penalize individuals who claim credentials from unauthorized institutions on employment applications. It also lists seven states where there may be problems with degree suppliers due to poor control systems and recommends that individuals confirm the standing of these institutions. This approach can best be characterized as 'buyer beware' in a market where information may not be readily available. It is also incumbent upon institutions to improve their transparency.

The US Higher Education Opportunities Act of 2008 sets out requirements to improve transparency in regard to tuition and fees by establishing criteria for net price calculations. As part of its cost-transparency measures, it requires the US Department of Education's free consumer information tool for students, parents, high school counsellors and others, College Navigator,[5] to develop a multi-year tuition and required-fees calculator for undergraduate programmes to inform first-time, full-time and Title IV aid recipients of the institutional net price of attendance. Other information in College Navigator includes estimated student expenses, enrolment, admissions requirements, retention and graduate rates, programmes and majors, accreditation and cohort default rates. It does not provide side-by-side comparisons or rating tables, but it has the virtue of being relatively comprehensive. Another tool is College Choices for Adults[6] which provides information about distance education courses for busy adults, what they entail, how other students have performed on these and reviews by leading organizations is in distance higher education. In Canada, the Council of Ontario Universities has a similar site, CUDO[7]. This offers key data, in a common format, about Ontario's universities:

- Number of degrees awarded, student enrolment and entering averages – all by programme.
- Number of students living on campus and activities offered.
- Student satisfaction.
- First-year tuition and ancillary fees by programme.
- Number of teaching faculty.
- Undergraduate class size, by year level.
- Research awards granted.
- Graduation rates and employment rates by programme.

Such online information can be invaluable for students, parents and the public, although not always suitable for distance education providers. However, such voluntary disclosure signals the willingness of the higher education sector to be accountable without tighter regulation by the federal, state or provincial governments.

Conclusion

The QA agenda for distance and online higher education in North America has a mixed pedigree. It reflects the interests of institutions working to preserve their autonomy in expanding and complex regulatory environments, competitive interests as new providers enter the market and concern for the legitimacy of the sector as a whole. While the public–private-profit nexus is not fully predicated on ownership classifications, recent questions about the efficacy of the regulatory and accrediting systems in North America have tended to focus on the impact of the for-profit sector.

The degree to which higher education can demonstrate success by being more accessible and inclusive runs counter to the longstanding claims of quality by the more elitist traditional institutions. Voluntary disclose initiatives include more throughput and output estimations but attempts to demonstrate 'return on investment' remain problematic. It is extremely difficult to define and monetize learning outcomes without curtailing some of the freedoms currently enjoyed by the academy. Many of these tensions are not unique to distance and online education. Higher education in general is repeatedly being challenged to demonstrate its value relative to the investments of both tax and tuition payers – and the transparency of the Internet makes retreating behind ivy-covered walls a doubtful proposition.

Notes

1 http://www2.ed.gov/about/bdscomm/list/hiedfuture/reports/final-report.pdf
2 http://www.detc.org/downloads/bulletins/2011/No.%202%20-%20Report%20from%20the%20Accrediting%20Commission.pdf
3 http://www2.ed.gov/policy/highered/leg/hea08/index.html
4 http://www.osac.state.or.us/oda/unaccredited.aspx
5 http://nces.ed.gov/collegenavigator/
6 http://www.collegechoicesforadults.org/
7 http://www.cou.on.ca/statistics.aspx

References

Apollo Group. (2010a, August 16). *Report of unscheduled material events or corporate event (SEC Form 8-K).* Retrieved from http://phx.corporate-ir.net/phoenix.zhtml?c=79624&p=irol-sec

Apollo Group. (2010b, August 23). *Higher education at a crossroads.* Retrieved from http://www.apollogrp.edu/Investor/Reports/Higher_Education_at_a_Crossroads_FINALv2%5B1%5D.pdf

Dillon, S. (2006, March 1). Online colleges receive a boost from Congress. *The New York Times.* Retrieved from http://www.nytimes.com/2006/03/01/national/01educ.html

Eaton, J. S. (2008). US accreditation: Bridging the international and national dialogue gap. *International Higher Education, 50*(53), 16–17. Retrieved from http://www.bc.edu/research/cihe/ihe/issues/2008.html

Ezell, A., & Bear, J. (2005). *Degree mills: The billion-dollar industry that has sold over a million fake diplomas.* Amherst, NY: Prometheus Books.

Gallagher, M. (2010). *The accountability for quality agenda in higher education.* Canberra: Group of Eight Australia. Retrieved from http://www.go8.edu.au/__documents/go8-policy-analysis/2010/accountability-for-quality-agenda/0_introduction.pdf

Government Accountability Office. (2010, August 4). *For-profit colleges: Undercover testing finds colleges encouraged fraud and engaged in deceptive and questionable marketing practices.* Retrieved from http://www.gao.gov/products/GAO-10-948T

Government of New Brunswick, Post-Secondary Education, Training and Labour. (2010, August 20). *Government takes action to protect students.* Retrieved from http://www2.gnb.ca/content/gnb/en/news/news_release.2010.08.1479.html

Gruver, M. (2007, March 15). New law prompts online school changes. *Casper Star Tribune.* Retrieved from http://trib.com/news/state-and-regional/article_833757cb-3c6b-5a35-a89f-b5265b392a56.html

Higher Learning Commission of the North Central Association of Colleges and Schools. (2010, August 13). *Commission statement on marketing practices at for-profit institutions.* Retrieved from http://www.ncahlc.org/

IES. (2008). *Fast facts.* Washington, DC: National Center for Educational Statistics. Retrieved from http://nces.ed.gov/fastfacts/display.asp?id=80

Kelderman, E. (2010a, April 18). Online educators balk at proposal requiring state authorizations. *The Chronicle of Higher Education.* Retrieved from http://chronicle.com/article/Online-Educators-Balk-at-Pr/65160/

Kelderman, E. (2010b, March 27). Inspector general keeps pressure on a regional accreditor. *The Chronicle of Higher Education.* Retrieved from http://chronicle.com/article/Inspector-General-Keeps-the/65691/

Lederman, D. (2010, January 27). Assessment disconnect. *Inside Higher Education.* Retrieved from http://www.insidehighered.com/news/2010/01/27/aacu

Pina, A. A. (2010). Online diploma mills: Implications for legitimate distance education. *Distance Education, 31*(1). 121–126.

Schmidt, S. (2007, January 18). China demands Canada protect its students from educational rip-offs. *CanWest News Service.* Retrieved from http://www.canada.com/nationalpost/story.html?id=a0f3e151-49b2-4153-bb82-2288720fb689&k=0

Steffenhagen, J. (2006, October 23). We feel betrayed: Kingston College Students. *The Vancouver Sun.* Retrieved from http://www.canada.com/vancouversun/story.html?id=99fd13cb-3e93-44b9-bde4-a42d3179631f&k=18701

Steffenhagen, J. (2007, February 9). Lansbridge University told to close over violations. *The Vancouver Sun.* Retrieved from http://www2.canada.com/vancouversun/news/story.html?id=725a5296-e1bf-4368-8846-baab4eeedb83&k=81405

US Department of Education. (2010a). *Fiscal Year 2011 Budget Summary – February 1, 2010.* Retrieved from http://www2.ed.gov/about/overview/budget/budget11/summary/edlite-section3d.html#tables

US Department of Education. (2010b, September 13). *Student loan default rates increase borrowers at for-profit school represent large and growing share of loan defaults.* Retrieved from http://www.ed.gov/news/press-releases/student-loan-default-rates-increase-0

7

QUALITY ASSURANCE AND ACCREDITATION FOR DISTANCE EDUCATION IN THE UNITED KINGDOM

Denise Kirkpatrick

Introduction

The UK uses an integrated approach to assuring quality in higher education, applying the same processes and standards to all institutions and, importantly in the context of this book, across all modes of delivery. Being a unitary state, the UK has a single national quality assurance (QA) system for higher education with some adaptations to take account of the three devolved national administrations of Scotland, Wales and Northern Ireland. This chapter outlines the work of the main agencies involved in this work – the Quality Assurance Agency (QAA) for Higher Education, the British Standards Institute (BSI), the British Accreditation Council (BAC) and the Open and Distance Learning Quality Council (ODL QC). It also considers the UK's approaches to QA and accreditation within the context of the EU.

The QAA and Higher Education

All universities and colleges that provide higher education in the UK are considered to be independent and self-governing. They are not owned by the state, but most receive government funding distributed by the separate higher education funding councils for England, Scotland and Wales, and the Department for Employment and Learning in Northern Ireland. Being autonomous, the individual institutions have the primary responsibility for assuring academic standards and quality. How well they meet these responsibilities is the responsibility of the QAA.[1]

The QAA is an independent body which is funded by the higher education institutions themselves and works closely with the major UK funding bodies, UK government departments and representative bodies such as Universities UK, Universities Scotland and GuildHE (an organization representing the heads of higher education institutions, formerly known as the Standing Conference of Principals). The QAA is responsible for checking how well the various institutions meet their responsibilities through a regular cycle of audit and review, identifying good practice, making recommendations for improvement and publishing guidelines to help institutions develop effective systems to ensure students have high quality experiences. The QAA approach to assuring academic quality and standards does not identify, nor does it consider the provision of distance education separately from the provision of on–campus education.

Each university and college of higher education is responsible for the standards of the awards it makes and the quality of the education it provides to its students. To achieve this, each has its own internal QA procedures and these are guided by the QAA's Academic Infrastructure.[2] The Academic Infrastructure is a set of nationally agreed reference points which give all institutions a shared starting point for setting, describing and assuring the quality and standards of their higher education courses. It has four interrelated elements: the code of practice, programme specifications, subject benchmark statements and frameworks for higher education qualifications (in England, Wales and Northern Ireland; and in Scotland). The code of practice for the assurance of academic quality and standards in higher education is concerned with the management of quality and the other three elements provide advice to institutions about the setting of standards. The use of the Academic Infrastructure contributes to a high level of confidence in the coherence of academic programmes and greater comparability across degree courses at different higher education institutions.

The QAA's *Code of Practice for the Assurance of Academic Quality and Standards in Higher Education*[3] comprises ten sections and provides guidance on maintaining quality and standards for those universities and colleges that subscribe to the QAA. It provides a framework within which a higher education institution can consider the effectiveness of its approach to a range of activities that contribute to academic standards and quality. The areas covered by this code of practice include: postgraduate research programmes; collaborative provision and flexible and distributed learning (including e-learning); disabled students; external examining; academic appeals and student complaints on academic matters; assessment of students; programme design, approval, monitoring and review; career education, information, advice and guidance; work-based and placement learning and admissions to higher education.

This code of practice was developed in consultation with the higher education sector and with the participation of key stakeholder groups and consequently reflects the concerns and views of both the users and providers of higher education in the UK. It was originally prepared between 1998–2001. Revisions of individual sections began in 2004 to reflect changing circumstances and sections of the code are regularly revised.

Each section of the code of practice identifies the key issues that an institution should consider in the respective area of activity. The QAA's precepts (expectations/principles) summarize those matters that an institution could reasonably be expected to address through its own internal QA arrangements. The accompanying guidance and explanation suggest possible ways by which these expectations may be met and demonstrated. The code of practice is underpinned by a set of principles related to the assurance of quality and standards to which all institutions are expected to comply. It is intended to provide broad guidance and is neither prescriptive nor exhaustive.

Of particular relevance to this book is *Section 2: Collaborative provision and flexible and distributed learning (including e-learning).*[4] This document serves as a code of practice for the academic management of learning delivered, supported and/or assessed through flexible and distributed arrangements at an awarding institution or in collaboration with other institutions. It was first published in 1999, revised in 2004 and amplified in 2010. The inclusion of a section relating to flexible and distributed learning is an acknowledgement of the expansion of the use of information and communications technology (ICT)-based and blended learning in higher education. Moreover, as stressed within this code, the revision may be characterized as moving from the process-based style of the earlier version to a more outcomes-based approach. It is clear that the distance education methodologies are to be included, as the QAA definition of distributed and flexible learning includes approaches to learning, teaching and assessment that do not require a student's place of study to be physically located within the institution and do not necessarily require that assessment of a student's achievements should take place at the location of the awarding institution.

The code of practice acknowledges that there are particular aspects specific to the academic management of the delivery, support and assessment of flexible and distance learning programmes that should be considered. In recognition of the myriad forms that flexible and distributed learning may take, the code of practice is not organized according to traditional academic functions. Instead, it takes the perspective of the student and is structured around: the delivery of a flexible and distributed programme of study, the support of students of that programme and the security of academic standards of the award and assessment of the achievements of those students. This inclusive approach allows for consideration of the various ways in which an institution may offer flexible or distance education without making assumptions about preferred models or organizational structures. And it signifies the importance of the student experience.

The code of practice is based on the underpinning principle that flexible provision should widen learning opportunities without damaging or compromising the academic standard of the award or the quality of what is experienced by students. In addition, the arrangements for assuring quality and standards should be as rigorous, secure and open to scrutiny as those for programmes through traditional campus-based modes of teaching. The code acknowledges the challenges involved in managing the potential risks associated with flexible and distributed learning which include security of information and assessment/grades, 'distance' between the student and the institution and assuring the identity of the learner.

The precepts that comprise the section of the code that relates to flexible and distributed learning are concerned with a student's experience of study. The code highlights the importance of the provision of information to students about the mode of study, requirements, assessment and reliability of the delivery system used, and emphasizes that the study materials will be subject to the same rigorous QA as in any other programme of study. Many of the dimensions mirror points made elsewhere in the code in relation to on-campus delivery but with specific reference to the particular demands presented by flexible and distributed provision. Therefore, this section of the code identifies support provided to learners, including the provision of feedback and guidance and the skills of those providing the support. It also identifies the need for an awarding institution to have mechanisms that allow the correct attribution of work to an individual student and for the confirmation that the work submitted is that of the individual student. This of course is a particularly salient consideration in distance and e-learning contexts as is the need for security and authentication in situations where remote or distributed assessment practices are utilized.

QAA and Collaborative Provision

The code of practice addresses both collaborative provision and flexible and distributed e-learning arrangements because, in practice, collaborative provision with a partner organization is often enabled or supported by the use of flexible and distributed learning. The QAA uses the term collaborative provision to denote 'educational provision leading to an award, or to specific credit toward an award, of an awarding institution delivered and/or supported and/or assessed through an arrangement with a partner organization'. Prior to 2004, collaborative provision mostly involved an awarding higher education institution with another publicly funded or overseas provider as a partner. UK institutions are now increasing their stake in the global marketplace and the UK government is encouraging new forms of collaborative provision and new types of provider in order to widen participation, promote lifelong learning and increase student employability. As a result, collaboration now has a broader and more diverse meaning. The October 2010 amplified version of *Section 2a* reflects the broader and more diverse portfolios of collaborative provision that institutions are now likely to have. The code of practice contains the QAA's precepts (expectations/principles) for the management of academic standards and quality in collaborative provision. The current approach is outcomes-based, focusing on ends rather than means, and institutions are encouraged to consider how the learning opportunities available to students compare between the collaborative provision and the 'home' provision.

The management of collaborative provision is included in QAA audits, either within the institutional audit process, through a separate audit of the institution's management of collaborative provision, or through a hybrid institutional audit. The approach is determined by the scale and variety of collaborative provision. In all cases, the audits are evidence based and conducted through peer review. The aim is to determine the reliability of the evidence on which an institution satisfies itself that the academic standards of its awards and credits are secure and that no problems exist in its partnership links.

QAA and Overseas Provision

Many UK universities and colleges also offer programmes to students studying outside the country, either at campuses directly run by the UK institutions or through collaborative arrangements with foreign partners. The QAA reviews both collaborative provision and programmes delivered on overseas campuses through the audit of overseas provision process. QAA's overseas audit is intended to improve confidence in the work of UK universities and colleges operating internationally. The audits of overseas provision are conducted on a whole-of-country basis and provide information about the way in which a group of UK universities and colleges maintain academic standards and the quality of provision in a designated country.

QAA Scotland

While the QAA works across the whole of the UK, it has a separate Scottish office, QAA Scotland.[5] This works closely with the Scottish Government, Universities Scotland, the Scottish Funding Council and other Scottish higher education organizations to develop and operate arrangements that reflect the needs of higher education north of the border. Much of its work centres on the Quality Enhancement Framework (QEF). It is this feature that distinguishes the Scottish approach from QA in the rest of the UK and is considered to be of interest to readers as it may be seen as the next logical step in QA. The QEF brings right to the fore the simple but powerful idea that the purpose of QA systems is to improve student experiences and consequently, their learning. This radical approach to QA and enhancement in higher education was introduced in Scotland in 2003. It involves the use of enhancement-led institutional review (ELIR),[6] which focuses on an institution's ability to manage the standards of its academic awards and the quality of the learning opportunities it provides for its students. Again, no distinction is made on the basis of modes of delivery employed by the institution.

The QAA Scotland *Enhancement-led Institutional Review Handbook*[7] has five key themes:

1. Enhancement includes assurance – seeking to learn from current activities and assurance and enhancement inextricably linked within the quality cultures of institutions.
2. Looking forward – how an institution learns from the past in order to inform the future.
3. Enhancement and risk – enhancement, change and innovation frequently involve risk. Institutions are expected to manage this risk in a way that provides reasonable safeguards for current students. The review process will recognize and support effective risk management and adopt a supportive and not punitive role in this context.
4. Supporting diversity – the review process will support the rich diversity of higher education institutions in Scotland and consequently engage with the enhancement of the learning experiences of students in the context of their own institution.
5. The UK and international context – the review process and outcomes will be used to promote the high standing of Scottish higher education internationally.

The ELIR is based on a comprehensive programme of subject reviews run by the institutions themselves. This is supported by the external review of all Scottish higher education institutions over a 4-year cycle. A high level of attention is given to improving and expanding the provision of public information about quality for a range of stakeholders including students, parents and employers. The role of students in the process is acknowledged through the provision of a stronger voice for student representatives in institutional quality systems, supported by a new national development service. QAA Scotland also operates a national programme of enhancement themes, designed to encourage academic and support staff and students to share good practice and work together to generate ideas and models for innovation in learning and teaching.

Working closely with the institutions, QAA Scotland places more weight on consensual approaches than on the more coercive stances embedded in some QA regimes, moves away from audit and towards improvement, balances QA and enhancement, emphasizes the student experience and focuses on learning rather than teaching. In common with QAA approaches elsewhere in the UK, it focuses on the academic management of delivery, support and evaluation of teaching, learning and assessment rather than the mode of delivery and views the quality of outcomes as of greater significance than the processes or methods that comprise the inputs.

The British Accreditation Council and Independent Further and Higher Education

While the QAA assures the quality and standards of UK-funded higher education, the British Accreditation Council (BAC)[8] is responsible for QA in the independent further and higher education sector. It works in conjunction with the British Council, whose Accreditation UK scheme serves as the definitive guide to UK English language centres,[9] and the ODL QC, described later in this chapter. The system of accreditation maintained by these three bodies provides a public guarantee of standards in the independent UK colleges.

The BAC oversees the inspection of, and accredits, private colleges preparing students for university entry, offering vocational and professional education and working in partnership with university or awarding bodies to offer fully validated higher education courses.[10] In common with the QAA approach, BAC accreditation does not separate out the primary or supplementary use of flexible, distance or e-learning. It conducts site visits to review matters central to quality management including the quality of staff, institutional procedures to monitor and respond to student progress/attendance, institutional responses to external examiner/moderator comments and staff development and appraisal. It also engages in other procedures to monitor and enhance performance. Accreditation is dependent on institutions demonstrating that they meet statutory requirements in a number of areas and the minimum standards for premises and health and safety; management, staffing and administration; student welfare; teaching, learning and assessment and management of quality. This approach is more focused on the establishment and operation of quality management systems, with greater emphasis on processes and statutory compliance than outcomes.

British Standards Institute, International Organization for Standardization and European Committee for Standardization

In addition to the bodies described above, some providers of distance learning, or more often e-learning, find it useful to refer to the standards developed and promulgated by the British Standards Institute (BSI)[11] or the International Organization for Standardization (ISO)[12] to evidence the quality of their business processes. The QAA refers to relevant BSI publications regarding those aspects of QA of e-learning that are concerned with purely technical matters.

BSI was the world's first national standards body. It is a non-profit organization that works closely with manufacturing and service industries, businesses, governments and consumers and has a close working relationship with the UK government, primarily through the UK Department for Business, Innovation and Skills. The BSI considers that standards are a vehicle for the sharing of knowledge, technology and good practices and it seeks to encourage standardization of activities. Its influence extends well beyond the fields of education and training, and its primary role is to ensure that British standards, European standards and ISO international standards are useful, relevant and authoritative. It is a leading participant in international work by ISO and European Committee for Standardization (CEN)[13] in developing e-learning standards.

ISO is an international standard-setting body composed of representatives from various national standards organizations. In collaboration with the International Electrotechnical Commission,[14] it has developed the ISO/IEC 19796-1:2005 standard, *Information Technology – Learning, education and training – Quality management, assurance and metrics Part 1 – General Approach.*[15] This provides an overall framework to assist in introducing QA in all provider and user organizations of e-learning. For a better understanding of ISO/IEC 19796-1:2005, several annexes show samples of its use. Additionally, an annex, Reference Quality Criteria is included. This provides a framework for comparing different QA approaches. Several examples of use are shown, such as specific quality objectives (e.g. metadata quality) and guidelines. ISO is working towards developing a harmonized quality framework, which will include specific quality instruments and metrics.

A number of the standards supported by BSI and ISO specifically address the needs of learners with disabilities and provide a framework for specifying learner needs and digital resources for the delivery of education. For example, ISO/IEC 24751-3:2008[16] provides a common language for describing digital learning resources to facilitate the matching of these resources to learners' accessibility needs and preferences.

The Open and Distance Learning Quality Council and QA of Private Educational Provision

The independent body, the Open and Distance Learning Quality Council (ODL QC)[17] was originally established by the UK government in 1969 as the Council for the Accreditation of Correspondence Colleges. Now an independent body, the ODL QC aims to identify and enhance quality in education and training and to protect the interests of learners. Its target audience is a broad range of private education and training providers which offer courses or modules at various educational levels, predominantly below higher education level. The ODL QC standards guarantee quality in all open or distance learning, including home study, correspondence courses, e-learning, blended and work-based learning. They were first adopted in 1998, revised in 2000 and the more extensively revised standards came into force in 2006. The standards are subdivided into six sections: outcomes, resources, support, selling, providers and collaborative provision.[18] These standards apply to any ODL provision, though their implementation may differ from case to case. When applying for accreditation, providers are required to address all the standards and give evidence that each has been met. Where a standard is not applicable, an explanatory statement to that effect should be included in the submission. If that standard has not been met, a clear statement of the reasons should be given and how the provider intends to remedy this situation. Failure to meet standards may not necessarily debar a provider from accreditation, but will highlight an area needing improvement for continuing accreditation. Providers who meet the standards are considered eligible to apply for accreditation by the Council. The process of accreditation involves assessment of a provider's administrative and tutorial methods, educational materials and publicity methods to ensure that all standards are met. Once accredited, providers are monitored and are reassessed at least once every 3 years.

Conclusion

Concerns in recent years over academic standards in the UK have not been over the mode of delivery but the equivalence of qualifications awarded by different institutions, a perception that teaching and learning standards and the value of awards have fallen, and the quality of the new private, for-profit entrants into the market. The approach to QA has moved away from assuring the quality of educational provision (the inputs) to a greater emphasis on the systemic enhancement of quality in the student experience and the learning outcomes. As public confidence in the quality of education grows, the move towards an enhancement focus is likely to continue. However, if there continues to be a growing sentiment that questions the quality and standards of higher education this may be reflected in a variation from this approach.

The UK has a long history of higher education provision and has an international reputation for the quality of its universities and colleges. Some may argue that this is based on the international reputation of a few high-profile, long-established universities, but it is fair to say that there is a high level of confidence in the quality of education provided by those institutions which are overseen by the QAA. The QAA has been extremely influential in developing a shared language of quality, QA and enhancement and directing the attention of institutions to its academic infrastructure. In its consideration of academic standards and quality, the QAA does not specifically identify distance education or e-learning, but as more and more institutions have adopted these modes, there has been increased attention to the quality of such provision. In part this has been due to the fact that these approaches are viewed as new and untested. However, the successful track record of UK distance education providers such as the Open University, the University of London with its International Programmes[19] and Birkbeck College[20] demonstrates that the UK has a proven history of quality distance learning provision that results in quality learning outcomes.

In the UK system, the universities and colleges lead the robust arrangements for ensuring quality and securing standards. Each institution is expected to have its own systems for independent verification of its quality and standards and of the effectiveness of its QA systems. Through internal processes, rigorous external review and a commitment to continuous improvement, the approach is designed to safeguard quality and standards and assist higher education institutions in enhancing the student learning experience. This approach has been extremely influential internationally, with aspects being adopted by the QA bodies of other jurisdictions, including Australia, Singapore and Africa. The broad QA activities of UK higher education providers are aligned with European developments that promote greater student involvement in quality processes. These are part of the process encapsulated in the standards and guidelines for QA in the European Higher Education Area which is meant to ensure more comparable, compatible and coherent systems of higher education in Europe. Unlike the countries of the EU, however, the UK has maintained a mode-blind approach and has not devoted the same amount of time and resources to developing benchmarking systems and QA processes targeting e-learning in particular. It has taken a more integrated view, focusing on the broad principles of academic quality and standards in the learning opportunities, teaching, support and assessment made available to students to help them to achieve their awards.

Notes

1   http://qaa.ac.uk
2   http://qaa.ac.uk/academicinfrastructure/default.asp
3   http://qaa.ac.uk/academicinfrastructure/codeOfPractice/default.asp
4   http://www.qaa.ac.uk/academicinfrastructure/codeOfPractice/section2/default.asp
5   http://www.qaa.ac.uk/scotland/
6   http://www.qaa.ac.uk/reviews/ELIR/default.asp
7   http://www.qaa.ac.uk/reviews/ELIR/handbook08final/default.asp
8   http://www.the-bac.org
9   http://www.britishcouncil.org/accreditation.htm
10 http://www.the-bac.org/accreditation
11 http://www.bsigroup.co.uk/en/?gcid=S17014x025&keyword=british%20standards%
12 http://www.iso.org
13 http://www.cen.eu/cen/pages/default.aspx
14 http://www.iec.ch
15 http://www.iso.org/iso/pressrelease.htm?refid=Ref992
16 http://www.iso.org/iso/catalogue_detail.htm?csnumber=43604
17 http://www.odlqc.org.uk
18 http://www.odlqc.org.uk/standard.htm
19 http://www.londoninternational.ac.uk
20 http://www.bbk.ac.uk

8

QUALITY ASSURANCE POLICIES AND GUIDELINES IN EUROPEAN DISTANCE AND E-LEARNING

Ulf-Daniel Ehlers

Introduction

New demands, new markets and new opportunities offered by information and communications technology (ICT) have all contributed to the open and distance learning (ODL) agenda in Europe. The 1970s and 1980s saw the establishment of such providers as the University of Hagen in Germany, Open University of the Netherlands, National University of Distance Education and Open University of Catalonia in Spain and Portuguese Open University. Since the early 1990s, many more European universities have adopted this mode of delivery to raise their profiles, provide education more flexibly and serve new target groups and for-profit private ODL providers have also emerged. Many conventional universities now provide blended learning programmes on campus. The Internet enables institutions to distribute courses and learning materials across national borders and Web 2.0 technologies such as wikis, blogs and social networks allow students to interact and collaborate in learning and generate and share ideas and content. The strong emphasis on lifelong learning in Europe only furthers the demand for e-learning.

Quality assurance (QA) has become a pressing issue. In 2000, the European Association for Quality Assurance in Higher Education (ENQA) was established to promote cooperation in QA in higher education in all of the Bologna signatory countries. At the time of writing, 24 QA agencies in 23 European countries feature on the European Quality Assurance Register for Higher Education (EQAR).

To foster understanding and improve standards in ODL in Europe and beyond, new networks, associations and professional bodies have also been established. The European Foundation for Quality in e-Learning plays a key role in providing various stakeholders with QA frameworks for e-learning and the European Association of Distance Teaching Universities (EADTU) and European Distance and e-Learning Network offer methods and means of QA in ODL to their member institutions. All of these contribute to the debate on, and development of guidelines for, QA in ODL and achievement of best practice. This chapter outlines these developments and issues and concludes with the lessons learned in regard to QA in ODL and in particular, e-learning.

The Bologna Process and QA

The Bologna Process has had a major influence on establishing transnational quality standards, for both conventional and ODL university providers. The Bologna Declaration (CRE, 1999) aimed for a European Higher Education Area (EHEA), the objective of which was to create more comparable, compatible and coherent systems of higher education across Europe. It also identified the need for European cooperation in developing comparable QA criteria and methodologies. Other goals agreed to were: easily comparable degrees, a system based on two main degree cycles (a third cycle has since been included), a common European system of credits and student and staff mobility.

In May 2001, the Ministers of Higher Education of the signatory countries met in Prague, reaffirmed their commitment to the objectives of the Bologna Declaration and invited ENQA to collaborate in establishing a common framework of reference for QA by 2010. With the growth of the Socrates and Erasmus[1] exchange programmes, the National Unions of Students in Europe (later to be known as the European Students' Union or ESU) formed into a political organization promoting the educational, social, economic and cultural interests of students through all relevant European bodies and in particular, the European Union, Council of Europe and UNESCO. At the Prague meeting, the ESU became an official observer in the Bologna Process, and it is now a consultative member to the Bologna Process, representing European students in various working groups, and its Academic Affairs Committee deals with such issues as the European Credit Transfer and Accumulation System (ECTS)[2] and qualification frameworks.

In 2003, in Berlin, the European Ministers of Education recommended that ENQA, in collaboration with the European Association of Institutions in Higher Education, European University Association and other bodies, should develop standards, procedures and guidelines for internal and external QA in European higher education. They also stressed that, consistent with the principle of institutional autonomy, the primary responsibility for QA should lie with the institutions themselves, albeit within the respective national quality agency frameworks.

At the meeting in Bergen in May 2005, the Ministers of Education adopted ENQA's *Standards and Guidelines for Quality Assurance in the European Higher Education Area*.[3] ENQA's main recommendations were that:

- There would be European standards for internal and external QA agencies.
- European external QA agencies would submit themselves to a cyclical review within 5 years.
- There would be an emphasis on subsidiarity, with reviews undertaken nationally where possible.
- A European register of QA agencies would be produced.
- A European register committee would act as a gatekeeper for the inclusion of QA agencies in the register.
- A European consultative forum for QA in higher education would be established.

The standards developed concerned a set of norms for fitness-for-purpose of rather than such criteria as excellence, value for money or transformation.

Meeting in London in 2007, the European Ministers of Education agreed to establish EQAR. The purposes of this were to:

- Promote student mobility by providing a basis for increased trust among higher education institutions.
- Reduce opportunities for 'accreditation mills' to gain credibility.
- Provide a basis for governments to authorize higher education institutions to choose any agency from the register compatible with national arrangements.
- Serve as an instrument to improve the quality of and promote mutual trust among QA agencies.

EQAR invites QA agencies operating in the EHEA which can evidence their credibility and reliability in a review against the *European Standards and Guidelines for Quality Assurance*[4] to apply for inclusion in the register. At the time of writing, EQAR is undertaking a self-evaluation process and preparing for its external evaluation, as requested by the Ministers of Education at the London Summit.

Another transnational agency is the European Consortium for Accreditation in Higher Education. This was founded in 2003 with the primary aim of mutual recognition of accreditation decisions. The European University Association (EUA), which represents and supports higher education institutions in 46 countries, is the official representative of the university sector in the Bologna Process and as such, participates in numerous working groups or consultative bodies within that framework. The EUA works on a broad range of topics important to its members, including quality and funding issues and university management practices.

This brief summary shows that considerable progress has been made in QA and accreditation in European higher education (see Qrossroads[5]). A position paper on the principles and priorities has been published by ENQA (2009). However, what is missing in all of these developments is a broadly acceptable QA system for ODL and e-learning. Let us now examine the organizations contributing to this field.

Organizations offering QA Guidelines for Open, Distance and e-Learning

Various national and transnational initiatives have been undertaken in regard to QA in ODL and e-learning. To take an example of work by a national QA agency, the UK Quality Assurance Agency's (QAA) (see also Chapter 7) *1999 Guidelines on the Quality Assurance of Distance Learning*[6] covered:

- System design – the development of an integrated approach.
- The establishment of academic standards and quality in programme design, approval and review procedures.
- The assurance of quality and standards in the management of programme delivery.
- Student development and support.
- Student communication and representation.
- Student assessment.

The QAA observed that the term 'distance learning' is now routinely applied to a wide spectrum of activities and these guidelines provided the starting point for a code of practice for such provision. In 2010, the QAA published its amplified *Code of Practice for the Assurance of Academic Quality and Standards in Higher Education: Section 2, Collaborative provision and flexible and distributed learning (including e-learning).*[7] This considers:

- Responsibility for, and equivalence of, academic standards.
- Policies, procedures and information.
- Selecting a partner organization or agent.
- Written agreements with a partner organization or agent.
- Assuring academic standards and the quality of programmes and awards.
- Assessment requirements.
- External examining.
- Certificates and transcripts.
- Information for students.
- Publicity and marketing.

It also includes elements specific to flexible and distributed learning:

- e-Learning.
- Delivery.

- Learner support.
- Assessment of students.

An example of work undertaken by a national distance education organization is the Norwegian Association for Distance Education's *Quality Standards for Distance Education.*[8] Developed in 1993, these have been twice revised, are approved by the Ministry of Education and Research in Oslo and must be signed up to by all members of the Association. They concern information and guidance, course development, instruction and organization. Each of these categories is then divided into:

- Conditions and constraints.
- Implementation.
- Results.
- Follow–up.

The quality factors (with related standards) are then articulated – for example, in regard to course development (implementation):

- Supervision, management and cooperation.
- Follow–up and guidance of authors.
- Choice of media and learning material.
- Different study situations.
- Evaluation of product underdevelopment with respect to the content methodology, target groups and circumstances of study (Bø, 2003).

At the transnational level, the European Association for Distance Learning (EADL) has produced the *EADL Code of Conduct for Members,*[9] based on the principles of proper care, legal security, reasonableness, reliability and due publicity. EADL guarantees to students that they will receive from its members the quality of service defined in this code of conduct. EADL members must sign up to it and renew their commitment every 3 years. They must also comply with the *Minimum Standards of Quality for EADL Members.*[10] These cover quality practice in regard to pre-enrolment, enrolment and contracts, counselling (other than direct lesson tutorials), examinations, face-to-face teaching, product management, tutorials and technology use. For example, under counselling practices, EADL members must sign up to the following:

- There shall always be, within normal office hours, someone readily available in the institute to handle enquiries of a counselling nature.
- Communications about administrative and tutorial matters should be answered within 7 working days of receipt.

- Where a longer timescale is required, communications should be acknowledged within 3 working days, the delay explained and an indication given of when the full answer can be expected.

Let us now consider QA in e-learning.

QA in e-Learning

A survey by the European Quality Observatory (Ehlers, Hildebrandt, Goertz, & Pawlowski, 2005) shows that, because of European higher education's different circumstances, cultures and quality needs, different QA models are being applied in e-learning across the continent. More than 650 models were reported to be in use. The most frequently used are the ISO 9000, EFQM Excellence model, SCORM and Total Quality Management.

The JISC Innovation Group, which is funded by the UK government and assists universities and colleges in employing innovative uses of digital technology, has published *Effective Practice in a Digital Age: A Guide to Technology-enhanced Learning and Teaching*.[11] This combines the outcomes of research with examples of current practice and suggests 'key points for best practice' in e-learning.

In 2005, the European Association of Distance Teaching Universities (EADTU) embarked on a 2-year project called Excellence.[12] This web-based instrument, developed in collaboration with experts from 12 higher education institutions, was designed to be used with other QA processes to assess the e-learning dimensions of curriculum and course design, course delivery, student and staff support services and institutional management. EADTU has also developed a *Quality Manual for e-Learning in Higher Education*[13] which lists the key factors and benchmarks for QA of e-learning.

Two QA models agreed to by a number of European higher education providers are the European Foundation for Management Development (EFMD) Certification of e-Learning (CEL), which concerns programmes, and the European University Quality in e-Learning (UNIQUe) label which concerns institutional accreditation.

EFMD is a non-profit organization funded through membership fees, grants, contracts, fee-based services and sale of publications. With 730 member organizations from academia, business, public service and consultancy in 82 countries, EFMD is well placed to provide a forum for information, research, networking and debate on innovation and best practice in management development. It is also well positioned to accredit management e-learning programmes through CEL. This joint initiative between EFMD, the Swiss Centre for Innovations in Learning at the University of St Gallen and Spirus Applied Learning Solutions, aims to improve e-learning management programmes through standards setting, benchmarking, collaboration and sharing best practice. The standards of such programmes vary widely and the introduction of accreditation signals that quality is something very much to be aimed for (Anderson, 2005).

The CEL accreditation process is shown in Figure 8.1. A university or other management education provider seeking accreditation for its programme is first advised on the criteria by which its eligibility will be judged. The programme must involve at least 100 hours of learning, operate on a durable basis and conclude with an assessment or examination. The provider then makes a formal application, providing information about their programme for initial assessment.

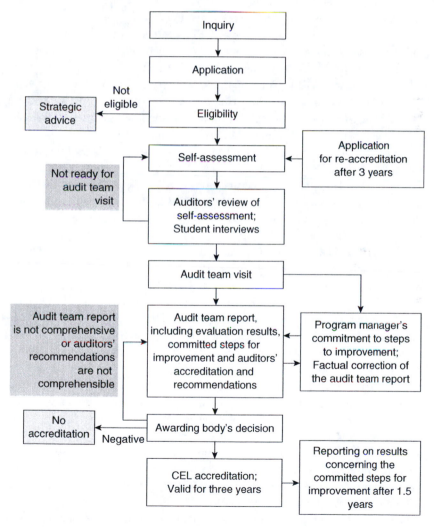

FIGURE 8.1   The EFMD CEL accreditation process

If the data are insufficient, further information is requested. If the provider and programme are considered eligible, and if there is a realistic possibility of accreditation, the provider is then issued with self-assessment guidelines and asked to develop a report in accord with the specified criteria, method of data collection, performance indicators and quality evaluation standards.[14] This self-assessment is then reviewed by the auditors. If it does not meet the required standards, further details are requested. The auditors then carry out a site visit. If the programme meets the criteria, CEL accreditation is granted. This is valid for 3 years. Eighteen months later, the provider must report on whether the recommendations agreed to with the auditors have been fulfilled. The results of this interim review are taken into account if re-accreditation is sought after 3 years.

The first programme to receive CEL accreditation was The Open University's Business School Diploma in Management. Other programmes receiving accreditation include the Curtin University of Technology Graduate School of Business MBA (Australia), University of Liverpool online MBA (UK), MBA programme of Universitas 21 Global (Singapore), Kavrakoglu Management Institute online MBA (Turkey), Global Management Challenge SDG (Portugal), ESIC Business Marketing Game (Spain), L'Oréal e-Strat Challenge Business Game (global) and Caterpillar University Sales Effectiveness Process Programme (global).

The UNIQUe label[15] is a certification system offered by the European Foundation for Quality in e-Learning (EFQUEL). It is designed for assessing e-learning quality in universities and colleges (Bijnens & Nascimbeni, 2007; Dondi & Moretti, 2007). EFQUEL builds its expertise on many projects and initiatives such as Self Evaluation Quality (SEVAQ),[16] a self-evaluation tool for e-learning which combines Kirkpatrick's (1998) four-level evaluation model for learning and the EFQM Excellence model.[17] UNIQUe's certification process follows much the same steps as the EFMD CEL system and involves self-assessment as well as peer review and site visits. However, its focus is on institutional, not programme certification. Institutions are certified on the basis of their learning resources, management of learning processes, research and development, standing in the e-learning community, connections with the business world, contributions to the community and internationally – and commitment to innovation. UNIQUe is currently the only global institutional certification system taking the latter into account. The UNIQUe peer review group recommends to an independent awarding body that an institution should be certified. Eighteen months after certification, the institution must report on its progress in assuring and improving quality in its e-provision and may seek re-accreditation after 3 years. The interim report and re-accreditation are seen as extremely important features of this QA process. They demonstrate that QA must be regular and cyclical, not simply a one-off review, and designed to achieve a balance between improvement and accountability (Vroeijenstijn, 1995).

UNIQUe was officially launched in 2009 after a 2-year pilot phase and certificates have already been awarded to the University of Leicester (UK), Helsinki University of Technology (Finland), Metodi E Tecnologie Innovative per la Didattica, Politecnico di Milano and University of Macerata (Italy), Moscow University of Industry and Finance (Russia), School of Humanities at the University of the Aegean (Greece) and University of Granada (Spain).

Conclusion

From Reception to Participation

QA in ODL and e-learning are undergoing considerable change and diversification in Europe. Regional and national QA approaches are encouraging and supporting common frameworks for assuring and improving all forms of ODL. There is greater valuing of bottom-up approaches to QA. There is a trend away from QA which is primarily concerned with input variables towards assessing and assuring outcomes, and from indicator-based approaches to more participatory and responsive approaches. Greater emphasis is being placed on learners' perspectives of quality and a culture of quality development and improvement, rather than reliance on external control.

In regard to e-learning, it would be argued that further paradigm shifts are required in applying QA. As Downes (2005) observes, e-learning has emerged from being a radical idea and is now widely regarded as mainstream. In what he terms 'e-learning 2.0', online learning ceases to be a medium used by institutional or commercial publishers or other providers to 'deliver' learning which is 'consumed' by students. It becomes a platform where learning is created by students as well as courseware creators and lecturers. It is more akin to a conversation or process of enquiry rather than a didactic text. Such fundamental changes require different questions to be asked during the QA process, different objects and processes to be evaluated, different quality criteria to be applied and different approaches to be adopted in seeking improvement.

From Prescriptive Evaluation to Learning Processes and Outcomes

In e-learning 2.0 environments, QA can no longer be limited to the evaluation of pre-determined objectives and learning environments or learning content produced by faculty. The learning arises not only through the reception of information provided, but the active participation of the learners, individually and collaboratively. So quality in e-learning 2.0 needs to be measured by how far a particular learning scenario or process stimulates the learners, motivates them to find, remix and repurpose content to accord with their own intentions and share their content and ideas with others – and not necessarily in the same institution or same country.

From Product Orientation Through Process Orientation to Performance and Competence Orientation

In e-learning 2.0, the focus of QA is not the pre-determined products but the learners' performance and development of learning products which can be recorded in e-portfolios during the course of the learning. Therefore, encouragement and support for learners' decision-making and responsibility for their own learning become important factors.

From Planning Education for the Learner to Planning Education by the Learner

In traditional ODL QA scenarios, the providers' judge the educational needs, design of the learning materials, methods of instructional design, uses of technology and quality and extent of the learning outcomes. In e-learning 2.0 scenarios, the learners need to participate in these processes, becoming partners in planning, designing, implementing and evaluating instruction. Thus QA also needs to focus on how well the providers are encouraging and supporting the learners in reflecting on quality, embracing learner-oriented forms of evaluation and using evaluation tools to personalize and develop the quality of the learning outcomes.

From Receiver to Developer of Learning Materials

QA in ODL scenarios should not follow the business model which assesses how customers accept, value and use the products or services on offer. Instead it should focus on the development and validation processes of personal learning, social communication and appropriate use of the tools for learning, again regarding the learners as developers of learning materials and experiences.

From Closed Learning Island to Open Learning Environment

As Kerres (2006) points out, learning management systems (LMS) function as islands in the enormous ocean of material on the Web. e-Learning 2.0 scenarios regard the LMS as a mere starting point, a signpost to help learners further search and research materials on the Internet and find and utilize other tools to develop personal learning portals. Thus QA can no longer focus on the materials and activities within the LMS, but needs to be concerned with the products and processes documented in these personal learning portals.

From Tests to Performance and Reflection

In today's e-learning 2.0 scenarios, learning progress and outcomes should be measured, not only by testing, but throughout the whole learning process, and the social interactions should be documented in e-portfolios or personal learning portals.

The greatest challenge now facing QA is how to measure the extent to which e-learning transforms the total educational experience, leads to lifelong learning and brings about other long-term benefits to the learners, institutions and society as a whole.

Notes

1 http://ec.europa.eu/education/lifelong-learning-programme/doc80_en.htm
2 http://ec.europa.eu/education/lifelong-learning-policy/doc48_en.htm
3 http://www.enqa.eu/files/ENQA%20Bergen%20Report.pdf
4 http://www.eqar.eu/application/requirements/european-standards-and-guidelines.html
5 http://www.qrossroads.eu/home
6 http://www.qaa.ac.uk/academicinfrastructure/codeofpractice/distancelearning/contents.asp
7 http://www.qaa.ac.uk/academicinfrastructure/codeOfPractice/section2/collab2010.pdf
8 http://nettskolen.nki.no/forskning/DISTUMQualityAssurance.pdf
9 http://www.eadl.org/documents/Code%20of%20Conduct%20nov%202005%20edition.pdf
10 http://www.eadl.org/aboutus/mission.php
11 http://www.jisc.ac.uk/media/documents/publications/effectivepracticedigitalage.pdf
12 http://www.eadtu.nl/e-xcellenceqs/
13 http://www.eadtu.nl/e-xcellenceQS/files/members/E-xcellenceManualGrey/index.html
14 http://www.efmd.org/images/stories/efmd/downloadables/Criteria-Indicators-Standards.pdf
15 http://www.qualityfoundation.org/unique-certification/
16 http://www.sevaq.eu/
17 http://www.efqm.org/en/

References

Anderson, L. (2005, March 21). Clicks and bricks work together in the world of corporate teaching. *Financial Times*. Retrieved from http://www.efmd.org/attachments/tmpl_1_art_041027wszf_att_050323jhbl.pdf

Bijnens, H., & Nascimbeni, F. (2007). *UNIQUe – European University Quality in Elearning*. Retrieved from http://unique.europace.org/pdf/eden_unique%20abstract.pdf

Bø, I. (2003, June 15–18). *E-learning, flexible and distance learning – The Norwegian approach and experience with quality* [PowerPoint presentation]. Paper presented at the *European Distance and E-learning Network Conference*, Rhodes, Greece. Retrieved from http://www.eden-online.org/contents/conferences/annual/Rhodes/images/IngeborgBo.ppt

CRE. (1999). *The Bologna Declaration on the European space for higher education: An explanation*. The Confederation of EU Rectors' Conferences and the Association of European

Universities. Retrieved from http://ec.europa.eu/education/policies/educ/bologna/bologna.pdf

Dondi, C., & Moretti, M. (Eds.). (2007). *Quality for e-learning in higher education Europe: Different approaches for different purposes.* UNIQUe. Retrieved from http://unique.euro-pace.org/pdf/WP1-report-v5_FINAL.pdf

Downes, S. (2005, October). *E-learning 2.0. Stephen's Web.* Retrieved from http://www.downes.ca/post/31741

Ehlers, U. D., Hildebrandt, B., Goertz, L., & Pawlowski, J. M. (2005). *Use and distribution of quality approaches in European e-learning.* CEDEFOP. Retrieved from http://www2.trainingvillage.gr/etv/publication/download/panorama/5162_en.pdf

ENQA. (2009). *ENQA position paper on quality assurance in the EHEA.* Helsinki: European Association for Quality Assurance in Higher Education. Retrieved from http://www.enqa.eu/files/ENQA_position_paper%20(3).pdf

Kerres, M. (2006). *Web 2.0 und seine implikationen für e-learning.* Retrieved from http://mediendidaktik.uni-duisburg-essen.de/web20

Kirkpatrick, D. L. (1998). *Evaluating training programs: The four levels.* San Francisco, CA: Berrett-Koehler Publishers, Inc.

Vroeijenstijn, A. I. (1995). Improvement and accountability: Navigating between Scylla and Charybdis. Guide for external quality assessment in higher education. *Higher Education Policy Series 30.* Bristol, PA: Taylor & Francis.

9

QUALITY ASSURANCE POLICIES AND GUIDELINES FOR DISTANCE EDUCATION IN AUSTRALIA AND NEW ZEALAND

Yoni Ryan and Mark Brown

Introduction

This chapter examines QA in Australian and New Zealand distance education (DE) over the past quarter century and the shifts occurring as digital technologies progressively replace print. A 'perfect storm' of force fields complicate the narrative, for example:

- The lack of an accrediting body for DE institutions or regulatory standards for DE providers or programmes to help assure quality.
- The rapid substitution of e-learning for correspondence/print-based DE.
- A disconnect between benchmarking exercises designed for quality enhancement at institutional level and individual practices.
- The transnational provision of higher education courses/programmes wholly or partly by means of DE and Australian universities working with overseas partners.
- A persistent and underlying perception by academics and researchers that DE is a 'fifth column' in management drives to reduce costs, limit academic autonomy, standardize programmes and convert university study into the business of borderless education.

The chapter argues the case for the Australian Tertiary Education Quality and Standards Agency, which is to be launched in 2012, and Universities New Zealand-Te Pokai Tara Committee on University Academic Programmes to establish practical and verifiable standards for DE based on more than commercial considerations of competitive risk to the universities.

DE in Australia and New Zealand

Australia and New Zealand have a long and distinguished history in DE. By 1995, the proportion of DE students in Australian universities was around 13%. With the exponential growth in e-learning, this proportion has grown. In the first half of 2009, almost 12% of all public university students, or over 108,000 students, were classified as external, an increase of 3% over 2008. A further 71,086 students were studying in mixed mode, another 8,700 external or mixed-mode students were enrolled in private universities (Department Education, Employment and Workplace Relations, 2010), and many more thousands were taking single online subjects rather than whole courses through Open Universities Australia (see Chapter 12). In New Zealand, the proportion of external students is even higher, at around 17% (Education Counts, 2010). The flexibility and convenience of e-learning are clearly proving attractive, especially to time-poor adults. Notwithstanding these two nations' long experience in DE, the large number of students involved, and the increasingly regulatory and auditing regimes, QA specifically concerning DE has largely escaped the attention of the QA agencies.

Emerging QA Issues in DE

In the 1980s, Australia's main providers of DE, the colleges of advanced education (CAEs), later to become universities, established procedures to ensure consistency and quality in their DE operations. This led commentators such as Campion (1990), Campion and Renner (1992) and Evans and Nation (1989) to criticize the emergence of 'Fordism' or 'instructional industrialism' in DE development and delivery. Their objections were primarily a response to what they, and many academics, perceived as an ideology which sought to reduce academic autonomy, and teaching to an atomized, mechanistic assembly line of 'resources' dependent on 'a maximum division of labour' (Campion & Renner, 1992). Tait (1993, p. 303) warned that the 'technocratic and managerial imposition of QA . . . runs the danger of diminishing rather than supporting quality'. Campion and Renner also argued that the drive to more flexible and open learning reinforced the Fordist paradigm by extending DE methods to on-campus teaching. Indeed, the Minister for Higher Education and Employment Services of that time, Peter Baldwin (1991), actually recommended the use of DE materials as a substitute for lecturers.

The CAEs were subject to state-based regulatory regimes, inexperienced in systematic auditing procedures, and familiar only with the teacher training programmes that dominated their offerings. With the implementation of Minister for Employment, Education and Training John Dawkins' 1987 and 1988 reforms via a 'Unified National System', some amalgamated to become new universities, while others became universities in their own right. Several of these had strong reputations in DE, for example, Gippsland CAE, which became part of Monash

University, and the Darling Downs Institute of Advanced Education, which became the University of Southern Queensland. Later, the government attempted to limit DE provision to eight so-called Distance Education Centres (DECs), more because of the political need to shore up the largely regional DE-providing universities than any concern for quality and efficiency. However, such was the extent of interest in DE across the sector that this DEC model did not survive for long.

In 1991, federal government concerns about the capacity of these new universities and rising costs of funding university study for an ever-growing number of students led to the establishment of the Committee for Quality Assurance in Higher Education which in 2001 became the Australian Universities Quality Agency (AUQA). Concerns over quality in DE led to Nunan and Calvert (1992) being commissioned to report on DE standards and this led to the establishment of an advisory body, the National Council for Open and Distance Education (NCODE). Another Government-commissioned report on costs and quality in 'resource-based learning' was undertaken by Jevons and Northcott (1994). In New Zealand, a mid-1990s attempt to create a 'virtual university' outside the national system by a group of e-enthusiasts led to close interest in DE by the then NZ Academic Audit Unit (Butterfield et al., 1999).

Throughout the 1990s, NCODE remained the peak body for advising on DE policy and sponsoring best practice and cooperation in this field. In 2002, it became the Australasian Council on Open, Distance and e-Learning (ACODE). ACODE's mission is to enhance policy and practice in open, distance, flexible and e-learning in Australasian higher education by:

- Disseminating and sharing knowledge and expertise.
- Supporting professional development and providing networking opportunities.
- Investigating, developing and evaluating new approaches.
- Advising and influencing key bodies in higher education.
- Promoting best practice.

ACODE does not accredit or monitor the quality of DE providers or programmes. It provides a set of benchmarks for DE and e-learning and associated scoping and good practice statements and performance indicators regarding:

- Institution policy and governance for technology-supported learning and teaching.
- Planning for, and quality improvement in, the integration of technologies for learning and teaching.
- Information technology infrastructure to support learning and teaching.
- Pedagogical application of information and communications technology.
- Professional/staff development for the effective use of technologies for learning and teaching.

- Staff support for the use of technologies for learning and teaching.
- Student training for the effective use of technologies for learning.
- Student support for the use of technologies for learning.

The ACODE benchmarks[1] were developed in collaboration with DE and non-DE providers in Australia and New Zealand. They also drew on the Australian Business Excellence Framework,[2] a non-prescriptive leadership and management system that describes the essential elements of organizational systems in seven categories and is based on 12 quality principles, and McKinnon, Walker, and Davis's (2000) *Benchmarking: A manual for Australian universities*. The latter assumes that excellence and value adding are goals sought by all universities. It also assumes that those aspects of excellence and value adding that can be easily quantified are not the only ones worth taking into account.

With the enthusiastic promotion of its executive and an environment in which 'quality' was assuming increasing significance, these benchmarks were rapidly adopted by higher education institutions. In 2010, 36 of Australia's 38 public universities and nine New Zealand universities were subscribing to ACODE and the non-member Australian Catholic University was also using its benchmarks. Led by the University of Southern Queensland, several Australian universities, New Zealand's Massey University, Malaysia's Sultan Idris University and The Open University are now engaged in a Pilot International Inter-Institutional Benchmarking Project using ACODE's eight benchmarks. These benchmarks are comprehensive and reflect ACODE's philosophy that 'quality education' is as much about the capacities of the people responsible for the learning and teaching as the 'business side' of education. However, they do not address the issue of graduate attributes, now a feature of AUQA audits. Which raises the question, if distance and online learning are to be judged as being of the same quality as on-campus education, how are skills such as oral communication, manipulative/clinical abilities and team work to be developed and assessed? ACODE's work also provokes thinking on the differences between quality enhancement, QA and benchmarking (Inglis, 2005).

Some DE-providing universities have adopted business-oriented QA approaches such as ISO certification. Sometimes this has been done for the purposes of political manoeuvring rather than any conviction that this is particularly appropriate to DE operations. For example, a former Director of the DE Centre at Gippsland sought ISO 9001 certification to counter disparagement by Monash University's Melbourne-based senior management by evidencing the Centre's strong record of instructional design and student support services.

DE has largely escaped the specific attention of AUQA. Its concerns have been more with adherence to regulatory requirements, academic governance, the financial health of institutions, ensuring academic standards in course development and review and the provision of facilities for on-campus students.

Challenges in Applying QA to DE

Institutional adoption of quality principles does not necessarily equate with specific quality processes and outcomes in DE. As Tait (1993) observed, QA procedures may detect poor performance such as slow turnaround times but cannot assure excellence in learning design or tutorial support. The quality of instructional design is largely invisible to all but the content specialists and distance/e-learning specialists responsible for the course/courseware development and delivery. This is particularly so with online learning. 'Flick through tests' may reveal something of the production values of the learning resources when print is the medium, but it is much harder to gauge the value of e-learning environments where the links and online interactions play such important roles in knowledge building.

Two further problems regarding QA and DE are the resistance of many academics to quality regimes and procedures, and the tendency for QA agencies and universities (even those with strong DE missions and reputations) to focus on the commercial risk factors associated with DE. We are witnessing what we might call the appropriation of DE to the 'enterprise university'. Writing about the University of Melbourne, one of Australia's oldest and most prestigious universities, Cain and Hewitt (2004) voiced concerns about what they described as the conversion of the academic institution to a corporation and a community of scholars to disempowered knowledge workers – a trend they also observed in other Australian universities. One of the university's entrepreneurial plunges into the world marketplace was the online Universitas 21 Global, a joint venture with the Canadian corporation, Thomson Learning. The Vice-Chancellor at the time believed that the online learning market had prodigious money-making capacity and represented the future of tertiary education. He also envisaged a shift of interest away from statutory authority towards the idea of 'brand'. Earning money for the faculty or department became a required activity.

When NCODE was outlining quality guidelines for institutions entering the DE market in 1996, it warned of factors militating against quality such as staff and student conservatism and 'packaging' learning. Similar concerns were being voiced in Europe by Field (1995). Following two major studies in the implications of media and borderless education for Australian higher education (Cunningham et al., 1998, 2000), Marginson and Considine (2000) published an influential critique of the commercialization of Australian universities, portraying globalized DE as a manifestation of the absorption of universities into the capitalist maw. Analyzing the submissions for the AUQA audits of the University of Southern Queensland, a significant DE provider, and the 'sandstone' University of Adelaide, a non-DE provider with aspirations in e-learning, Reid (2005, p. 4) concluded that the pervasive social ideology was 'constructing Australian universities as entrepreneurial businesses in an education marketplace'. As shown later, this resonates with the parameters laid down by AUQA.

In the larger DE operations, the traditional practice was to centralize opera-tions. The instructional designers, media specialists and technologists collaborated with the teaching staff in providing pedagogic expertise, a student learning per-spective and technical know-how in the development and delivery of pro-grammes. And by subjecting the entire DE process to a quality framework, the legitimacy of DE as fulfilling educational experience was validated. However, this came to be regarded by academics as a bureaucratic imposition with inordinately lengthy timelines that disrupted the rhythm of the academic year (Inglis, 2005). In recent years, the trend has been to dismantle these central services. For exam-ple, despite its ISO certification and internal QA procedures, the highly successful Monash Gippsland DE operation fell victim to its size. The unit of over 120 peo-ple was disbanded in 2005 and its functions were devolved to the faculties. A sim-ilar fate befell the Centre for University Extramural Studies at Massey University, New Zealand's leading DE provider. Growing acceptance of DE, the removal of differentiated government funding for delivery modes and the migration of tech-nology to the desktop led to the dismantling of this centre and the re-location of its instructional designers to a small training and development unit (Prebble, 2010). Decentralization in other Australian and New Zealand universities has led to a failure to ensure DE and e-learning standards. The consequences of this are examined in the next section.

AUQA Audits and DE Quality

AUQA conducts audits of all Australian self-accrediting higher education institu-tions, Commonwealth, State and Territory government accreditation authorities, non-self-accrediting institutions approved as higher education providers under the Commonwealth Higher Education Support Act of 2003 and other higher education institutions under contract. In 2007, AUQA finished its first 5-year cycle of audits. In 2008, it began a second cycle, with some changes to the scope and nature of the audits, as explained in the AUQA Audit Manual.[3] AUQA's audit methods are concerned with the institutions' QA arrangements in the fol-lowing dimensions: objectives, approach, deployment, results and improvement. AUQA does not impose an externally prescribed set of standards upon auditees, but uses each institution's mission and goals as its primary starting point for the audit. The audits are also based on critical self-reviews by the institutions. This not only enables the auditee to supply the information required by AUQA, but can lead to improvements in procedures and practices, even without AUQA's involvement. All of AUQA's audit reports are published in full on the Web.[4]

AUQA's audits focus on two themes. The first, 'Internationalization', is man-datory. The second is negotiable between AUQA and the auditees. The first theme reflects the heavy reliance of Australian universities on the international student dollar (Marginson & Considine, 2000). There have been increasing reports of quality being compromised in transnational provision (Fion Lim, 2007), whether by means of 'fly-in, fly-out', twinning programmes, branch campuses, partnerships, franchising or DE. There have been reports of students graduating without adequate English language skills, staff being pressured to pass under-performing international students, and poor supervision of international partners. These programmes are often perceived by enthusiastic, but unbusinesslike, academics as 'cash-cow' opportunities. And the expansion of online means of delivery not only increases the apparent attraction of DE as a means of generating offshore income, but growth in private providers. AUQA has warned of the damage to the nation's educational reputation by questionable practices in the stampede into the global market (Ryan, 2008). Similar concerns have been expressed in New Zealand. Unfortunately, with a market-driven philosophy and the abandoning of centralized DE provision, the lessons learned across the years about ensuring quality in off-campus and technology-based provision are being largely disregarded.

Two recent reports on Australian universities with long and honourable traditions in DE, large numbers of external students and involvement in offshore provision reinforce Reid's (2005) concerns over the business focus of universities and QA agencies.

University A, a multi-campus institution, was audited in 'Internationalization' and 'Professional education and practice-based learning'. With 60% of its students external and 4% offshore, the intersection of these themes was apposite. The audit report is telling in regard to DE and QA at this university. It observes:

> [The university] needs to give greater attention to the competitive risks it faces in flexible and online delivery, and to improving the consistency and quality of the academic experience for all students. Given the number of initiatives under way, the university needs to develop explicit change management strategies to ensure that all its academic staff are able to improve their ability to develop curricula and to teach in ways that are appropriate [to the University's] aims.

Having noted that the university seeks to maintain a leadership role among Australian universities in flexible learning and professional education, the report observes that the university has clarified responsibilities for online learning and flexible delivery, established a new division responsible for learning and teaching services and successfully implemented its online learning platform. It also commends the university for establishing its Flexible Learning Institute. However, it comments:

> [The university] needs to do more to increase academic staff knowledge of, and take-up of, online learning capabilities [and] more systematically to

plan for this to occur . . . consider the adequacy of the information it provides to prospective and current students, particularly for external students and . . . the strategic risks of its goals of leadership in flexible learning, given the presence of many other competitors, and to business continuity risks, particularly for IT infrastructure.

In regard to Internationalization, the report concludes:

[The university] has an Internationalization Strategy but acknowledges that staff across the University do not yet have the multidimensional understanding of internationalization that this strategy aims for. This finding was reflected in a 2008 critical self-review of internationalization undertaken by the university. The self-review revealed a number of recommendations from the 2004 AUQA Audit Report that had not been addressed, particularly in regard to the monitoring and evaluation of the performance of off-shore and onshore partners. While some strategic action has been taken . . . including the rationalization of offshore teaching partnerships, not all operational aspects of QA were attended to.

Clearly, for the auditors, the quality of DE at this university was in question, notwithstanding the university's stated commitment to ACODE's benchmarks for the provision and support of e-learning. However, it is particularly significant that the comments refer to the 'competitive risks' faced in flexible and online delivery. This is a marked departure from the intention of QA to 'guarantee that the quality of product or service meets some predetermined standard' (Inglis, 2005).

The audit report on University B, 80% of whose students are external, focused on 'Flexible learning' and 'Internationalization'. It observed:

[The university] is a university of contrasts. Pockets of innovation contrast with rigid adherence to past practices in other areas. The energetic and enthusiastic embrace of the university's bold vision for the future by heads of school and other senior staff contrasts with the apparent satisfaction of others with the status quo.

It went on to say:

Although [the university] has a history of leadership in DE, the first AUQA audit in 2003 was unable to find convincing evidence for the university's claim at that time that it was 'at the forefront of online learning'. The university's Cycle 2 audit portfolio refers to [the university] being in 'a declining distance education position within the sector'. After the AUQA Cycle 1 audit, [the university] established a Distance Education Review 'to develop proposals for [a new model of distance education] that was credible in the 21st century'. This produced over 100 recommendations [but] overall the recommendations of the DE review 'lacked a clear vision or direction' (as mentioned in the Self-Review Report), and they were not gathered up into a new strategic vision. In consequence, a 'new model' did not emerge at that time. This Advisory Committee was disbanded in 2007. [The university] drew up a Strategic Plan for 2007–2010. It is perhaps indicative of the extent to which the University's explicit attention to DE had waned that there are only two brief mentions of DE in the Plan, both about restoring off-campus enrolments to their 2005 level, and without comment on the contemporary electronic environment for DE.

AUQA did acknowledge that this inattention to University B's core business was due partly to internal upheaval. However, the agency's observations on the uneven quality of DE planning and implementation at these two universities suggest that the prevailing discourse is more concerned with the business of education rather than the quality of the student experience. On the internationalization issue, Australia is the only developed nation with falling numbers of international students. Phillimore and Koshy (2010) observe that the government now needs to address the impact on the entire international education sector of its policies – including *regulation of quality issues in the sector* (italics added). The AUQA reports reveal a gap between the rhetoric and reality with regard to quality. Institutional quality principles and procedures are not necessarily reflected in the efforts of individual staff struggling with ever-increasing workloads and the effects of decentralizing or totally dismantling the previously available academic and technical support services.

Conclusion

QA for DE in Australasia is a 'perfect storm' because so many government bodies, semi-autonomous agencies, universities and professional associations are involved and are operating in an era dominated by economic considerations and the metrics of accountability. Yet in the end, the translation of regulations and benchmarks into quality learning design and delivery is down to institutions and individuals.

Looking to the future, the International Council for Open and Distance Education has launched a pilot project[5] to examine international regulatory frameworks, identify best practice and examine the rules and regulations hindering DE development. This project involves the International Network for Quality Assurance Agencies in Higher Education, AUQA, ACODE and the newly formed Distance Education Hub (DEHub) based at the University of New England (UNE). This may provide guidance in establishing QA standards for

Australian and New Zealand DE and e-learning. If this and ACODE's bench-marking project, the new Australian Tertiary Education Quality and Standards Agency and Universities New Zealand-Te Pokai Tara Committee on University Academic Programmes, can establish practical and verifiable standards for DE, based on more than commercial considerations, DE could finally become a worthy component of the higher education landscape.

Notes

1 http://acode.edu.au/resources/ACODE_benchmarks.pdf
2 http://www.saiglobal.com/PDFTemp/Previews/OSH/as/misc/gb/GB002.pdf
3 http://www.auqa.edu.au/qualityaudit/auditmanuals
4 http://www.auqa.edu.au/qualityaudit/universities/
5 http://www.icde.org/?module=Articles;action=Article.publicShow;ID=1765

References

Baldwin, P. (1991). *Higher education: Quality and diversity in the 1990s.* Canberra: Australian Government Publishing Service.

Butterfield, S., Chambers, M., Moseley, B., Prebble, T., Uys, P., & Woodhouse, D. (1999). *External quality assurance for the virtual institution (AAU Series on Quality, 4).* Wellington: NZ Universities Academic Audit Unit.

Cain, J., & Hewitt, J. (2004). *Off course: From public place to marketplace at Melbourne University.* Carlton North, VIC, Australia: Scribe Publications.

Campion, M. (1990). Post-Fordism and research in distance education. In T. Evans (Ed.), *Research in distance education* (pp. 44–51). Geelong, Australia: Deakin University Geelong, Institute of Distance Education.

Campion, M., & Renner, W. (1992). The supposed demise of Fordism: Implications for distance education and higher education. *Distance Education, 13*(1), 7–28.

Cunningham, S., Ryan, Y., Stedman, L., Tapsall, S., Bagdon, K., Flew, T., & Coaldrake, P. (2000). *The business of borderless education* (Published under the Evaluations and Investigations Program). Canberra: DETYA.

Cunningham, S., Tapsall, S., Ryan, Y., Stedman, L., Bagdon, K., & Flew, T. (1998). *New media and borderless education* (Published under the Evaluations and Investigations Program). Canberra: AGPS.

Department Education, Employment and Workplace Relations. (2010). *2009 Higher Education Student Statistics.* Canberra: Department Education, Employment and Workplace Relations. Retrieved from http://www.deewr.gov.au/HigherEducation/Publications/HEStatistics/Publications/Pages/2009FullYear.aspx0.

Education Counts. (2010). Retrieved from http://www.educationcounts.govt.nz/statistics/tertiary_education/participation

Evans, T., & Nation, D. (1989). *Critical reflections on distance education.* London: Falmer Press.

Field, J. (1995). Globalisation, consumption and the learning business. *Distance Education, 16,* 270–283.

Fion Lim, C. B. (2007). Quality assurance of Australian offshore education: The complexity and possible frameworks for understanding the issues. *Journal of Education Research, 8*(1), 19–36. Retrieved from http://www.edfac.unimelb.edu.au/research/resources/student_res/postscriptfiles/vol8/Fion_Lim.pdf

Inglis, A. (2005). Quality, quality assurance and benchmarking: Comparing frameworks for managing quality processes in open and distance learning. *International Review of Research in Open and Distance Learning, 6*(1). Retrieved from http://www.irrodl.org/index.php/irrodl/article/view/221/304

Jevons, F., & Northcott, P. (1994). *Costs and quality in resource-based learning on- and off-campus*. Canberra: National Board of Employment, Education and Training.

Marginson, S., & Considine, M. (2000). *The enterprise university: Power, governance and reinvention in Australia*. Cambridge: Cambridge University Press.

McKinnon, K. R., Walker, S. H., & Davis, D. (2000). *Benchmarking: A manual for Australian universities*. Canberra: DEETYA. Retrieved from http://www.dest.gov.au/archive/highered/otherpub/bench.pdf

Nunan, T., & Calvert, J. (1992). *Report of the project to investigate quality and standards in distance education*. Australia: University South Australia and Deakin University.

Phillimore, J., & Koshy, P. (2010). *The economic implications of fewer international higher education students in Australia: Final report to the Australian Technology Network of Universities*. Perth, WA: The John Curtin Institute of Public Policy. Retrieved from http://www.atn.edu.au/newsroom/Docs/2010/August_2010_Economic_implications_of_fewer_international_higher_education_students_in_Australia.pdf

Prebble, T. (2010). *From a distance: 50th Jubilee of distance learning*. Retrieved from http://www.massey.ac.nz/massey/fms/AVC%20Academic/50th%20Jubilee/From_a_Distance.pdf

Reid, I. (2005). Quality assurance, open and distance learning, and Australian universities. *International Review of Research in Open and Distance learning, 6*(1), 1–12.

Ryan, Y. (2008). Borderless education and business prospects. In T. Evans, M. Haughey, & D. Murphy (Eds.), *International handbook of distance education* (pp. 741–763). Bingley: Emerald.

Tait, A. (1993). Systems, values and dissent: QA for open and distance learning. *Distance Education, 14*, 303–314.

10

QUALITY ASSURANCE IN OPEN UNIVERSITIES

Asha Kanwar and Kate Clarke

The Rise of the Open Universities

In 1988, there were 10 open universities in the 54 countries of the Commonwealth. Today, there are 27. There are four in Africa, with four more in planning, India has 14, catering to 25% of all enrolments in higher education, and Asia has over 70 open universities and the largest number of adult open and distance learners in the world. This trend is likely to continue. Half the world's population of 6.5 billion is aged under 20 years and there are two billion teenagers in the developing world. By 2020, the World Bank predicts that to achieve sustainable economic development, 40–50% of the global workforce will need to be tertiary qualified 'knowledge-workers'. With access to tertiary education currently at less than 10% of the relevant age group in, for example, South Asia and sub-Saharan Africa, existing institutions simply cannot cater for the rising demand. Universities that are open to people without formal academic qualifications and which teach by means of distance education, online learning or mixed-mode study will continue to be the only viable option for millions. The issues of the quality of these open universities become ever more pressing.

Perceptions of the Open Universities

There is still a perception barrier to be overcome in regard to both the open entry and open and distance learning methods of the open universities, especially in the developing world where they are considered second rate and second chance. Unfortunately, all open universities are tarred with the same brush, despite substantive independent evidence of quality in some of these institutions. It is therefore in the interests of all providers to ensure that the QA arrangements are sufficiently robust and rigorous to counter prejudice and criticism. There is a constant struggle for recognition and parity of esteem. A number of institutions and courses lack the governmental, regulatory and legal support to ensure that their degrees are equivalent to those of the conventional universities in their countries. Many graduates find that their qualifications are not deemed to be on par with conventional degrees by professional associations or employers. Clearly, there is need to demonstrate that the qualifications gained through ODL and the knowledge and skills of the graduates are the same as those from the more conventional institutions. To achieve this, strong evidence of quality is needed.

Trends in QA in ODL

There was no discussion of QA as it is now understood when the first open universities were established – the University of South Africa in 1946 and The Open University (OU) in the UK in 1969. The term used in the 1960s and 1970s was 'standards', which Mills (2006) with some prescience, defined as 'objective measurable outcomes'. The criteria used to measure standards were the process of course preparation and the quality of study materials; feedback and interactivity in the guise of counselling, tutorials and assignments; and the usability of ODL for the subject concerned. The reference point was the conventional system where high standards were upheld in terms of well-qualified faculty, adequate infrastructure and facilities, regulated entry requirements, prescribed curriculum, classroom attendance and evaluation procedures.

It was in the 1990s that QA began to dominate the ODL agenda. The discussion shifted quickly from developing and applying QA systems for distance education in developed countries such as the UK, Australia, Canada and New Zealand to how these could be adapted to different contexts, for example in India and Hong Kong.

In the first decade of the new millennium, the emphasis has shifted to the integration of external and internal QA measures, institutions developing a culture of quality and more recently, a focus on self-evaluation and improvement rather than accountability. Self-evaluation requires the institution to find evidence to answer the following questions:

- How effectively does it communicate with its stakeholders?
- How well does it provide the outcomes that its stakeholders need and value?
- How effectively does it engage with local and international communities?
- How effective are its innovative and creative responses to a changing environment?

- How effectively does it develop the capacity of its people to provide valued outcomes for stakeholders?
- How well does it monitor and improve its performance? (Kanwar, 2010).

A model based upon self-evaluation is particularly helpful in resource-poor nations without the luxury of national QA agencies or the resources necessary to opt for regional or international accreditation. This is why The Commonwealth of Learning has developed the Review and Improvement Model (COL RIM)[1] (see Chapter 15). COL RIM provides higher education institutions with the knowledge and tools they need to conduct effective 'do-it-yourself' quality audits and avoid the costs of QA and dependency upon external evaluators in asking and answering the critically important questions set out above.

Models of QA in Various Open Universities

Countries such as the UK, India, Malaysia and Turkey require compliance by ODL providers with national quality frameworks. Thus institutions such as the OU and India's Indira Gandhi National Open University (IGNOU) operate in accord with guidelines set by the national bodies: the Quality Assurance Agency for Higher Education (QAA) in the UK and the Distance Education Council (DEC) in the case of India. Other countries such as Pakistan, South Korea and China offer no, or only general, guidelines, allowing institutions such as the Allama Iqbal Open University (AIOU), Korean National Open University (KNOU) and Open University of China (OUC), considerable leeway in their QA policies and procedures. Some countries with a long-standing tradition of ODL tend to assure quality in ODL and conventional institutions alike through national accrediting bodies, as in Malaysia, Taiwan, Sri Lanka and Bangladesh. Others, as in Indonesia, employ different instruments for accrediting on- and off-campus programmes.

A range of different models applies at the institutional level. Some universities, such as the Open University of Hong Kong (OUHK), Indonesia's Universitas Terbuka (UT), Open University of Malaysia (OUM), Open University of Sri Lanka (OUSL) and AIOU adopt a centralized approach to QA with dedicated QA units operating in accord with national or institutional policies and responsible for coordinating and implementing QA across the institutions. An account of how UT established and operates its QA system is given in Chapter 11. It is worth noting that it and OUM have both gained ISO certification, while the former has also received international accreditation from the International Council for Open and Distance Education. Other institutions, such as Turkey's Anadolu University, IGNOU and OUHK operate a 'collective model', assigning responsibility to various boards, councils and committees at the various levels and stages of operations. Others, like KNOU, OUC and the University of the Philippines

Open University (UPOU) might operate with what might be called a 'dispersed' model, expecting all academic divisions and administrative and support units to assure quality in their programmes and services (Latchem & Jung, 2009).

Case Studies of QA in Open Universities

Open universities adopt different approaches to QA according to their governance structures, cultural contexts and other circumstances. We consider four case studies.

Open University of Sri Lanka

In 2004, OUSL was reviewed by the Quality Assurance and Accreditation Council of the University Grants Commission (UGC), Sri Lanka, which used the same criteria for external QA as for the conventional universities. The outcome of the institutional and subject reviews was 'Confidence' (which is the highest category followed by 'Limited confidence' and 'No confidence'). However, the Senate and Council of OUSL believed that this QA review had not taken sufficient account of the specific features of ODL in the institution, namely, design, development and production of multi-media self-learning materials, flexible entry requirements for a diverse target audience, learner-centred teaching, efficient student support centres, multi-tasking faculty with ongoing staff development, multiple delivery modes using ICT, appropriate infrastructure, and geographically distributed study centres. A year later, OUSL therefore proceeded to develop a QA framework for ODL in partnership with the UGC and COL. In 2006, this framework was field-tested and amended to accord with the national Asia Development Bank-funded Distance Education Modernization Project (DEMP).[2] The resultant QA national guidelines for ODL defined the criteria for evaluation under the following headings: vision, mission and planning, management, organizational culture and leadership, learners, human resource development, programme design and development, learner support and progression, learner assessment and evaluation, learning infrastructure and resources, research, and consultancy and extension services. Accreditation standards and performance indicators were developed to help ODL providers engage in critical self-reflection and encourage and support a culture of quality within institutions.

In 2008, the standards and performance indicators developed by OUSL and COL in the DEMP project were amended to make them internationally applicable, with inputs from open and dual-mode institutions in Canada, India, Jamaica, Hong Kong, Malaysia, Pakistan, Papua New Guinea, South Africa, the UK, COL and UNESCO. These resulted in COL's *Quality Assurance Toolkit for Distance Higher Education Institutions and Programmes* (COL, 2009). This is an example of an open university in a developing country taking the lead in developing standards and quality measures for ODL that are applicable to other institutions in other countries.

A similar leadership role in assuring quality in ODL has been performed by UPOU. In recognition of its achievements in pushing the frontiers of learning provision, the Commission on Higher Education of the Philippines has designated it as the National Centre of Excellence in Open Learning and Distance Education and uses UPOU's QA policies and approaches for its own *Policies and Guidelines on Distance Education.*[3]

Open University of Malaysia

OUM is a private university owned by Multimedia Technology Enhancement Operations (METEOR) Sdn. Bhd and a consortium of 11 of the country's public universities. It is accredited by the Malaysian Qualifications Agency (formerly the National Accreditation Board) which accredits both conventional and ODL institutions. OUM is designed to leverage the quality, prestige and capabilities of its owners, but it has also developed its own QA system for its courses and courseware and the Institute of Quality, Research and Innovation conducts annual audits to confirm quality in these. OUM has used the *QA Guidelines for Multi-Media Learning Materials*[4] developed by COL's Asian office, the Commonwealth Educational Media Centre for Asia and, according to the COL Quality Performance Indicators,[5] on a 1–5 scale, its course design and development rate at 3.8 points and its instructional design procedures at 4.5. Furthermore, four of OUM's departments have ISO 9001:2000 certification from the Standard and Industrial Research Institute of Malaysia. Here we see an example of an open university constantly trying to improve its performance and outcomes through internal and external QA measures, the latter pertaining to international as well as national standards.

National Open University of Nigeria

NOUN was initially established in 1983. It was suspended by the government a year later but its potential for providing access, equity and education for all became so self-evident that it had its second coming in 2001–2002. NOUN aims to adopt the best practices of different ODL institutions across the world while developing its own unique character. Thus, for most disciplines, instead of developing its own courses, the university purchases course materials from institutions in the UK, Australia, India and South Africa which have already been subject to QA and/or evaluation. The Directorate of Instructional Resources Development, which is responsible for course development and providing contextually relevant self-learning instructional materials in various formats, also carries out quality auditing to ensure that NOUN's course materials meet global standards and the instructional objectives.

In large countries such as India and Nigeria, where students are scattered over vast distances, timely dispatch and receipt of materials can be a major challenge. NOUN endeavours to address this problem by distributing materials through study centres and offering over 500 courses on the university's website, so that students may access them without delay wherever they may be. There is an emphasis on the use of ICTs, especially in relation to e-Examinations so that the turnaround time between examinations and announcement of results can be greatly reduced. NOUN also invests in continuous professional development of staff through its Regional Training and Research Institute for Distance and Open Learning which was established with support from COL.

NOUN is an example of a new open university which, rather than attempting to develop everything from scratch, draws on the products and practices of other open universities which have been tested and found to be successful in other jurisdictions and integrates them into its own operations and QA processes.

The Open University

The Open University (OU) is judged by the UK QAA using exactly the same criteria and reference points as with all of the UK universities. The OU remains faithful to its mission of openness and, despite one third of its degree students possessing lower entry qualifications than those usually required by the conventional universities, it ranks among the top UK universities for the quality of its teaching and research.

The OU operates transnationally. Through OpenLearn and iTunes University it makes its educational resources available globally. It supports its students throughout Europe, just as in the UK, through regional centres and locally appointed coordinators and tutors. In some parts of the world, direct OU delivery of courses has evolved to include partnership with local organizations and, because the OU holds its degree-awarding powers by virtue of a royal charter, the UK QAA Academic Infrastructure (see Chapter 7) is the reference point for any partnership, anywhere in the world. The OU has developed a *Guide to Quality and Standards in the Open University*[6] and a *Handbook for Validated Awards*[7] to inform and support such partnerships. It approves, monitors and evaluates its partner institutions and their programmes of study for OU-validated awards through its Validation Services (OUVS). The approach is both judgmental and developmental and, because the OU is the awarding partner, the partnership is in some respects unequal. Nevertheless, the network of partners represents an international academic community of practice, learning from one another and sharing quality practice. Two examples follow.

The OU's original partnership with what was then the Singapore Institute of Management (SIM) arose through an expressed need at government level for improved initial training for teachers in Singapore. Starting with teacher education, SIM became an OU Centre in Singapore and, with SIM's local knowledge, the OU then successfully launched additional programmes in Business and Management, IT and Computing, and Humanities. Initially, the OU retained overall responsibility for all operations. However, over time, as SIM developed as an institution, it began to propose changes to the operations and programmes to make them better suited for Singapore, and some of these measures were in turn adopted by the OU. The partnership helped the OU to become alert to indicators about the 'market' and local circumstances and was as much about building local capacity as exploiting market opportunities. SIM designed and delivered its own courses as well as OU courses, and in 1998 it became an accredited institution of the OU. Eventually, as SIM University, it became Singapore's first private university with its own degree-awarding powers.

The OU also partners with the non-profit private Arab Open University (AOU). The AOU is headquartered in Kuwait and operates through branches in Kuwait, Jordan, Lebanon, Egypt, Bahrain, Saudi Arabia and Oman. It is an autonomous institution with its own degree-awarding powers, is licenced to use OU learning materials in its own programmes and has acquired both institutional accreditation and validation of its programmes by the OUVS. However, it is subject to the requirements of local accrediting bodies which vary from one country to another, for example, in the amount of contact time required. One of the important lessons learned from this initiative has been awareness of cultural sensitivities, an issue addressed elsewhere in this book. Cultural awareness and cultural appropriateness are not only valuable in the transnational context, but in serving the multi-cultural student population in the UK. In both Singapore and the Arab countries, the OU's partners have had to offer a different blend of ODL and conventional face-to-face tuition. Neither is able to adopt the OU's open entry policy. If they did, they would not achieve local accreditation. As mentioned above, conservative attitudes and perceptions to 'open' higher education constrains the capacity of open universities to benefit from the distinctive model of quality at a scale that has been the hallmark of the OU.

Conclusion

There is still great need and scope and for rigorous QA in many of the world's open universities. It is important that they ensure quality for the students, have parity of esteem nationally and internationally, and achieve transnational accreditation, credit transfer and recognition of qualifications. How might this be achieved?

There is potential for the open universities to agree to, and monitor, generic threshold standards for their distance and e-learning. There are existing models that can be adapted and developed for this purpose. These include the European Association of Distance Teaching Universities (EADTU) *Excellence benchmarks for e-learning*,[8] the UK QAA's *Code of Practice Section 2: Collaborative provision and flexible and distributed learning (including e-learning)*,[9] the standards set by the UK Open and Distance Learning Quality Council and other accrediting agencies' expectations and guidance for those validating ODL programmes.

Through the good offices of such organizations as UNESCO, the International Network for Quality Assurance Agencies in Higher Education (INQAAHE) and COL, it should be possible to arrive at a set of principles and standards that regulators and government bodies across the world can use to benchmark ODL in their jurisdictions. Rather than proceeding on the assumption that most ODL is of poor quality, regulatory bodies would have some benchmarks against which to test such assumptions. And the open universities would be able to demonstrate that they are setting, moderating and achieving standards that are benchmarked against those of all other higher education institutions.

The OU views its fundamental purpose as no different from the other universities in the UK, even though its mission and mode of delivery is distinctive. It has been supported and encouraged in this approach by the QAA which frames its expectations and benchmarks around outcomes rather than inputs. Thus, unlike the regulations which bind many other open universities, there are no judgments based upon the number or size of classrooms, classes, physically located libraries and so on. Rather, the requirement is to demonstrate the quality of the courses and programmes, learning resources and support – and fitness for purpose.

Far too many institutions around the world are constrained in providing ODL and reaching out into their communities by time-honoured and misguided regulations. Undoubtedly, regulations such as the amount of face-to-face teaching or on-campus attendance required in ODL provision are framed with the very best intention of protecting the students' interests and safeguarding academic standards. Unfortunately, their impact on organizations that aspire to deliver quality ODL programmes is frequently counterproductive. Resources that would otherwise be used to achieve excellence in distance and online learning have to be deployed in satisfying the requirements for face-to-face teaching.

Across the world, the growth of private providers of higher education prompts much debate. There is an increasing tendency to regulate private and/ or overseas providers and impose rules over recognition of qualifications. Here again, the motive is commendable where it protects the learner, but actions sometimes appear to be motivated more by uninformed prejudice against distance or e-learning or by political concerns. Certainly it is important that students in one country should be guaranteed teaching, services and awards that are equivalent to those applying in their own and/or their providers' countries. And it is entirely appropriate for local regulation and accreditation to address local needs and concerns. But the current proliferation of often very local, very prescriptive and very detailed regulations runs counter to the wider development of consensus and harmonization across geographical regions. In a higher education landscape that is increasingly transnational, higher education institutions in many countries are finding that it is becoming more, rather than less, challenging to navigate issues of regulation and recognition.

Whilst there seems to be significant consensus about principles, there is little evidence of any real mutual recognition of the outcomes of accreditation or other kinds of QA processes. Here again, international and regional bodies have an important role to play. The Bologna Process, UNESCO and INQAAHE are encouraging the harmonization of QA principles and, to a lesser extent, practices, to foster mutual recognition of the outcomes of accreditation and other comparable processes. But it is often not possible for developing countries to muster the human and financial resources to develop such protocols on their own. However, there are resources to help these countries in this work. For example, COL has developed a *Transnational Qualifications Framework*[10] for use by the 32 small states of the Commonwealth, which is now freely available for adoption and adaptation by any country. COL's toolkits, instruments and publications, as well as a QA micro-site,[11] are other free resources available to all. And the Asia Pacific Accreditation and Certification Commission (APACC) has published its *Accreditation Manual* and *Handbook for Accreditors and Regional Skills Standards for TVET.*[12] APACC seeks to promote the comparability of education and training systems among concurring countries, enable harmonization and standardization of their curricular programmes and qualifications, and accelerate the competitiveness of workforces by facilitating mobility across national borders.

Most ODL QA systems focus mainly on input and process measures. A survey of nine mega-universities by Jung (2005), lists the key QA areas identified by these institutions. Most of them share three common themes: content, learner support, and learner assessment. Only one mentioned 'outcomes of courses and programmes' and only one identified 'accountability to stakeholders' as key areas of QA. Most of the criteria related to inputs and processes rather than to results and outcomes.

In 2010, Rediff.com undertook a ranking project in which it examined all the ODL institutions in India. It was only able to obtain enrolment data from 114 out of the 176 institutions, showing that India has a long way to go in ensuring comparable data availability. The 30 top institutions were also examined under three broad domains: reach and resources, learning experience, and results and efficiency. The top 10 comprised five open universities, three private players and two dual-mode state-level universities. IGNOU, the leviathan with 2.8 million students, convincingly topped the overall ranking, but dropped to 15th place in the results and efficiency category, revealing the need to improve its pass percentage and customer service. By contrast, Mumbai University, with its Institute of Distance and Open Learning, and the Symbiosis Centre for Distance Learning were rated 27th and 20th respectively in reach and resources, but 3rd and 6th respectively in terms of learning experience. Very few of the ODL providers rated consistently across all three categories, showing that if they wish to achieve credibility and quality, they must be open to more such surveys, provide much more evidence of their outcomes and shift the emphasis in their QA systems from inputs to outcomes.

The need for strong advocacy for, and evidence of, equitable, viable, effective and quality ODL is greater today than it was 40 years ago. The content and tone of the above recommendations may lead the reader to conclude that the efforts of the past four decades have failed to establish the credibility of ODL conclusively since it continues to be a matter of debate. But it needs to be appreciated that the reference point for the quality and effectiveness of ODL, still a fledgling educational/training modality in many countries, lies in a higher education system that has developed over almost a thousand years. Such esteem by virtue of so long a practice and association is not likely to be easily dented, much less completely erased by the newcomers. The going will be tough, but the ODL providers are on the right track and will get closer to their goal of reaching the unreached and gaining better recognition by guaranteeing quality education.

Notes

1 http://www.col.org/resources/speeches/2010presentation/2010-01-28/Pages/default.aspx
2 http://www.adb.org/documents/rrps/sri/rrp_sri_33251.pdf
3 http://202.57.63.198/chedwww/index.php/eng/Information/CHED-Memorandum-Orders/2005-CHED-Memorandum-Orders
4 http://www.cemca.org/finalQAMLM.pdf
5 http://www.col.org/SiteCollectionDocuments/HE_QA_Toolkit_web.pdf
6 http://www.open.ac.uk/pdg/lto/qa/p3.shtml
7 http://www.open.ac.uk/validate/documents/004-ou-handbook-for-validated-awards.pdf
8 http://www.eadtu.nl/e-xcellenceqs
9 http://www.qaa.ac.uk/academicinfrastructure/codeOfPractice/section2/default.asp
10 http://www.colfinder.org/vussc/VUSSC_TQF_document_procedures_and_guidelines_Final_April2010.pdf
11 http://www.col.org/resources/micrositeQA
12 http://www.springerlink.com/content/v8v007854484n723/

References

COL. (2009). *Quality assurance toolkit for distance higher education institutions and programmes.* Vancouver: Commonwealth of Learning. Retrieved from http://www.col.org/SiteCollectionDocuments/HE_QA_Toolkit_web.pdf

Jung, I. S. (2005). Quality assurance survey of mega-universities. In C. McIntosh (Ed.), *Lifelong learning and distance higher education* (pp. 79–95). Paris/Vancouver: UNESCO-COL.

Kanwar, A. (2010, April). *Review and improvement model (COL RIM)*. Paper presented at the *meeting of the University of Guyana*, Georgetown. Retrieved from http://www.col.org/SiteCollectionDocuments/Kanwar100409_COLRIM.pdf

Latchem, C., & Jung, I. S. (2009). *Distance and blended learning in Asia*. New York: Routledge.

Mills, R. (2006). A case study of the Open University, United Kingdom. In B. Koul, & A. Kanwar (Eds.), *Towards a culture of quality* (pp. 135–148). Vancouver: Commonwealth of Learning.

11

QUALITY ASSURANCE IN A MEGA-UNIVERSITY: UNIVERSITAS TERBUKA

Tian Belawati, Aminudin Zuhairi and I.G.A.K. Wardani

Introduction

Indonesia first embarked on correspondence education in the 1950s. In 1984, the Indonesia Open University or Universitas Terbuka (UT) was inaugurated by Presidential Decree as the 45th university in Indonesia. It had two main missions: to broaden access to higher education and to improve teacher training standards and qualifications. With a population of around 230 million people – Indonesia is the world's fourth most populous country – and with less than 20% of the relevant age group able to attend conventional universities, the open access provided by UT is seen as most important for the Indonesian people. The university now offers almost 1,000 courses to 646,467 students, 84% of whom are teachers. The majority of its students reside in Sumatra, Java, Kalimantan, Bali, West Nusa Tenggara, Sulawesi, Maluku, East Nusa Tenggara and Papua. UT also operates in Saudi Arabia, Singapore and Johor, Malaysia, and in 2011, will also start teaching students in Hong Kong, Taiwan, Macau and South Korea.

UT's Head Office is in Kota Tangerang Selatan, a satellite city of the capital Jakarta. It has 37 Regional Offices in 32 provinces and has Faculties of Economics and Developmental Studies, Social and Political Sciences, Mathematics and Natural Sciences, Teacher Training and Educational Studies, and one Graduate School. Delivery is by means of print supplemented by audio/video, computer/ UT Online and some broadcast television and radio programmes. UT's learning materials are developed by recognized content experts who are lecturers in reputable Indonesian universities. Their quality is demonstrated by their wide use by other Indonesian universities, and they are accessible to both UT students and the general public through the Karunika e-Bookstore. The university also provides the off-campus learners with tutorials and practical learning facilitated by qualified tutors, instructors and/or supervisors from UT and various well-known public and private universities. For some courses, resource persons are invited in from business, industry and other sectors.

UT operates an open policy for enrolment and flexible arrangements for study. Apart from the Teacher Training and Educational Studies programmes, which are only for in-service early childhood, primary and secondary school teachers, all of UT's programmes are open to any holders of a high school diploma, regardless of age or whether they are recent school leavers or working adults. Thirty-seven percent of the students are male and 63% are female. The fees are set low and the students may register for any of the courses on offer, take time off from their studies or resume their studies at any time of the year, and study at their own pace according to their needs and circumstances. There is no time limit to completing the studies: once students enrol on at least one course, their personal data are entered into the student record system and only transferred out of this into the alumni record system on completion or graduation. Students not taking courses within four consecutive semesters are categorized as non-active, but are re-activated as soon as they re-register for a course. Students may apply for credit transfer for courses previously taken at other accredited universities. They are expected to study independently or in study/tutorial groups, and the course materials are designed specifically for these purposes.

The number of students continues to increase. Operating an open policy for such a large number of students and over such a large and divided landmass, requires a very strong and well-articulated management system. The Head Office is responsible for the academic and administrative policies and developing academic programmes and materials, while the daily operational activities to serve the students are devolved to the Regional Offices. To provide optimal educational services to students, UT collaborates with many institutions and organizations including:

- Local public and private universities which help with the writing of course and examination materials and providing tutors, practicum instructors, examination supervisors and facilities and support for the students.
- Local government agencies and offices for conducting tutorials and examinations and providing student scholarships.
- Q-Channel and TV-Edukasi for televising tutorial and promotional materials and RRI for broadcasting radio tutorials.
- Bank Rakyat Indonesia and Bank Tabungan Negara for payment of tuition fees and purchase of course materials by students.

Developing and Implementing the QA system

The sheer scale and nature of the UT enterprise and complexity of logistics presents enormous challenges in terms of assuring quality. Prior to 2001, a number of key policy documents had stressed the need for quality, but it was only in UT's 2001–2005 Operational Plan that the need for QA was explicitly expressed. This led to the establishment of a Quality Assurance Committee which was answerable to the Rector and Vice Rectors and mandated to develop a QA framework. The Asian Association of Open Universities (AAOU) had just formulated a QA framework and since UT was a founding member of the AAOU, the QA Committee decided that rather than re-inventing the wheel, it would base its system on this. Through a process of university-wide consultation, the Committee developed a draft QA Policy Manual comprising 107 statements of best practice regarding:

- Policy and planning.
- Human resource recruitment and development.
- Management and administration.
- Learners.
- Programme design and development.
- Course design and development.
- Learning support.
- Learner assessment.
- Media for learning.

All members of staff were then invited to comment on this Manual with the aim of generating a sense of ownership and obtaining further inputs regarding the steps taken and needed. The Manual was then converted into a self-evaluation instrument by adding quality indicators, using a 1–4 Likert scale, to gain university-wide self-judgments on the extent to which these indicators were being fulfilled and to measure attitudes towards the best practice statements. When this self-evaluation was first carried out in 2002, the average rating score for all 107 best practice statements was 2.46. When it was repeated in 2005, the results showed an increase to 3.83. It had been anticipated that the 2005 ratings would be higher than this, but it transpired that introduction of the QA process had led to greater understanding and higher expectations on the part of the managers and staff.

The next step was the development of QA Job Manuals to encourage and support continuous improvement. These defined the required performance standards for all systems, mechanisms and procedures, the intended outcomes, and the resources and competencies needed for their realization. These standards were not imposed by senior management, but developed by many small teams of academic, technical and administrative staff in the various operational units of the university. This approach enabled the staff to provide constructive guidelines for the various activities and ensured that the reference standards were understood, realistic, achievable and respected. It also helped to develop the sense of a learning organization within which people could readily learn from the ideas and practices of others.

In March 2003, by Rector's Decree, the QA framework, QA Policy Manual and QA Job Manuals were formally adopted by UT. Given the scale and complexity of the university and planned QA system, it was decided that it would be best to have a special unit to co-ordinate and oversee the university-wide implementation of QA activities based on the policies and guidelines formulated by the QA Committee, rather than a 'collective' or 'dispersed' QA system as at some other mega and open universities (Jung, 2005; Latchem & Jung, 2009). The year 2004 was named the 'Year of the Spirit of Quality Assurance'. Thus UT embarked on establishing a quality culture in ODL (Koul & Kanwar, 2006) and from this point on it was committed to:

- Continuous and consistent use of the QA Policy and Job Manuals.
- Establishing a quality-oriented work culture in line with the documented QA systems and procedures.
- Integrating the QA system in annual action plans for continuous improvement.
- Encouraging and supporting staff to achieve the specified quality targets.

As might be expected in any change or innovation, these approaches met with some initial resistance. Clear direction, supervision and resource commitment were needed from senior management to win over the hearts and minds of the staff. Another critical step was establishing the link between QA and human performance management. The Job Manuals helped to generate a quality-oriented work culture in line with systems and procedures documented in the QA Policy Manual. These explained the job descriptions and performance standards/criteria, how feedback would be provided, the appeals process and how various incentive systems related to performance. It was found that these not only helped staff in performing their daily tasks, but also triggered the realization that their knowledge and skills could always be improved upon and that targets and performance indicators could always be raised. These Manuals have since been revised several times, on each occasion reflecting the increasing belief of staff that 'quality begins with us'. In all administrative, academic and service units, the staff are bound by work contracts which they agree to at the start of each year, their performance is monitored throughout the year, and at year's end, their performance and achievements are assessed. Quality performers receive some reward or incentive in the following year. Underachievers receive training and support.

After almost a decade of continuous effort, all UT staff can now be considered to be aware of, and committed to, continuous improvement. QA has become integral and routine and UT's quality culture received special mention in the granting of the Certificate of Quality by the International Council for Open and Distance Education (ICDE).

QA in the In-service Teacher Education Programmes

It may be instructive to drill down to see the university's QA system at work. As mentioned earlier, the need for improved and more widely available teacher education for early childhood, elementary and secondary teachers was one of the main drivers for Indonesia adopting ODL. These teacher education programmes are by far the most popular of UT's courses, attracting 500,000 students per semester.

It may be recalled that four of the components in the QA Policy Manual were programme design and development; course design and development; learning support and learner assessment. These apply to all of UT's study programmes, so let us see how the Faculty of Teacher Training and Educational Studies operates in accord with these requirements.

Programme Design and Development

The first three best practice statements in this component read:

1. The programmes are developed on the basis of needs of learners either through market research or consultation with industry/professions.
2. The programmes reflect the institutional mission and objectives.
3. Access is as open as possible with flexible entry and exit points.

The bachelor programmes for teachers were developed in response to the Government's December 2005 Teacher Law[1] which aimed to improve the qualifications and classroom performance of Indonesia's 2.7 million teachers who constitute at least 70% of the country's public service. Only about half of Indonesian students are taught by teachers holding a university degree. The programmes had to offer the same curriculum and same competencies as the conventional teacher education institutions. And because of variations in the teachers' qualifications and experience, the programmes had to be multi-entry and designed to accommodate these differences. Depending on their prior training and years of experience, the teachers can start their studies at different levels and can gain exemption by having taken earlier courses.

Course Design and Development

The first three best practice statements in this component read:

1.   The course is designed according to the programme objectives as well as the needs of prospective learners and employers.
2.   The content and assessment processes are determined by the learning outcomes.
3.   The methods of learner support are built into the design of the course.

The documentation for the teacher education programmes clearly and comprehensively describes the curriculum, aims and objectives, target groups, expected competences, teaching and learning processes, learner assessment methods, delivery modes, support services and credit and time requirements. The curriculum is regularly evaluated and revised to meet the changing needs and demands of the national education system, school curricula, teachers and society at large. The new policies and expectations mean that the expectations of graduate competencies/attributes also need to be reviewed and revised in consultation with the stakeholders. Teaching practicums are crucial to these programmes, for it is only in the classroom that the teachers can demonstrate their teaching competencies and reflect on the theories, principles and research they have been exposed to. Such activity-based learning must be well designed, planned, managed, supervised and evaluated. Failure to ensure this will result in poor or failed teachers. So the programme is designed to allow teachers to take the practicums in their own classrooms supervised and mentored by their principals or more experienced colleagues. At the end of each week, the teachers and their supervisors or mentors share their ideas and experiences. Where necessary, micro-teaching is also used to reinforce or improve teaching skills.

Learner Support

The first three best practice statements in this component read:

1.   Academic support is considered during programme development and built into the design of the course/materials.
2.   The tutors are selected and trained for their role of facilitating learning both before and during the offering of the course.
3.   Sufficient group tutoring opportunities are provided to enable learners to investigate and expand their understanding of the content.

It may have been a considerable number of years since many of these in-service teachers last engaged in formal education and most find difficulty in wholly independent study. So these programmes include face-to-face tutorials to help them with their learning, use of the learning materials and managing their often limited time for study. The many hundreds of tutors needed to support these teachers are carefully selected according to strict criteria. Most of them are senior lecturers in conventional public universities who, being familiar with only face-to-face teaching and learning, need special training in tutoring distance education students and the course content, after which they are accredited as UT's tutors. Despite the large numbers of teachers taking these courses, the tutorial sessions are so organized as to involve groups of 30 or less. The teachers are also encouraged and enabled to form their own study groups, and these have been shown to be teachers' most valued and important support system.

Learner Assessment

The first three of best practice statements in this component read:

1. Assessment is integral to every learning and teaching strategy adopted and includes formative as well as summative processes.
2. Self-assessment should be extensively used throughout a course to enable independent learners to gauge and adjust their progress.
3. Where appropriate, assessment involves a measurement of the achievement of learning outcomes.

In these in-service teacher training programmes, it is important to assess both the academic and professional competencies of the teachers. The former are assessed through written assignments, tests and examination. The latter are assessed through practicums, the use of portfolios and supervisors' or mentors' observations. During the practicums, using live classroom observation or videoconferencing, the teachers are assessed for their abilities in planning, preparing and evaluating their lesson plans, teaching and learning, and uses of resources, classroom management, and inspiring and motivating students. Their professional capacities in such matters as reflecting on their teaching, assessing pupils' work and maintaining records are assessed by examining their teaching portfolios. Their capacities to interact with their colleagues, other professionals and the families of their pupils are also observed and recorded by the supervisors and mentors. The commitment and integrity of these supervisors and mentors is clearly critical to assuring quality, and so each teacher is evaluated by two supervisors who receive special training in the use of the assessment manual, instruments and methods.

To assess the longer-term outcomes of these in-service courses, UT conducts studies into the graduates' performance. A 2001–2002 study concerned 344 elementary school teachers in six provinces who were graduates of the Diploma II programme. Data were collected through classroom observation, the use of a teacher performance assessment instrument, a questionnaire, and interviews with stakeholders. The mean score of the teachers' performance was 3.7 (in a 1–5 scale), or 74% of the ideal performance. A 2008 study involved 200 graduates of the elementary and early childhood teacher education programmes, again from the six provinces and using the same survey methods. In this case, the mean score of the elementary teachers' performance was 4.16 (83.2%) and the early child-hood teachers' performance, 4.32 (86.4%). The school principals and other stake-holders reported that the performance of these teachers was not only comparable with that of teachers graduating from the face-to-face teacher education institu-tions, but often revealed greater independence, more creativity and a stronger work ethic. Some of these teachers have received Teacher of the Year Awards from their local education authorities, some have become pioneers in classroom-based action research, and some have become leaders of teachers' working groups. Such outcomes help UT evidence that distance education can be comparable with face-to-face continuing professional development.

External Assessment and Accreditation

QA at UT is essentially an internal process, conducted in the spirit of continuous improvement to better satisfy the stakeholders. But it is also acknowledged that UT can never claim to be a high-quality institution on the basis of its own inter-nal quality audits. It needs validation from external auditors or assessors, not only to convince the stakeholders who are not involved with or persuaded by the internal QA process, but to provide feedback to the institution on whether it is achieving acknowledged and recognized quality standards. External QA also forces the institution to verify the soundness of its internal QA system. For all of those reasons, UT has invited external assessment by the International Council for Open and Distance Education (ICDE), International Organization for Standardisation (ISO), and National Accreditation Board for Indonesian Higher Education (BAN-PT), an independent body accountable to the Minister of National Education.

The ICDE assessment was not concerned with the academic standards of UT's courses or qualifications, since these are regulated nationally and there are no agreed international standards for qualifications, curriculum and aca-demic content. It focused on the internal QA procedures, reviews and out-comes, the QA Centre's use of external reference points for the quality and standards of services, the internal systems for the management of quality and standards, the experiences of students as learners, and the quality of the teach-ing staff, including appointment criteria and the ways in which teaching effec-tiveness is appraised, improved and rewarded. The granting of the ICDE Certificate of Quality in 2005 and 2010 helped to re-assure UT's stakeholders of the university's ability to provide quality distance education throughout

Indonesia. The procedure also provided management and staff with useful feedback on their achievements and the matters needing further improvement. The commendations for the instructionally sound learning materials, effective materials distribution systems, extensive and well-conducted systems for handling examination manuscripts and quality of the tutors and their training and support system also helped to boost staff morale and motivation. The ICDE review team also noted a deep commitment to quality and QA in the various departments that it visited, including the Regional Offices. It also saw UT's venturing into online learning as offering tremendous opportunities for the university to participate in new areas of human resource development in the country.

Seeking ISO certification was another attempt to verify the largely self-developed QA procedures. In 2006, UT received ISO 9001:2000 and ISO 9001:2008 certification for the quality management of course materials distribution from the headquarters to the Regional Offices. At the time of writing, UT has obtained 10 ISO 9001:2008 individual certificates for the quality of the learner support systems in 10 of the 37 Regional Offices, one ISO 9001:2008 certificate for the combined learner support of 25 of the Regional Offices, and a further ISO 9001:2008 certificate for teaching, learning and examination materials development and distribution and academic administration services.

BAN-PT is concerned with the quality of the educational inputs, processses and outcomes at the programme level. Assessment is carried out by examining the course documentation, self-evaluation methods and reports and site visits. The site visits provide opportunities for classroom and learning support observation and for interviews with the university's and faculty's senior managers, teachers, tutors, support staff and students. If a study programme fulfils the performance indicators set by the Accreditation Board, accreditation is granted and is valid for 5 years. All of UT's programmes that were established before 2005 have been accredited and at the time of writing, UT is about to renew the accreditation status of these programmes and embark on the accreditation of all newly established programmes.

Applying for certification and accreditation from these three external quality agencies has forced UT to follow national and international standardized procedures. It has involved a steep learning curve, but it has also helped UT to gain confidence in its own internal QA system and ability to satisfy its stakeholders. The external quality audit is therefore considered as important as the internal QA process. But the most important aspect of all this is not the attainment of accreditation, or certification but the courses of action involved in achieving these.

Conclusion

Implementing QA in a large institution such as UT is a monumental task. It is all too easy to talk about quality, but it requires explicit and consistent commitment by senior and middle managers, a systematic approach and a great deal of commitment, effort, patience, awareness raising and training to ensure that every unit and every staff member is committed to changing the work culture. So, what are the main lessons to be learned from the UT experience? Our experience is that:

- Quality is not just a question of rhetoric by senior managers, grandiose mission statements or policymaking that is intended for show but never implemented. Quality needs to be embedded in the planning and operations of every part and at every level of the institution.
- QA needs to be looked upon as an investment and senior management needs to evidence its commitment to QA by investing major resources in its implementation.
- Transparency and accountability are essential. Every unit in the university needs to be honest in appraising what outcomes it has, and has not, achieved and which systems and procedures do, and do not, work. Such findings then provide the basis for continuous improvement and, in the case of units functioning less well, encouraging and supporting them to do better.
- It takes time for the concepts and practices of QA to be fully internalized by an entire institution. As in any change process, there will be cynicism, indifference and resistance. This is only to be expected, since QA challenges and threatens time-honoured attitudes and practices.
- All decisions about QA should be arrived at through a participative process of 'upstream management', organizing and adding value whenever a problem, opportunity or new idea is identified.
- QA involves team building, building morale, improving work systems and procedures, and changing the work culture.
- Only people make things happen and everyone's work in the institution should be assumed to have a direct impact on stakeholder satisfaction. From this it follows that improving unit and institutional performance depends upon improving individual performance.
- Embracing QA can help institutions become learning organizations, more open and adaptable to change and innovation, more prepared for global partnership and competition and more able to benchmark themselves against other institutions in other nations, share best practice and achieve a quality brand for ODL.

With the changing times and educational and technological advances, UT recognizes that its efforts regarding QA have only just begun, but by being able to evidence the various external and internal QA measures and outcomes, it is now in a better position to convince its stakeholders of its commitment to quality. It will take time to see what impact this has on other distance education providers and conventional institutions in Indonesia.

Note

1 http://web.worldbank.org/external/default/main?page PK=34370&piPK=34424&theSite PK=4607&menuPK=34463& contentMDK=21400192

References

Jung, I. S. (2005). Quality assurance survey of mega-universities. In C. McIntosh, & V. Zeynep (Eds.), *Perspectives on distance education: Lifelong learning and distance higher education* (pp. 79–98). Vancouver: Commonwealth of Learning and Paris: UNESCO.

Koul, B. N., & Kanwar, A. (Eds.). (2006). *Perspectives on distance education: Towards a quality culture.* Vancouver: Commonwealth of Learning.

Latchem, C., & Jung, I. S. (2009). *Distance and blended learning in Asia.* New York: Routledge.

12

QUALITY ASSURANCE IN A CONSORTIUM: OPEN UNIVERSITIES AUSTRALIA

Teresa De Fazio, John Ketonen and Michael Crock

Introduction

Open Universities Australia (OUA) is Australia's largest online higher education provider. It is a broker for seven shareholder universities (Curtin University, Griffith University, Macquarie University, Monash University, RMIT University, Swinburne University of Technology and University of South Australia) and 11 other public and private education and training providers. Offering more than 1,040 units and 131 qualifications from these quality-assured providers, OUA arranges for a very wide range of study options in Arts, Business, Education, Health, IT and Law and Justice. Since its inception in 1993, it has had over 120,000 enrolments and over the past 3 years has grown at a rate of over 25%. Quality assurance (QA) is a vital concern of OUA and this chapter details the steps taken to meet the stakeholders' requirements, assure and improve the quality of the courses and services and operate in a fiscally responsible way.

Open Universities Australia

OUA had its origins in a 1993 Commonwealth (Federal) Department of Employment, Education and Training (DEET)-funded open learning initiative to make university study available to all intending students unable to gain places in other systems on a fee-for-service basis. Australia's public universities were invited to tender to establish a company to administer this system and, following negotiations between DEET and the various competing universities, a deal was struck. The Monash University-owned Open Learning Agency of Australia (OLAA) was funded for 3 years on the understanding that it would then become self-funding and operate for a minimum of 10 years (Latchem & Pritchard, 1994).

OLAA's courses and units derived from existing accredited degree programmes. Any Australian university tendering to provide these had to subject their proposals to a rigorous and independent selection process to ensure quality in content, educational design, student services and fit within the curriculum framework. They also had to offer credit recognition and degree pathways for the OLAA students. There were no prerequisite academic standards; the only requirement was payment of a fee. Despite being somewhat disadvantaged financially and some early scepticism over the credibility and sustainability of this initiative, OLAA thrived. Meeting a hitherto untapped demand, its successes encouraged many of the universities to adopt similar flexible approaches. So what became the OUA had to reinvent itself, find new markets and above all, assure quality in its products and services.

The number of OUA preparatory, vocational, undergraduate and postgraduate programmes is continually increasing.[1] OUA students may enrol in any first-year undergraduate unit without the normal entry requirements applying in the universities. All they put at risk is the fees they pay. OUA helps them identify the courses appropriate to their needs, advises them on the costs of study and their eligibility for various government financial assistance schemes such as Austudy and scholarship and award schemes. OUA also operates its own scholarship scheme. In the academic year 2011, it awarded scholarships totalling A$120,000 to seven undergraduates, one postgraduate student and one indigenous student. The OUA scholarship recipients are selected on the basis of outstanding academic achievement.

The students are guided and assisted through the enrolment process. Credit transfer and recognition of prior learning are assessed on an individual basis and OUA also assists students wishing to change courses, defer studies and so on. Students are enabled to get in touch with each other to discuss their studies through a student network called My OUA. Students who feel that they are unprepared for the rigour of academic study may also choose from a range of non-accredited study skills preparation programmes (Figure 12.1, overleaf).

OUA students may study and take exams anywhere in the world but they graduate from a participating Australian university, not OUA. Most of the courses have no quotas. The students study at their own pace according to their work, family or personal circumstances. If their exam/assignment results are of the required standard, they gain credits which accumulate to permit university entry. The courses and units they study, their tutors and the assessment methods are identical to the equivalent on- and off-campus courses of the providing universities. While the universities operate on a semester basis, OUA's undergraduate programmes operate on a 13-week basis and its postgraduate programmes on a 14-week basis. The vocational units are offered on a continuous basis and differ

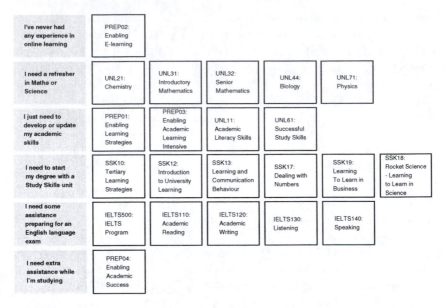

FIGURE 12.1   Helping students prepare for study at OUA

Source: Open Universities Australia 2010 Handbook (2010).

in duration. Online is the main means of delivery but print and correspondence are still used for students with special needs or who are incarcerated. An undergraduate degree comprises 24 units. Students who complete of all of the course requirements are then able to graduate alongside all of the students who have studied by conventional means at the awarding university of their choice.

About two-thirds of the students are female, and most of the students are in the 18–29 age group and take the Arts and Social Science courses. There are also students in prisons, students with special needs, students studying through special arrangements with their employers and students studying under special scholarship schemes such as the Thai–Burma Refugee Programme. The wide range of backgrounds, characteristics and reasons for study presents OUA with interesting challenges in responding to students' needs and ensuring quality inputs and outcomes.

OUA's QA System

OUA is acutely aware of the need to ensure quality in the students' learning and engaging with tutors, advisors, third-party service providers and other students (De Fazio, 2008, 2010). It also has to ensure quality in its brokering role and value-add to the contributions of the participating universities, all of which have their own QA systems. It must also conform to the Higher Education Support

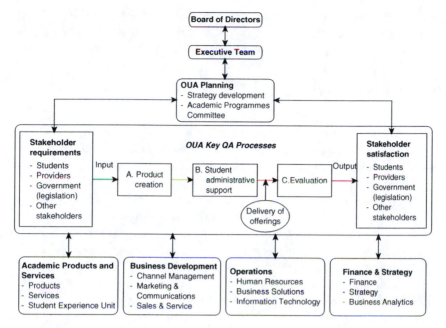

FIGURE 12.2   OUA's QA system

Act, failure to comply with which can have serious consequences. For all of these reasons, OUA requires a QA system as shown in Figure 12.2.

There are four main operational areas. Academic Products and Services is responsible for the portfolio of courses and units on offer, evaluating student satisfaction and overseeing learning pathways and retention initiatives. The Business Development group deals with the various client groups, marketing, communications and sales. The Operations group is concerned with professional development, business solutions and IT. The Finance and Strategy group oversees the financial and strategic directions of the organization.

OUA operates to a 3-year strategic plan. The strategic planning involves determining the stakeholders' needs, the requirements for new or revised products, procedures and services and the funding and resource implications of these. The implementation and monitoring of the strategic plan is the responsibility of the Executive Team but the provider institutions participate in this process through the Academic Programmes Committee. Each of the operational groups is responsible for devising its annual plan consistent with the strategic plan. Each of these groups sets key performance indicators and there are half-yearly reviews of all staff to see how their performance accords with these. The entire system is designed to ensure consistency, synergy and a sense of ownership in the ways in which the operational groups work towards the agreed outcomes. The final stage of the process is evaluation. Unit Satisfaction Surveys and portfolio reviews are employed to gauge stakeholder satisfaction and the results are fed back into the planning process to continuously improve the quality of the operations.

OUA's Stakeholders

OUA regards the students as its prime stakeholders, both in an academic and a business sense. Not only are the students affected by the quality of the OUA's programmes and services, but they contribute to these by bringing their knowledge, skills, experience and enthusiasm to the learning and providing feedback on their needs, circumstances, experiences in and satisfaction with the courses and units.

The relationship between OUA and the other stakeholders is rather more complex. Lendrum (1995) identifies three levels of provider–customer relationship. At the lowest level is the *vendor relationship*. Here transactions are basic, communications are limited and the provider–customer relationship is not strong and may be temporary. At the next level is the *supplier relationship*. This involves value-adding initiatives, fuller communications and stronger multifunctional relationships that may be of longer term or permanent. At the highest level, there is *partnership*. Here there is the sharing of visions and strategies and mutual interest in achieving strong and open communications, quality products and services and trust.

OUA has to identify and develop the appropriate level of relationship with its various stakeholders in order to assure quality in its management, products and services. The major providers of courses and units are regarded as partners. They have representation on the Academic Programmes Committee which meets quarterly to make recommendations on the programmes to be provided and modes of delivery, assessment and accreditation to be employed. Consultation and communications with the providing institutions also occur through forums and conferences held throughout the year. These events also help to strengthen working relationships, consider ways of improving operations and collaboration, examine trends in technology and online learning and showcase achievements in teaching, learning and student services. There are also annual provider portfolio reviews which evidence quality and best practice pertinent to each provider.

The relationship with the third-party suppliers, those who provide services such as counselling and career services, supply textbooks, materials and IT services and generally help to ensure that OUA's processes are responsive to requirements, is more than that of a supplier or a vendor. The OUA sets key performance indicators and regularly monitors these third-party suppliers' performance against these to ensure that the terms of agreement are met.

OUA also regards its own staff as an important stakeholder group. Employee satisfaction and motivation are essential to quality in operations, and so human resource policies and strategies are designed to ensure clarity in roles and functions, cross-departmental collaboration and the provision of staff training. OUA also regards society as a whole as a stakeholder group. It considers good and responsible corporate citizenship as integral to its mission, and it seeks to ensure that its policies and processes address environmental, economic, societal and community needs. For example, it has a commitment to a green building initiative which has resulted in installing a vegetated roof cover on the OUA building to increase resilience to climate change as well as provide additional outdoor amenities for the staff.

A major part of assuring student and other stakeholder satisfaction is ensuring that all of the processes leading up to the delivery of the products and services for which OUA is directly and indirectly responsible are managed efficiently and effectively. These processes include ensuring adequate provision of funding for new or revised courses and units, ensuring that these accord with OUA's own quality criteria and ensuring that all the tutors are adequately trained for the work. The OUA also ensures that its website, handbook, student advisory services and one-stop study management hub are up-to-date and user-friendly for all potential and existing students.

Product Reviews and Satisfaction Reviews

To assure quality in the OUA 'product' and 'brand', the organization conducts reviews prior to the release of every new or revised and improved course as well as at strategic points throughout its lifespan. Funding to providing institutions is dependent upon successful achievement of successive milestones. The QA reviews are concerned with the quality of the learning resources, delivery strategies and pedagogy and are based upon the guidelines for auditing online courses and units suggested by Herrington, Herrington, Oliver, Stoney, and Willis (2001):

- The product (learning resources) criteria cover:

  - Accessibility. Ensuring that the learning resources are organized in such ways as to make them easy to locate and access.
  - Currency and richness of curriculum content. Ensuring that the learning resources are appropriate and reflect a rich variety of perspectives.
  - Strong use of media. Ensuring that the various technologies and media are selected and used in appropriate ways.
  - Inclusivity. Ensuring that the content and materials demonstrate cultural and gender inclusivity.

- The delivery strategy criteria cover:

  - Clear goals, directions and learning plans. Ensuring that the information and expectations of student roles are clear.

- Communication. Ensuring that the courses and units provide opportunities for, encourage and support dialogue between the students and their lecturers/tutors and the students and other students.
- Equity and access. Ensuring that the course and unit materials and activities are accessible and available to all students enroled in these programmes.

• The learning pedagogy criteria cover:

- Authenticity in tasks. Ensuring that learning activities involve tasks and contexts that reflect the ways in which the knowledge will be used in real-life settings.
- Opportunities for collaboration. Ensuring that the learning environment encourages and requires students to collaborate, thereby encouraging problem solving and critical thinking.
- Learner-centred environments. Ensuring that there is a focus on activities that provide degrees of freedom, decision making, reflection and self-regulation.
- Engaging. Ensuring that the learning activities challenge learners and provide some form of encouragement and motivation to support their engagement.
- Meaningful Assessment. Ensuring that authentic and integrated assessment is used to evaluate student achievement.
- Competencies. Ensuring that competencies are scaffolded well so that incremental tasks lead to major tasks and learning objectives.

Student Support

OUA ensures that the catalogue of courses and units is comprehensive and up-to-date, that there is appropriate cross-accreditation between providers, that articulation points are built in, and that its offerings and services provide students with every opportunity to achieve successful learning outcomes. The learners often need assistance to enable them to understand and rise to the challenge of academic level studies, so as shown earlier, the product range includes enabling and preparatory courses, both generic and discipline specific and accredited and non-accredited, to cater for the different needs of individuals and cohorts.

Throughout their studies, online tutoring support is available 24/7. This is provided by a third-party provider called Smarthinking.com. Through this service, students are entitled to 4 hours of academic skills tutoring for each unit undertaken. They can also apply for further assistance at a discounted rate. This system enables them to connect with tutors for live online tutoring sessions, check out sample online tutoring sessions and submit drafts of essays to the Online Writing Lab for detailed critiques on their writing skills. Personalized feedback is typically provided within 24 hours. Throughout the life of this service, 90% of OUA students have stated that they have found working with a Smarthinking tutor valuable in supplementing their learning and in helping to develop their confidence and academic skills. Additional support services, such as counselling of a more personal nature to assist students in regard to life issues that impinge upon their studies or well-being are also provided. Career advice such as resumé writing, developing interviewing skills and selecting career paths is also on offer.

OUA has also implemented a tutor support management system. Designed especially to provide online tutorial support in high enrolment units, particularly in the first year of undergraduate study, this involves:

- Ensuring that the student–tutor ratio in high enrolment units (typically 350–400) is no more than 200 students per tutor.
- Determining the required number of tutors and identifying and contracting the tutors.
- Organizing and delivering professional development programmes for those tutors who are employed by OUA and providing tutor guidelines for those tutors who are employed by the institutional providers. These set out the requirements – for example, the response times to student postings – clarify the key points and activities involved in the units of study and provide guidance on how to conduct the weekly, content-related online discussions, provide email support and manage interactions within the virtual learning environment. A system of online professional development for tutors which replicates the student learning experience to provide context and understanding has been in operation for several years. Because of increasing interest in such professional development, OUA is currently redesigning this programme and devising others to address other aspects of online teaching.

OUA recognizes outstanding achievement in the uses of online learning technologies through a peer-recognized award scheme called NOVA. The winners are selected on the basis of innovation and sound principles in instructional design, learner support and uses of technology. Students are also able to nominate academics for recognition as outstanding or exemplary teachers when completing the unit satisfaction survey.

Student Evaluation

Student evaluation is another critical component in OUA's QA system. Several survey systems are used to yield valuable feedback on the quality of the student experience:

- On completion of each unit, a student unit satisfaction survey is administered to provide feedback on the unit and inform OUA and providing institution on the experiences of the learners. These findings are carefully analyzed and their implications are considered and acted upon within OUA. They are also shared with the providers to help them continuously improve the quality of their offerings.
- Surveys of learner support interventions are also undertaken to gauge the students' uses and levels of satisfaction with these. For example, one survey is used to gain feedback on the Smarthinking services.
- A leavers' survey is sent out to all students who are no longer studying through the OUA to gauge the circumstances that currently prevent them from studying or have led to their discontinuing their studies. This information is then used to inform the various intervention strategies that can be provided by OUA, for example, by making clearer the expectations of learners and fine-tuning or improving information and learner support services to help learners realize their expectations.
- OUA also operates a system for documenting, analyzing and resolving student complaints. This is another invaluable source of information for continuous improvement by OUA and the institutional providers.

These surveys are critical, but they do not take account of the whole student experience or the other stakeholders' needs. This is why OUA also reviews the quality of, and need for improvement in, such critical processes as the print, telephone and online information services for students and intending students, the management of student enquiries and complaints, the admission of students into courses and units and the funding and other resourcing of new or revised offerings. These various QA processes must all interlink to achieve a common goal – to meet, or better still, exceed, stakeholder needs. For example, in response to student requests for greater flexibility when making enquiries, OUA has recently extended the closing time for the student advisory office to 10.00 p.m. (Australian Eastern Standard Time) between Monday and Thursday each week. Friday operating hours remain 8.30 a.m.–5.00 p.m. (AEST). These extended operating hours allow the student advisors to assist students in the various time zones across Australia and those who find it difficult to call during working hours. This is but one example of OUA's commitment to continuously improving its student support services.

By ensuring that all of the various stakeholders' needs are met, other benefits are achieved, such as improving student retention rates, ensuring that provision is in line with market demand and stakeholder expectations, breaking down any barriers or impediments in cross-functional, cross-institutional and cross-sector operations and helping to improve the OUA brand.

Benchmarking

OUA is constantly reviewing opportunities to benchmark its products and services. While some benchmarking occurs within the internal review processes, external benchmarking is seen as most beneficial as this reveals the competitive standing of the organization. No external accreditation authority carries out audits of OUA but the providers themselves are audited by the Australian Universities Quality Agency (AUQA) and so it is critical to ensure alignment between OUA's operations and standards with the AUQA guidelines.

OUA operates in accord with Standards Australia (1996), which suggests that best practice and generic benchmarking should involve:

- Analyzing process(es) and deciding what is to be benchmarked.
- Defining and measuring selected processes and formulating a benchmarking plan.
- Selecting benchmarking partner(s) and agreeing on benchmarking parameters.
- Carrying out the benchmarking.
- Analyzing the results.
- Recalibrating operations and measuring results and effects.

Being a unique organization, both in Australia and globally, it is not possible for OUA to benchmark its operations against those of its competitors or peers. However, it is able to benchmark itself (through QA specialists employed by OUA) against the eight sets of criteria devised by the Australasian Council on Open, Distance and e-Learning (ACODE) (see also Chapter 9). These criteria refer to:

- Institution policy and governance for technology-supported learning and teaching.
- Planning for, and quality improvement of, the integration of technologies for learning and teaching.
- Information technology infrastructure to support learning and teaching.
- Pedagogical application of information and communications technology.
- Professional/staff development for the effective use of technologies for learning and teaching.
- Staff support for the use of technologies for learning and teaching.
- Student training for the effective use of technologies for learning.
- Student support for the use of technologies for learning.

The ISO 9001:2008 Quality Management Systems – Requirements[2] and Baldridge National Quality Programme Criteria for Performance Excellence[3] also help to inform OUA in focusing on the quality of its products and services and endeavouring to satisfy all stakeholders' requirements.

Conclusion

OUA is unlike any of the other open and distant learning providers described in this book. It is a leading Australian distance education provider, but a private company, owned by a consortium of public universities. It acts as a broker in providing open entry distance education courses and units and providing access to study pathways that enable students to transfer to on- and/or off-campus programmes and gain a degree from a leading Australian university of their choice. It offers a comprehensive list of courses and units from many different universities and it enables students to 'mix and match' these. And it requires all of the providers, which are autonomous institutions, to undergo a rigorous QA process in regard to their course content, instructional design and service delivery.

The major challenges for OUA are making sure that it can value-add to what the individual institutions can achieve on their own, ensuring that all of the various stakeholders' needs and expectations are not only met, but exceeded. Moreover, OUA is required to predict future market demand and act upon the insights gained to proactively achieve better outcomes. All of its management systems, products, processes and services must be rigorous, robust, transparent, accountable and under constant review. Where there are concerns, these must be responded to and ameliorated. But ensuring quality for OUA is like aiming for a moving target. There is always call for further improvement in supplier and customer relationships, products, services and feedback mechanisms to ensure quality. This is an ongoing challenge, a critical task.

Notes

1 http://www.open.edu.au/public/courses-and-units
2 http://www.iso.org/iso/catalogue_detail?csnumber=46486
3 http://www.nist.gov/baldrige/

References

De Fazio, T. (2008). *Academic conversations in cyberspace: A model of trialogic engagement*. Paper presented at *ASCILITE 2008 30*, Melbourne. Retrieved from http://www.ascilite.org.au/conferences/melbourne08/procs/defazio-1.pdf

De Fazio, T. (2010). *Thinking smart: Conversations with students in developing their academic skills*. Paper presented at *BlackBoard Summit*, Cairns. Retrieved from http://www.bbworld.com/2010/australasia/content.asp?id=1641

Herrington, A., Herrington, J., Oliver, R., Stoney, S., & Willis, J. (2001). Quality guidelines for online courses: The development of an instrument to audit online units. In G. Kennedy, M. Keppell, C. McNaught, & T. Petrovic (Eds.), *Meeting at the Crossroads: Proceedings of the 18th Annual Conference of the Australian Society for Computers in Learning in Tertiary Education* (pp. 263–270). Melbourne: ASCILITE.

Latchem, C., & Pritchard, T. (1994). Open learning: The unique Australian option. *OpenLearning, 9*(3), 18–26.

Lendrum, T. (1995). *The strategic partnering handbook.* Sydney: McGraw-Hill.

Open Universities Australia. (2010). *Open Universities Australia 2010 Handbook.* Melbourne, Australia: Open Universities Australia.

Standards Australia. (1996). *Benchmarking explained – A guide for undertaking and implementing benchmarking.* SAA/SZZ HB80:1996. Homebush, NSW: Standards Australia and Standards New Zealand.

13

QUALITY ASSURANCE IN REGIONAL DUAL-MODE UNIVERSITIES

The University of the South Pacific and The University of the West Indies

Rajesh Chandra, Dianne Thurab-Nkhosi and Stewart Marshall

Introduction

The quality assurance (QA) approaches adopted by The University of the South Pacific (USP) and The University of the West Indies (UWI) reflect the experiences of two institutions that not only have to cope with the tyranny of distance but are jointly owned by the governments of their member countries. These regional universities must provide teaching, learning, research and support services across both physical and virtual locations, in the context of increasing competition from offshore universities, with limited resources and with a keen awareness of the importance of quality in differentiating higher education providers. This chapter reviews and reflects on the QA processes and procedures implemented at these institutions, the challenges experienced and the lessons learnt.

ODL at USP

Established in 1968, USP is a regional university, serving 12 Pacific island countries: Cook Islands, Fiji, Kiribati, Marshall Islands, Nauru, Niue, Solomon Islands, Tokelau, Tonga, Tuvalu, Vanuatu and Samoa. It has campuses in all member countries. The main campus, Laucala, is in Fiji. The Alafua Campus in Samoa is the location of the School of Agriculture and Food Technology and the Emalus Campus in Vanuatu is the location for the School of Law.

USP is the premier higher learning institution in a region of extraordinary physical, social and economic diversity. Its programmes are widely accepted internationally and recognized as equivalent to those in Australian and New Zealand universities and all its programmes are externally evaluated. The current

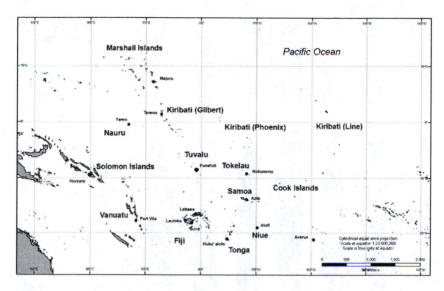

FIGURE 13.1   Countries served by USP

enrolment is just over 20,000 students [equivalent full-time student (EFTS) 10,623 in 2010] spread over 14 campuses across an area of 33 million km^2 (Figure 13.1). USP graduates over 2,500 students annually, 25% with postgraduate qualifications. Member governments fund about 39% of the university's recurrent expenditure, the balance coming from student fees, development partners, philanthropic organizations and the university's own entrepreneurial activities.

USP's founders recognized that only a small number of students would be able to attend the main Laucala campus in Fiji. The Morris Report (1966), which investigated the need for higher education in the South Pacific and recommended the establishment of USP, also proposed that:

> The University should have an Extra-mural Department to enable it to carry university studies to towns and villages through the Region, and to promote understanding of and affection for the University in the people of distant areas.
>
> *(p. 48)*

The university embarked on distance education in 1971. Since then, this mode of delivery has expanded and now constitutes an important priority area for the university as reflected in its 2010–2012 Strategic Plan (USP, 2009). Figure 13.2 illustrates the different modes of study at USP between 2004–2009.

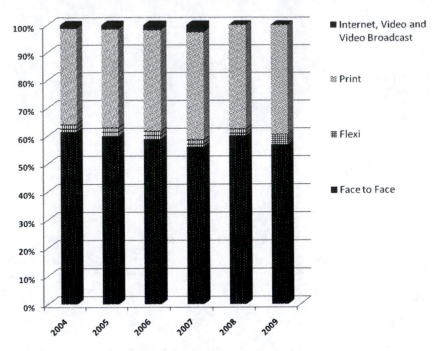

FIGURE 13.2 USP EFTS by mode of study 2004–2009

Source: USP (2009).

Multi-modal, multi-entry, multi-exit and flexible delivery characterizes the USP approach. The Centre for Flexible and Distance Learning (CFDL) provides overall leadership and is in charge of three units: Student Learning Support, Multimedia and Course Design and Development. It is also responsible for the bulk of the course design and materials production. However, the open and distance learning (ODL) programmes are owned and operated by the various faculties and are taught by the same lecturers who teach the face-to-face versions of these courses, thus ensuring that ODL is mainstreamed into the university's overall teaching and learning processes. The Deputy Vice-Chancellor (Learning, Teaching and Student Services) is in charge of ODL and the Director of CFDL reports to him/her. The Heads of School are responsible for the quality of the ODL teaching and learning. The Campus Directors are responsible for enrolment and registration and the quality of the teaching, learning and student support services provided at the various campuses.

Challenges in Developing and Delivering ODL at USP

USP faces many challenges in developing and delivering quality ODL products and services across such a vast region. For example:

- Most of the management and resourcing are concerned with face-to-face provision, and the regional campuses (formerly known as regional centres) lack lecture rooms, videoconferencing rooms and other essential facilities and learning resources.
- Lack of continuity in the leadership of ODL. There have been five Directors and three Vice-Chancellors in the last 8 years.
- The legacy of a lack of energetic leadership and advocacy for ODL shown by previous senior management.
- Most of the teaching staff are recruited from conventional universities, few have any experience of ODL, some are resistant to the rapid expansion of ODL and some departmental heads are philosophically opposed to ODL.
- Tensions between the faculties, whose staff feel that ODL is the business of CFDL and are thus reluctant to provide the necessary staffing and resources for the development of ODL, and the CFDL which feels that it 'owns' ODL.
- The USPNet satellite communications network linking the 12 member countries was for a long time rudimentary and inadequate in capacity, and until recently, the level of information and communications technology (ICT) provision in the South Pacific was low, preventing rapid deployment of technology-intensive ODL. The difficulties in managing technological change quickly, given the speed of technological change and emergence of other providers offering wholly online programmes.
- A lack of adequate student support, especially in the areas of orientation and tutorials (this is now being granted greater attention and resources).

However, the 2010–2012 Strategic Plan prioritizes ODL and significant resources are now being deployed. A major regional campus development plan is in preparation. The issue of tensions between the faculties and the CFDL is now being resolved and student support is now being granted greater attention and resources. These measures, and the conversion of programmes to online using Moodle as the Learning Management System will undoubtedly bring about positive change.

QA for ODL at USP

USP has always integrated ODL into its overall operations, so the QA procedures for ODL are the same as those applying to the university overall. USP uses a system of external examiners that has been widely adopted in the Commonwealth universities. In 2004, the university developed a new quality management framework[1] through which it commissioned the Australian Universities' Quality Agency and Academic Quality Audit Unit of the

New Zealand Vice-Chancellors' Committee to assure the university's quality. The first institutional quality audit was completed in March 2008.

The university also has a system of external advisors for all programmes and the university augments these with other more direct assessment of ODL programmes. USP has also commissioned periodic external reviews of ODL (e.g. Lockwood, Smith, & Yates, 2000).

Internally, all ODL programmes and courses go through the same quality processes as the face-to-face courses, that is to say, through the School Boards, Faculty Boards, Faculty Academic Standards and Quality Committee, University Academic Standards and Quality Committee and University Senate and Council. All of these programmes also now have Advisory Boards comprising the major stakeholders which provide an additional layer of QA and, as from 2010, all ODL courses are subject to external review for quality.

Other strategies to ensure quality include:

- The use of Turnitin software to help lecturers track plagiarism.
- The provision of an orientation programme for ODL students called Success@USP.[2]
- Travel by teaching staff from the main campus in Fiji to regional campuses to meet students, offer courses and tuition, inspect facilities and mentor regional campus staff.
- The conduct of a first-year course experience survey to identify student views of quality and address any shortcomings.
- The use of course evaluations by lecturers to review their courses and performance and by Heads of Schools to monitor the quality of the lecturers.
- Faculty members obtaining copyright clearances for their courses and the appointment of a copyright officer to ensure copyright compliance.
- Regular internal audits of campuses and centres through the normal internal audit system to help identify possible system failures.

ODL at UWI

UWI caters for the higher education needs of the 17 English-speaking countries and territories in the Caribbean: Anguilla, Antigua and Barbuda, the Bahamas, Barbados, Belize, Bermuda, the British Virgin Islands, the Cayman Islands, Dominica, Grenada, Jamaica, Montserrat, St. Kitts and Nevis, St. Lucia, St. Vincent and the Grenadines, Trinidad and Tobago and Turks and Caicos. UWI's mission is to unlock West Indian potential for economic and cultural growth by providing high-quality teaching and research aimed at meeting critical regional needs. The university was originally instituted in Jamaica in 1948 as an independent external college of the University of London. As with USP, UWI's students

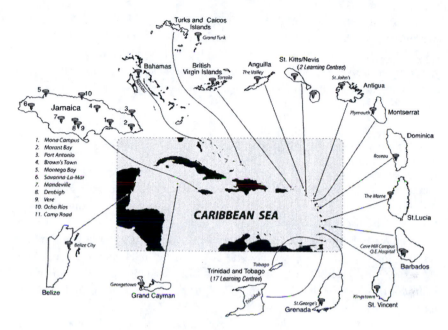

FIGURE 13.3   UWI distance education centres

Source: Thurab-Nkhosi and Marshall (2007, p. 99).

are from diverse cultural, social and economic backgrounds. Enrolment has grown from 33 students in 1948–1949 to 40,908 in 2007–2008 (UWI, 2008).

The university has four major campuses: three physical campuses at Mona in Jamaica, St. Augustine in Trinidad and Tobago and Cave Hill in Barbados and the virtual UWI Open Campus (UWIOC). The UWI Council approved the development of the UWIOC in 2007. This decision marked the implementation of an integral aspect of the university's 2007–2012 Strategic Plan, bringing together the previous Office of the Board for Non-campus Countries and Distance Education, School of Continuing Studies, UWI Distance Education Centres and Tertiary Level Institutions Unit. The UWIOC was formed to 'provide a leadership presence in the 12 non-campus countries and to reach out to the underserved communities by leading the charge in e-learning and multimode education' (Tewarie, 2009, p. 1). There are currently 42 UWIOC site locations in the region, as shown in Figure 13.3.

UWIOC is headed by a Principal and governed by a Campus Council in keeping with the statutes and ordinances of the UWI. It draws on the existing intellectual capacity of the three physical campuses and its organizational structure is driven by the operational functions of teaching, research and consultancy. Its academic operations are governed by an Academic Board, which is subject to the authority of the UWI Board for Undergraduate Studies and UWI Board for Graduate Studies and Research. UWIOC staff are distributed across the Caribbean and UWIOC currently offers programmes in university preparation, leisure and vocational skills, professional development and undergraduate and graduate studies. Figure 13.4 shows the UWIOC organizational structure.

Challenges to Developing and Delivering ODL at UWI

The challenges faced by UWI in developing and delivering ODL are multi-faceted. It is difficult to find content specialists with the expertise and will to develop courses in a timely fashion. It is also difficult to recruit suitable part-time staff to function as course coordinators to prepare course guides, set assignments, monitor tutors, facilitate students online and grade examination scripts. Some students are capable and ready to be independent learners but others are not, and this, coupled with a lack of understanding of the time commitment required for online learning, can result in 'absenteeism' online and in extreme cases, dropout.

The UWIOC centres in the islands have varying levels of technology capabilities for online teaching and learning. Further, UWIOC is faced with the ever-increasing costs of the constantly changing technology, finding and hiring multimedia specialists to exploit the new media and providing staff and infrastructure to ensure appropriate material distribution and student support.

A recent study by Thurab-Nkhosi (2010) found that the UWIOC staff and students also identified the following challenges:

- Being a new organization, UWIOC has yet to have total buy-in from staff regarding its vision and operations.
- There are issues of change management and communication.
- There are problems with the timing and provision of information regarding registrations, examinations and courses.
- Students feel that the course coordinators and tutors are not always as responsive as they should be and that access to library facilities at some locations is poor.

QA at UWI and the UWIOC

Attempts to put a QA system in place at UWI began in the 1950s and 1960s, when a generic pattern of QA was established in the Commonwealth Caribbean. This early QA system covered only course and programme approval and the appointment and promotion of staff. In keeping with global trends in the 1990s, UWI sought to enhance this by implementing a system of quality audit and

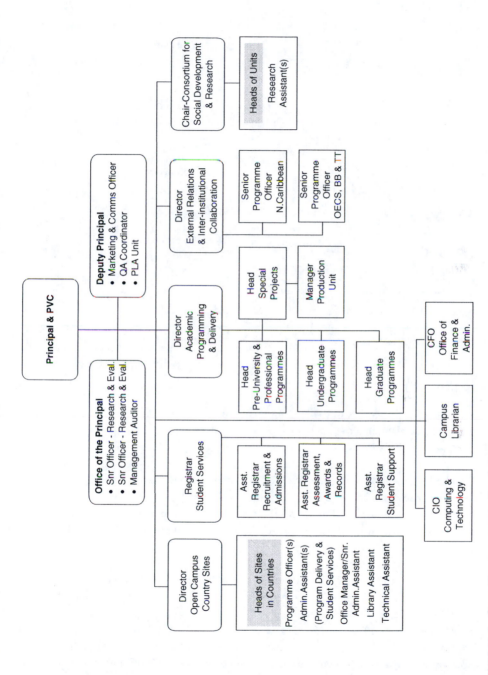

FIGURE 13.4 Open Campus organizational chart

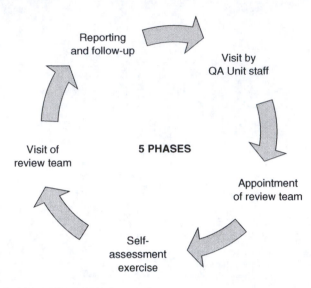

FIGURE 13.5   The UWI QA review cycle

Source: Re-printed with permission from Perry (2002).

assurance. A Board of Undergraduate Studies (BUS) was established in 1996 to conduct this. In 2001, the Office of the Board for Undergraduate Studies (OBUS) was established within BUS to implement the policies and directives of BUS. The QA Unit was established to:

- Improve the quality of the learning experience of UWI students.
- Provide assurance to stakeholders as to the quality of provision and standards at the university.

The definition of quality used by BUS is 'fitness for purpose' and the QA process comprises an internal assessment of the quality of the learning experience of the student and an external review of the teaching and learning outcomes. When a particular discipline is selected for review at UWI, it undergoes the five-phase process depicted in Figure 13.5.

UWIOC is currently developing its own QA process. While this needs to be in accord with the university's QA system, variations are needed to accommodate the different modes employed in the ODL environment. In the meanwhile, the UWIOC continues to implement the QA processes and procedures of the Distance Education Centre, the Unit responsible for the ODL programme prior to UWIOC's establishment (Thurab-Nkhosi & Marshall, 2007, 2009). Table 13.1 outlines the QA procedures currently used by the UWIOC but which are not yet part of an institutional plan.

TABLE 13.1 UWIOC processes for QA

Quality indicator	UWIOC process/procedure	Whether documented
Institutional support	Fees paid to academic staff and contract course writers as an incentive	Statement of policies and principles
	UWIOC courses recognized for assessment and promotions in the UWI	Annual departmental reports
	Staff providing course administration assistance and facilitating communication with country sites	
	Training provided for course coordinators and course developers	Training materials
Course development	Team approach	Course Development Template
	Course developer procedures in the form of a template	Course developer's Contract
	Work schedule with time lines attached to a contract for course development	
Course Structure/ design	Clear instructional design process	Course plan forms
	Use of graphics, photos and illustrations	Style guides
	Professional Page composition	Templates
	Built-in student practice opportunities	
Teaching/learning process and student support	e-Tutor support for students	Course coordinator guides
	Support for e-tutors through training and assistance from course delivery assistants	Tutor guides
	Audioconferencing, online discussion forums, chat and web conferencing including the use of Skype and Elluminate live	Course guides for students
	Staff and student orientations	
	Helpdesk support	
	Technicians at UWIOC centres	
Faculty Support	Course development training	Course development templates
	Course coordinator training	Training materials
	e-Tutor training	
	Course delivery assistants for monitoring online activity	
Evaluation and assessment	Course evaluation	

A QA Framework for ODL in Regional Universities

So what kind of QA framework can be employed in regional universities such as USP and UWI? Kirkpatrick (2005) suggests that a QA framework for ODL should concern:

- A general philosophy which includes the policy and mission statement, culture, attitudes of staff and staff commitment.
- Products: learning materials, course resources, media and outputs (retention rates, number of graduates, assessment outcomes, pass rates, standards of performance, etc.).
- Services: registration and advisory services, tutoring, counselling, feedback and guidance on learning, support for learner progress, provision and management of study centres and resources, customer service, ICT helpdesks and responsiveness to issues.
- Support processes: delivery systems, record keeping, scheduling, electronic backup, warehousing and stock control, and QA procedures.

Drawing on this model, a QA framework for a regional ODL provider could be as follows:

Vision, Mission and Guiding Philosophy Performance Indicators

There should be:

- Clear articulation of the ODL institution's vision, philosophy and understanding of a culture of quality, and communication of these throughout the institution and all member countries. The underlying philosophy should be one of creating a culture of quality and transformative learning and continuous improvement rather than one of compliance with standards.
- Concordance with regional and national QA and accreditation frameworks.
- Institutional policy on quality which takes account of the issues specific to ODL processes, procedures and modalities as well as the more general quality aspects of face-to-face teaching and learning.

Curriculum and Instruction Performance Indicators

There should be:

- Processes and procedures in accord with criteria agreed to by the institution and which take account of standards, research and stakeholder feedback.

- A specific individual or team responsible for these processes and procedures to ensure that quality-oriented activities are not neglected in the rush of day-to-day work.
- Specific guidelines for training course developers, tracking progress and addressing challenges in the system. There must also be a system of peer-review, evaluation and revision.
- Training and monitoring course coordinators, lecturers, tutors and students and evaluation and review of the delivery system.

Student Support Performance Indicators

There should be:

- Coordination among all the departments and units providing student support.
- Accurate, clear and user-friendly information for prospective students regarding ODL programmes and courses, the nature and requirements of ODL study and the learner support systems available.
- Accurate, clear and timely registration information and guidelines.
- Orientation to the ODL institution and ODL modes of study.
- Accuracy, clarity and timeliness in managing all administrative issues.
- Accuracy, clarity and timeliness in delivering courseware, academic counselling, effective tutorial support and effective technical support.
- An effective system for review and revision of the student support procedures and ensuring that changes and improvements are implemented in the light of feedback received.

Institutional Support Performance Indicators

There should be:

- Adequate allocation of resources to address at least basic student and staff needs.
- Transparent, consistent and appropriate policies for staff recruitment, appointment, professional development and recognition and reward.
- Up-to-date and effective policies regarding copyright and plagiarism.
- Opportunities for staff involvement in decision-making in regard to policies impacting on staff conditions of work.
- Adequate student input into teaching and learning policymaking.

Technology Support Performance Indicators

There should be:

- An up-to-date technology platform that will reach most students and be reliable and adequate for the tasks expected in ODL across the range of delivery modes from print based to fully online.
- Compatibility in the elements of technology and a tight policy to avoid unnecessary multiple platforms.
- Adequate numbers of computers and good broadband provision.
- Prioritization of open-source software to ensure sustainability and cost-effectiveness.
- Adequate staff and student orientation and training in the use of these technologies.
- Adequate technical personnel and support to ensure that staff are working as smartly as possible and that students do not experience difficulties that lead to loss of interest in the course or attrition.
- Adequate facilities for chats and networking among students.
- Mechanisms for course lecturers and tutors to monitor student participation.

Of course, these policies, procedures and performance indicators could well apply in any ODL institution. But the point in assuring quality in regional institutions such as USP and UWI is that not only must these be fully understood and acted upon by everyone, from senior managers to the most junior academic, administrative and technical staff, but across all regions and technological landscapes and the range of stakeholders, cultures and socio-economic circumstances. It is not enough to simply gain compliance. The need is for commitment to seamless, consistent and high-quality educational provision, by whatever mode(s), in all of the member countries served.

Conclusion

The world's two regional universities that are so similar in most respects have interestingly followed different models of ODL.

UWI has established a separate section, the UWIOC, to provide ODL working alongside and utilizing the academic resources of the other physical campuses. USP has followed a model in which the same faculties provide ODL with the support of a specialist unit, the CFDL, that assists with course design and production but does not employ academics to prepare these courses. All of these belong to the faculties.

USP has followed a strong policy of mainstreaming ODL so that the faculties are now hosting student support for ODL and in some cases, experimenting with new technologies before they are even adopted by the university. UWI initially located ODL within the faculties which provided student support while the separate campuses were responsible for registration, but after experiencing difficulties with this model with the introduction of online learning, it became necessary to centralize the management of ODL in the UWIOC.

At USP, the faculties have played a leading role in the use of Moodle and are being supported and empowered to become centres of excellence in educational innovation across the full spectrum of learning and teaching at the university and within a central technology and learning framework. At UWI, it is UWIOC that plays the leading role in the development of a single Moodle platform for the online offerings of the whole university. It would be interesting to undertake a more detailed comparative study of these two models, not only in regard to the QA systems, but the overall impact, efficiency and cost-effectiveness of these two approaches.

Both within USP and UWIOC, there is an understanding of the QA systems which need to be in place. Several systems have already been implemented, such as programme development guidelines, programme approval procedures including review by appropriate committees and boards, the appointment of QA staff to ensure that standards are met at the end of the production cycle and the establishment of QA committees. There is still a sense, however, that all of these activities could be better coordinated.

Notes

1 http://www.quality.usp.ac.fj/
2 http://www.usp.ac.fj/index.php?id=6269

References

Kirkpatrick, D. (2005). Quality assurance in open and distance learning. In *Commonwealth of learning knowledge series: A topical, start-up guide to distance education practice and delivery.* Vancouver: Commonwealth of Learning. Retrieved from http://www.col.org/SiteCollectionDocuments/KS2005_QA.pdf

Lockwood, F., Smith, A., & Yates, C. (2000). *Review of distance and flexible learning at the University of the South Pacific.* Suva: The University of the South Pacific.

Morris, C., Aitken, F. R. G., Collins, H. M., Hughes, P. W., & Christie, D. H. (1966). Report of the Higher Education Mission to the South Pacific. London: Her Majesty's Stationary Office.

Perry, A. (2002). The quality assurance system of UWI. In H. Beckles, A. Perry, & P. Whitely (Eds.), *The brain train: Quality higher education and Caribbean development* (pp. 67–77). West Indies: University of West Indies Press.

Tewarie, B. (2009, July 2–3). *The regional university model – Does it still stand? A perspective from the University of the West Indies.* Paper presented at the *IIEP Policy Forum, Tertiary Education in Small States: Planning in the context of Globalization.* Retrieved from http://www.iiep.unesco.org/fileadmin/user_upload/pol_forum_09/tewarie_TrinidadTobago.pdf

Thurab-Nkhosi, D. (2010). *Towards the development of a quality assurance framework* (Unpublished doctoral dissertation). University of Sheffield, UK.

Thurab-Nkhosi, D., & Marshall, S. (2007). Defining a quality assurance tool for web-based course development and delivery at the University of the West Indies. In B. N. Koul, & A. Kanwar (Eds.), *Perspectives on distance education: Towards a culture of quality* (pp. 99–112). Vancouver: Commonwealth of Learning.

Thurab-Nkhosi, D., & Marshall, S. (2009). Quality management in course development and delivery at the University of the West Indies Distance Education Centre. *Quality Assurance in Education, 17*(3), 264–280.

USP. (2009). *Strategic Plan 2010 – 2012: Quality, relevance sustainability.* Suva: Author.

UWI. (2008). *UWI statistical review academic year 2007–2008.* St Augustine, Trinidad: Author.

14

CONDUCTING AN EXTERNAL INSTITUTIONAL QUALITY REVIEW: THE PALESTINIAN AL-QUDS OPEN UNIVERSITY

Kathleen Matheos

Introduction

In 2006–2007, as part of a project aimed at improving the Palestinian higher education system,[1] the World Bank funded a review of the Palestinian Al-Quds Open University (QOU). The University of Manitoba (UM) was contracted to undertake this review through Education Management Europe. The international external evaluation team, led by the author, comprised four faculty members from Extended Education at UM who were well-versed in open and distance education, and two Palestinian lecturers in Business Administration and Continuing Education at Birzeit University, Palestine, one of whom had taught part-time at QOU. The comprehensive evaluation was concerned with the overall operation of QOU but with a special focus on the quality of QOU's open and distance teaching and learning.

The following chapter chronicles the evaluation process and concludes with a snapshot of QOU 3 years after the event, evidencing the outcomes to the evaluation.

The Context

Higher education in Palestine faces a range of challenges, foremost of which are the Israeli occupation, lack of mobility, security threats and extremely challenging socio-economic conditions. Figure 14.1 (overleaf) shows the two regions served by QOU – Gaza and the West Bank and East Jerusalem, which are separated by the State of Israel. All crossing points are controlled by the Israel Defence Forces. Entry into the Gaza Strip, with its well over one million inhabitants, needs a permit from the Israeli Army which can take months to acquire or may never

Jenin
Study Centre ▲

Tukam

Tubas

Qalquiliya   Nablus   **WEST BANK**

Bidya ▲   Salfit

Ramallah & Al-Bireh   Jericho

Al-Esariyeh ▲

JERUSALEM

ISRAEL

Bethlehem   ▲ Beit Sahour

Hebron

GAZA   North Gaza

Gaza

Dora   Yatta ▲

Middle Gaza

Khan Younes

Rafah

● = Educational Area
▲ = Study Centre

EDUCATIONAL REGIONAL CENTRES & STUDY CENTRES

FIGURE 14.1 Regional centres and study centres of QOU

eventuate. East Jerusalem is currently within Israel and only Palestinians holding Jerusalem identity cards can access this area without special permission from Israel. QOU staff holding Palestinian Authority identity cards cannot travel to the East Jerusalem centre, where there is a significant administrative arm of the university, without special permission from the Israeli authorities. And individuals crossing from the West Bank to Israel must pass through checkpoints, show identity documents and may be subject to searches.

There is an ever-increasing demand for higher education in Palestine. In addition to QOU, there are 12 conventional universities. Palestinian women participate in higher education at slightly lower rates than men, but their participation rates exceed those for other Middle Eastern countries and other developing regions of the world (Hashweh, Hashweh, & Berryman, 2003). Just over 50% of QOU's students are female.

Government funding for higher education is extremely limited, student fees must be set low and the universities have limited opportunities to generate any other income. The Israeli occupation and intifada have combined to undermine economic growth and responding to increasing demand with limited resources inevitably affects quality. Hashweh et al. (2003) concluded that quality was declining in most of the Palestinian universities and that the university administrators were aware of this. However, in none of the institutions they examined were there any institutionalized systematic programme evaluation and development procedures aimed at monitoring and improving academic quality. They found that the student/teacher ratios and percentage of part-time teachers were increasing and that faculty were often moonlighting or taking on overloads. World Bank studies have shown that higher education increases the likelihood of finding employment but, in contradiction with international evidence that such education is a profitable investment both at the country and individual level, the rates of return in the West Bank and Gaza are either negative or close to zero for college and undergraduate studies and just above zero for postgraduate studies. This is largely due to the closure of the country.

These unique circumstances have resulted in approximately 40% of the undergraduate students in the West Bank, Gaza and East Jerusalem being distance learners served by QOU. For the majority of these 60,000 constituents, QOU represents the only opportunity for higher education study.

Al-Quds Open University

Founded in 1991, QOU is the only institution mandated by the Ministry of Education and Higher Education (MOEHE) to provide distance education in Palestine. Initially a government university under the Palestinian Authority, it is now a public university. Its President is appointed by the President of the Palestinian National Authority for a 4-year term, renewable for one additional term. There are two Vice-Presidents, one responsible for Academic Affairs and the other for Administration. Curriculum decision-making follows that of the conventional universities with proposals for new courses and course changes originating at department or programme level and progressing up to the University Council and President.

QOU enrols mature-aged students who cannot attend conventional institutions but currently, 50% of the new admissions are high school graduates opting

for distance study. Studying through QOU is flexible, allows learning while earning, incurs slightly lower fees than those of the conventional universities and
makes it possible to study at, or closer to, home, so reducing the costs and incon-
veniences of travel.

QOU offers undergraduate degrees in Technology and Applied Sciences,
Agriculture, Social and Family Development, Administrative and Economic
Sciences and Education. All of these programmes use Arabic as the language of
instruction, making this the only fully Arabic medium higher education institution in Palestine.

QOU was based upon The Open University model. First established in
Amman, Jordan, its headquarters moved to East Jerusalem in 1991. The development of the university occurred in three phases:

- Phase 1 was concerned with providing open and distance education for
  Palestinians under the occupation and for the diaspora in the neighbouring
  countries. At this stage, the clientele was the older student whose studies
  had been interrupted or delayed by the political situation. This met a
  limited, albeit extremely important, need in Palestinian society.
- Phase 2 began in 1994, subsequent to the relocation of the university
  headquarters in East Jerusalem. This was marked by a growing number of
  high school completers requiring access to higher education, a need
  which QOU responded to by admitting sequential learners, a practice
  which remains in place today. The admission policies for these students
  are identical to those for mature learners – they must pass the *Tawjhe* (high
  school graduation) examinations. By 2000, QOU had 25,000 students,
  with much of the growth attributable to these high school entrants. While
  this change in clientele was acknowledged as meeting a recognized need,
  it was seen by some conventional universities as infringing upon their
  territory.
- Phase 3 began in 2000. With an expanded and transformed student body, the
  university focused on the development of its delivery mode, student services,
  library services and a student portal. The growth in enrolments continued
  throughout this period, doubling to 60,000 registrations in 2010. Over 50%
  of the new admissions are now sequential students, entering directly after
  completing their high school studies.

Planning the Evaluation

QOU had been operating in accord with the traditional correspondence model
augmented with optional face-to-face tutorials. Although this appeared to be
functional and was continuing to attract students, it was decided that a

comprehensive evaluation was needed to provide QOU with the tools and means to enhance the quality of its open, distance and online provision. The evaluation was conceived as a three-stage process:

- Conducting a preliminary environmental scan: viewing and trying to understand the educational, economic, political and social environments within which QOU operates, and considering the factors that would influence the goals, direction and processes of the evaluation.
- Carrying out an in-depth analysis of QOU: its governance and administration, teaching and learning, student services, technology and infrastructure and alignment with MOEHE policies. During this stage, policy and demographic documents were to be reviewed, interviews were to be conducted with senior administrators in QOU, the conventional Palestinian universities and the MOEHE and surveys and focus groups were to be undertaken with faculty and students. This consultation with the internal and external stakeholders was intended to provide information and insights into organizational and operational issues. A comparative gap analysis was then to be undertaken, assessing the strengths, weaknesses, opportunities and threats (SWOT) for QOU and benchmarking its operations against international best practice in open and distance learning, while paying particular heed to the unique and difficult environment in which the institution operated.
- Assembling all of these findings and developing and presenting the draft evaluation findings through dissemination workshops with the Palestinian Accreditation and Quality Assurance Commission (an autonomous body under the umbrella of the MOEHE), the MOEHE, QOU and the Tertiary Education Project at the World Bank.[2] The feedback from these sessions was then to be incorporated into a final report and a set of recommendations were to be submitted to QOU and the MOEHE in February 2007.

While all of the team members were experienced in evaluating open and distance courses, programmes, departments and institutions, it was clear that evaluating this system, which operated across the West Bank, Gaza and East Jerusalem, would require the team to rethink the process. It was also apparent that carrying out the evaluation was going to give the Canadian members of the team first-hand experience of the difficulties faced by QOU's administrators, faculty and students. At the outset of the study, one senior administrator observed, 'This is not a normal situation for higher education' – a statement that was certainly borne out. Other administrators corroborated and expanded on his comments, raising concerns about measuring QOU against international quality assurance (QA) frameworks and benchmarks for open and distance learning without understanding the unique circumstances in which the institution operated.

Conducting the Evaluation

Prior to undertaking the evaluation, the team members reviewed the limited available literature on open, distance and conventional higher education in Palestine and the Middle East, and familiarized themselves with the political and socio-economic situation in Palestine. Arriving in the country, the Canadians soon came to recognize the abnormality of the situation as they experienced the checkpoints, delays, closures and everyday frustrations experienced by the local populace. During the course of the evaluation, there was also the election of Hamas, the Israeli war with Lebanon/Hezbollah, and the resultant Fatah government in the West Bank and governing of Gaza by Hamas. It was truly a challenging environment, requiring the team to develop strategies to ameliorate as much as possible the constraints on carrying out the evaluation as planned.

For a start, issues of access and mobility presented some very real challenges in interviewing the wide range of QOU administrators, teaching staff and students. QOU is an attenuated institution, with the President and Deans located in the West Bank, the Vice-Presidents Academic and Administrative in East Jerusalem, the Associate Vice-President with responsibility for Gaza operations based in Gaza and the other administrators, faculty members and students distributed across these three regions. The preliminary face-to-face meetings with QOU administrators had to be held in Ramallah, due to the travel restrictions placed on West Bank residents. The Canadian team was able to travel throughout the West Bank and Jerusalem, but was required to provide passport identification at all checkpoints. The Palestinian consultants held Jerusalem identity cards, so they were also able to travel between the West Bank and Jerusalem. But travel time was uncertain, being dependent upon the opening and closing of checkpoints, and delays of several hours were not uncommon. Schedules continually had to be revised and, in some cases, cancelled as a consequence of checkpoint closures. Videoconferencing links were available between Ramallah and Gaza, but neither video- nor audio conferencing was available at the regional study centres. Telephone interviews were used in certain situations, but the team aimed to visit as many centres as possible to conduct interviews, run focus groups and gain first-hand understanding of the institutional processes and circumstances.

The Palestinian culture is a high-context culture, which means that information is shared much more readily and openly in face-to-face environments where contexts can be taken into account and closer personal relationships can be established. Therefore, despite the inconvenience and additional time requirements, wherever possible, the team travelled out to speak with the administrators and staff at the various locations. However, time constraints prevented the Canadian team members from attending all of these meetings and of course there was the language problem, so some of the regional study interviews and focus groups had to be conducted in Arabic by the Palestinian team members. Unfortunately, despite repeated requests by QOU for permission from the Israeli authorities for the evaluators to travel to Gaza, where 35% of the QOU student population resided, they were never authorized to do this. At the onset of the project, videoconferencing with Gaza was possible, but the subsequent bombing attacks destroyed the infrastructure and so later communications were limited to mobile phones. Couriered student and faculty surveys were also conducted by QOU staff in the regional study centres. The quantitative and qualitative data gained from these surveys were then translated into English for analysis and summarizing, after which, follow-up interviews and focus groups were conducted, again face-to-face. A SWOT analysis was conducted in Ramallah by inviting participants from the West Bank and East Jerusalem to attend and by videoconferencing with Gaza. Despite all of the challenges, the evaluation team was, for the most part, able to complete the tasks as planned.

Despite a limited budget for the administration and logistics of the evaluation, QOU gave the project very full support. This was the very first external evaluation ever undertaken at QOU and not surprisingly, it was regarded with some trepidation. QOU staff voiced concerns that the international team would not take into account the fact that the university was the only open and distance institution in the country, that it faced criticism from the conventional universities and that it was trying to serve an ever-growing student body in a particularly difficult political and economic environment. Also, although this was not directly said, it appeared that the QOU staff were apprehensive about the Palestinian members of the team being associated with the largest conventional university in the West Bank. This was shown in the constant offers of QOU personnel to make the team's arrangements, accompany the evaluators to the centres and so on. The review team members had to explain that, while these offers of help were very much appreciated, it was important for them to meet with the interviewees alone to ensure open and frank comments.

There were also larger political and social issues at play. As mentioned earlier, shortly after the team embarked on the evaluation, Hamas was elected in a general election, displacing the ruling Fatah Party of the Palestinian Authority. The actual formation of the Hamas government took some time, during which period the evaluation team continued working with the Fatah-appointed MOEHE officials. Eventually a new Hamas cabinet was appointed and all US and EU aid to Palestine was frozen, resulting in an unpaid civil service for several months and acute economic problems throughout the country. However, it was decided to press ahead with the evaluation and the new ministry officials agreed to support the team in completing the second and third stages of the evaluation. Then, midway through the evaluation, Israel and Lebanon went to war, Gaza was then continually bombed, the economic situation worsened and there were fears of civil war.

In early 2007, with the Hamas government now in place, the draft evaluation report was presented to the MOEHE and Council of Higher Education which comprises the presidents of all the Palestinian universities. Because travel restrictions were still in force, these sessions were held in Ramallah and so could be only attended by those in the West Bank. The final evaluation report incorporating feedback from the ministry and university leaders was submitted, as scheduled, in February 2007. The full report was posted in English and Arabic on the QOU website. Such openness and transparency was indicative of the sense of ownership of the process, the commitment of QOU's senior and middle management and their acceptance of the recommendations.

In the final report (Matheos et al., 2007), the key recommendation was the development of the scholarship of teaching within distance, open and online environments and to this end, the establishment of an Open and Distance Learning Centre (ODLC). The ODLC was seen as necessary to develop and enhance quality in distance teaching and learning, develop and apply a more interactive model of course delivery, provide faculty information and development resources and services and undertake research in order to revitalize QOU's teaching methods and courseware.

The secondary recommendations focused on the regional centres. QOU has 17 regional centres and additional study centres in certain regions, such as Bethlehem and Beit Sahour, to accommodate the growing demand for higher education in these regions. The regional centres are the face of the university in the community, so it is important that they have the capacity to develop and sustain the provision of high-quality teaching and learning, administrative and student services and information and communications technology (ICT). The evaluation highlighted the need to develop criteria, benchmarks and a model for these centres to engage in self-assessment, identify areas for improvement and develop the capacities of their managers and staff.

The Outcomes

Three years after the evaluation, it is salient to consider whether the evaluation did in fact achieve the intended outcomes.

QOU quickly established the ODLC. A Director with a PhD in education and graduate qualifications in computer engineering was appointed to be answerable to the Vice-President Academic Affairs and advise the university's President on all matters concerning e-learning.

The establishment of the ODLC provided the forum to revisit teaching and learning at QOU, and a Memorandum of Understanding for further collaboration between QOU and UM was signed in the Fall of 2007. One immediate outcome of this was that the author spent a 6-month sabbatical at QOU, co-conducting research into blended and online learning in the Palestinian context. The ODLC

Director and the author confirmed the need to move away from an essentially print-based correspondence model with optional study centre attendance, to a more interactive model of online course delivery. For most of QOU's instructors, this was something entirely new. Until this time, the curriculum was standardized, the course textbooks, assignments and exams were prepared centrally and the instructors' roles were confined to teaching the prescribed curriculum in bi-weekly tutorials and to grading assignments and examinations. In the proposed approach, they would be required to identify resources and develop activities and assignments to augment the textbooks. The online activities would require the students to explicitly interact with the content and with each other, and the marking schemes would need to be revised to take account of the students' participation in online activities.

The faculty members had reservations about the time commitment needed to not only develop the courses but also the instructional methods in the proposed formats. And the administrators were concerned that the students might not be receptive to the redesign of the courses and pedagogy. Many students, they believed, had enroled in the university to receive a credential in the traditional format. If the extra work demands led them to withdraw, this would present a problem for QOU which depended to a great extent upon tuition fees. However, both faculty and administration could see that technology could be a major driver in transforming pedagogy.

The QOU Academic Council considered these issues and then ratified a request to embark on a pilot project to redesign ten QOU courses to improve student engagement and learning. These courses and instructors were selected by the Academic Programme Directors from the various disciplines and geographic areas. The instructors responsible for redesigning these courses and materials received a stipend, were given ongoing online instructional technology support and attended a course redesign workshop focusing on:

- The use of a learning management system (Moodle) and virtual classroom (Elluminate).
- The use of online learning activities.
- The development of a course blueprint.
- How to redistribute marks to the online activities (the final exam remained as required in its institutional format).

After implementing the pilot programmes, the instructors and the students were asked for their views on these. The instructors responsible for developing and teaching the courses were interviewed individually for their views on using ICT for teaching, learning and administration, the conditions at QOU that would facilitate or impede the adoption of new technologies, how teaching the redesigned course compared with the more traditional approaches and how they envisaged QOU developing in future years. The students were interviewed in focus groups. They were asked to share their views and experiences in accessing and using ICT for their personal learning, the instructors' uses of the technology and how well they felt QOU facilitated the use of technology for learning. They were also asked whether they found the new online learning to be a positive experience and what recommendations they would like to make regarding teaching, learning and use of the technology. Both the instructors and students reported that this new form of teaching and learning was a positive experience and that, while it involved more work, the formative assessment and online discussions were invaluable learning tools. Both groups identified the need for more computers and better connectivity and raised concerns about costs of home computers and Internet connection for the more disadvantaged learners. The students also recommended expanding the hours of operation of the computer labs. Many of the students admitted that they had previously submitted copied assignments, rarely attended tutorials and often only looked at the self-study texts immediately before the mid-term and final exams. They recognized that the learning redesign, which required them to engage weekly with the content, instructor and other students promoted better learning. The redistribution of marks had led to concerns that the students in the redesigned courses might not be as well prepared for the final exams. However, the final grades reflected no difference between the new and traditional courses (Matheos, Rogoza, & Hamayil, 2009).

In the Fall of 2010, there were 133 blended learning courses on offer, ODLC had developed a resource centre of materials to support ODL and QOU had embarked on a project in which teachers from beyond the Middle East could teach undergraduate courses to students in Palestine. The first of these transnational courses occurred in 2009 in the form of a credit course in leadership for QOU students, offered in English by a UM professor, fully online and utilizing Moodle and Elluminate. All new faculty members are now required to undergo training in distance education methods and uses of technology and there are training opportunities for existing staff. By September 2010, 1,862 faculty members had been trained by the ODLC. In 2008, QOU undertook a capacity building initiative at the regional centres that included benchmarks and checklists for both administrators and faculty members.[3]

The information gained in the 3 years since the original evaluation indicates that it did make a difference in improving quality at QOU through reflection, capacity building and appropriate applications of technology.

Conclusion

Conducting this evaluation was a profound learning experience for the Canadian consultants, both professionally and personally, and they were impressed by the tenacity of the institution and its ability to deliver education in extremely difficult circumstances. The project taught them some invaluable lessons about conducting an external review to improve the quality of an overseas institution:

- Research the culture and context of the institution and environment.
- Be aware of the issues the institution faces in relationship to other institutions, government and community.
- Respect the environment and people with whom you work.
- Never underestimate the impact of the external political and social issues.
- Create a team of international and local personnel, but be sensitive to the issues local consultants face working in their own community.
- Develop a comprehensive evaluation plan based on the understanding of the institution and environment, but be flexible in adapting the plan to unexpected circumstances.
- Reflect on the literature and benchmarks, but remember that quality must be addressed relative to context.
- Build relationships through face-to-face contacts especially when working in a high-context culture.
- Make readily applicable suggestions towards improving the quality of education.
- Enjoy and learn from the process.

Notes

1 http://web.worldbank.org/external/projects/main?page PK=104231&piPK=73230;the SitePK=40941;menuPK=228424;Projectid=P08376
2 http://web.worldbank.org/WBSITE/EXTERNAL/TOPICS/EXTEDUCATION/ EXTEDUCATION/0,,contentMDK:20298183&menu PK:617592&pagePK:148956 &piPK:216618&theSitePK:282386,00.html
3 http://www.qou.edu/odlc/en/reports.jsp

References

Hashweh, M., Hashweh, M., & Berryman, S. (2003). *An assessment of higher education needs in the West Bank and Gaza.* Washington, DC: United States Agency for International Development. Retrieved from http://pdf.usaid.gov/pdf_docs/PNACW688.pdf
Matheos, K., MacDonald, M., McLean, C., Luterbach, B., Baidoun, S., & Nakashhian, S. (2007). *A comprehensive evaluation of Al-Quds Open University.* Retrieved from http:// www.qou.edu/english/manitobaReport/qouFullReport.pdf
Matheos, K., Rogoza, C., & Hamayil, M. (2009). Leapfrogging across generations of open and distance learning at Al-Quds Open University: A case study. *Online Journal of Distance Education Administration,* 12(4). Retrieved from http://www.westga.edu/~distance/ojdla/winter124/matheos124.html

15

LOWERING THE COST AND INCREASING THE EFFECTIVENESS OF QUALITY ASSURANCE: COL RIM

Geoff Plimmer, Willie Clarke-Okah, Caroline Donovan and Winsome Russell

Introduction

Imagine an institution fraught with quality problems, where the staff are too busy and too nervous to address them, and discussions about quality (or the lack of it) occur in surreptitious conversations, emails and phone calls. Imagine, too, an institution where understanding about management directions is unclear and bureaucracy is rife, where controversial proposals cannot receive endorsement by committees and where staff just keep their heads down and concentrate on their own work. Imagine also that there is a growing demand for institutional quality assurance (QA) but that the use of external quality assurance (EQA) is prohibitively expensive. This scenario is typical of many educational institutions across the globe, particularly in developing countries. It is the context in which the Commonwealth of Learning Review and Improvement Model (COL RIM) (Commonwealth of Learning, 2010) seeks to make a difference.

The use of QA has grown tremendously in the last 15 years, yet there are still tensions between internal improvement and accountability, compliance versus a quality culture, managerialism versus better teaching and learning and process versus outcomes (Harvey & Williams, 2010). We know that compliance with EQA has improved and that EQA accountability demands and processes are moving increasingly towards improvement regimes. But we also know that academics often see QA compliance as irrelevant to their core business of teaching and research. So while there is evidence of the positive effects of EQA, there are negative effects that exacerbate the characteristics of a poor quality environment, as described above, which result in problems of acceptance, legitimacy and effectiveness (Huisman & Westerheijden, 2010). Cost is another bugbear. Our experience is that institutions tend to over-prepare for QA, amassing vast quantities of data and evidence, only a fraction of which is ever used, while over-zealous evaluators give people the run-around for obscure and unnecessary details. All of which add unnecessarily to the costs of QA.

This is why the Commonwealth of Learning (COL), is trialling a new system, COL RIM, which focuses on capacity building and improvement and can be fully owned by the institutions. This system is particularly suited to developing countries which often suffer from a lack of QA capacity and resources and are not always helped by ill-fitting ideas and 'experts' from the West. COL's mission is to help improve access to quality education and training, especially in developing countries. Facilitating QA is one way to do this. In 2007, COL was involved in two expensive invitational audits at the University of South Africa (Unisa) and University of Ghana (UG). Unisa had requested a trial audit to prepare for an audit by the South African Council on Higher Education. The UG wished to establish what it needed to do to re-establish its former national eminence. In the case of the Unisa audit, a preliminary meeting of the external evaluators from six countries was held in the UK. The pre-prepared documentation filled wall-to-wall shelving in two rooms and over 400 interviews were carried out. In the case of the UG audit, the issues noted included the necessity for self-review (due to a lack of readiness, the panel had to make a return visit), the need for performance indicators as evaluation tools and the importance of rationalizing a clear audit scope. Both quality audit reports are available on the web.[1,2] The two audits served their purposes, but each cost over US$ 100,000, so COL decided to create a new model that would yield similar benefits but at much lower cost.

The two key lessons learned in the Unisa and UG audits were that much of the value of QA comes from self-assessment and that it is essential to have mechanisms in place to encourage staff, institution-wide, to take QA seriously. These findings were the starting point for the development of COL RIM. The challenge was to achieve a model that could be applied in environments similar to that described in the opening paragraph. The model subsequently developed was trialled at the University of Technology, Jamaica, in 2009. At the time of writing, a further trial had been completed in Sri Lanka, one was under way in Nigeria, a Memorandum of Understanding (MOU) was being signed with an institution in Lesotho, and the Commonwealth Secretariat was negotiating with COL to implement COL RIM in the Seychelles, Belize and Guyana in 2011. This chapter explains how COL RIM works and the lessons learnt to date in trialling this system.

COL RIM

COL RIM is offered to institutions on a voluntary basis and, unlike regulatory QA, requires no funding or licensing for its operation. There is, of course, some reputational risk to institutions undertaking the review, but the stakes are relatively low because the model emphasizes improvement over accountability. Rather than assessing an institution's performance against quality criteria, it is concerned with an institution's ability to investigate and analyze its own issues with integrity and rigour, arrive at reasonable evidence-based judgments and conclusions and make sound recommendations for improving its processes and outcomes. The status 'COL RIM verified' can then be used in communications with stakeholders. Table 15.1 shows how this model is designed to complement and help institutions meet the traditional QA requirements by addressing legitimacy diminishing common problems.

Let us examine how COL RIM works, drawing on our experience in trialling it at the University of Technology, Jamaica, and reflect on the lessons learned to date. The model comprises five steps: initiation, staff survey, self-review, verification and follow-up. The tools provided include readiness self-assessment questions, staff survey instruments, key evaluation questions, performance indicators, decision guides, staff training material, the *COL RIM Handbook*[3] and online support.

Initiation

This first step comprises readiness assessment and an MOU. The readiness self-assessment questions, developed in collaboration with representatives of Commonwealth institutions, are intended to be widely discussed throughout the institution. The senior management may be willing to sign up for evaluation, but the time and people requirements and level of transparency and openness required may not have been seriously considered. Readiness for COL RIM means that the senior managers must be wholly and continuously committed to leading and advocating the COL RIM process, releasing staff, allocating allied resources, being prepared to discuss openly what needs to be improved, being receptive to new ways of thinking and doing things, and quality of education. The institution's application to COL must evidence all of these.

COL and the institution seeking COL RIM then sign the MOU, which commits the institution to the COL RIM principles of transparency and rigorous analysis. This agreement also covers the resource commitments, timelines, arrangements for external verification and cost-sharing and so on. Agreed deadlines are a pre-condition. Without this, each stage is at risk of going overtime at considerable inconvenience to the external verifier. The strong position taken on this issue was a consequence of one lead verifier having the stressful experience of receiving a self-review report only one day before flying out for the on-campus verification. The second stage of implementation, the survey, does not commence until the MOU is signed and the institution has paid its share of the costs – a disincentive to pull out or delay.

TABLE 15.1 How features of COL RIM address the traditional problems with external QA

	Traditional problems with EQA	How these issues are addressed in COL RIM
Acceptance	High incentives to 'cover up' quality issues	No high stakes Incentives for high level of transparency and authentic self-review 'Verification' (the COL RIM 'quality mark') depends on quality of the self-review and not on organizational performance
	Emphasis on inputs and processes with low emphasis on results	COL RIM emphasizes results which show whether inputs and processes are working
	Low involvement of internal staff	All staff members have a voice in the survey Two distinct teams of internal staff play key roles (self-reviewers and internal verifiers) Internal staff are involved in making judgments [i.e., they influence the scope (from the survey) and own the outcomes]
	Limited QA capacity, poor self-review, and poor follow-up	Capacity building: preparation and training of the self-reviewers; centralizing and elevating and supporting the self-review process and using a team of internal verifiers trained by lead verifier
Effectiveness	Replication and duplication across multiple QA frameworks	Complements and supports preparation for external QA approaches
	Low impact on core business	Emphasis on teaching and learning outcomes COL RIM reduces compliance behaviour by focusing on what matters
	Encourages mechanistic compliance-driven behaviours Large numbers of prescriptive indicators	Fewer higher level indicators Six high-level evaluation questions guide a thematic big picture approach
	Fragmentation Especially traditional university EQA is oriented to	Whole of institution approach

(*Continued*)

TABLE 15.1 (Continued)

	Traditional problems with EQA	How these issues are addressed in COL RIM
	programmes/academic areas rather than whole institution	
	Judgmental rather than developmental	COL is not a regulatory body and the focus is on improvement rather than accountability, so the COL RIM approach includes developmental advice and support and builds capacity by training the staff
	Regulatory bodies make judgments but traditionally do not offer developmental advice or share good practice approaches	
Cost	Number of days of external intervention(s)	Combination of strengthened internal QA and periodic external institutional level audit is the least time-consuming/expensive approach
	Increased number of interventions for programme level EQA	
	More time needed without self-review (e.g., Ghana)	Good self-review and good scoping of external intervention reduces time/cost
	Amount of preparation Excessive paper-based preparation (e.g., Unisa)	COL RIM verification accesses institutional information in its usual location in electronic and paper-based systems on an 'as needed' basis
	Huge scope/big samples (e.g., Unisa with 400 interviews)	Systematic approach to scoping that starts wide and inclusive (the survey) and focuses progressively on issues of importance to stakeholders Sampling techniques
	Size of the external panel (e.g. Ghana and Unisa)	One external verifier trains and leads a team of internal verifiers
	Credibility depends on the high status of the external panel members	Credibility depends on rigorous implementation of valid and reliable methods
	External perspective increases perceived 'objectivity' and high rank increases perceived 'credibility'	Skills set of the external verifier is important

In recognition of the fact that institutions are at different stages of development, operate in different circumstances and have their own strategic directions, drivers, contexts and level of quality maturity, COL RIM can be customized to meet institutional needs. This is a matter for negotiation during the preparation

TABLE 15.2 Themes and evaluative questions

Themes	Evaluative question
Communication	How effectively does the institution communicate with its stakeholders?
Needs orientation	How well does the institution provide the outcomes that its stakeholders need and value?
Engagement (optional)	How effectively does the institution engage with local and international communities?
Quality management	How well does the institution monitor and improve its performance?
Innovation and creativity (optional)	How effective are the institution's innovative and creative responses to a changing environment?
Capacity building	How effectively does the institution develop the capacity of its people to provide valued outcomes for stakeholders?

of the MOU. COL RIM offers six thematic questions (Table 15.2) that broadly reflect the global consensus on quality indicators for education and training. The institution can opt out of two of these six themes and add its own. The finally agreed-to thematic questions are the centrepiece of the model. All lines of inquiry ultimately seek answers to these.

Staff Survey

Implementation begins with an online survey of all managerial, administrative, academic, technical and support staff. Referring to the quality indicators and performance descriptors, the managers and staff are asked to rate and comment on their perceptions of the practices in their own work areas. Their ratings and comments give voice to the informed but often voiceless stakeholders, and their identities are protected to ensure transparency and confidentiality. The results are processed by an independent agency. This democratizing process reveals hidden issues and pressure points and makes it harder for those in positions of power to conceal bad news.

The survey results signal areas of potential strength and weakness and are used by the self-review team to determine the scope of the self-review. Our early expectations were that the self-reviewers would themselves be able to examine the survey responses, identify cause-and-effect relationships and discern patterns that indicated systemic, interrelated problems across the different themes. We have found, however, that this expectation is unrealistic. The self-reviewers can become too absorbed in the details, partly because they already know their organizations so well.

COL RIM seeks a holistic view that steers away from the comfortable but common 'tick the box' approach which assumes that institutional performance can be meaningfully broken down into component parts and that rating each part will yield an aggregate score reflecting institutional performance. However, although the survey analysis is intended to provide a frame of reference for thinking, rather than a substitute for thinking, we have found that such systemic thinking can be harder to achieve than we originally thought. The thinking processes have tended to default to what Baser and Morgan (2008, p. 96) refer to as solving 'mechanistic capacity crossword puzzles'. Self-reviewers have told us that they spent considerable time cross-referencing between themes and indicators. Consequently, much of the cross-referencing information about how indicators related to each other has now been removed from the *COL RIM Handbook* in order to lift the level of enquiry from the indicator to the thematic questions. Now the survey results are reported directly on themes, to avoid self-reviewers wasting their time labouring over indicators that are really only meaningful in the context of the bigger picture.

Preparation Visit

In the original design of our model, the preparation visit was an optional component. The original cost-saving idea was that COL would hold periodic workshops and meetings on COL RIM for interested institutions and that the participants would then be able to return to their institutions fully informed, equipped with presentational material and able to introduce the model to their colleagues. But we found that workshop participants did not feel able to introduce the model adequately, that the self-reviewers needed more training for their role than was originally envisaged, and that preparation visits were requested by all institutions. So we now offer the preparation visit immediately after the delivery of the survey report together with more in-depth training (of the self-review team in particular) so that introduction of the model and the training are focused on actual and emergent issues rather than theoretical concepts.

Self-review

The self-review team comprises senior managers of the key operational areas. This formal ownership by senior management ensures that the QA process and outcomes cannot be palmed off as the work of subordinates. In reality, getting senior management to give time and political capital to hands-on investigation and in-depth consideration of quality issues is not easy. In our first trial, the self-review team was small and under-resourced. When it came time to do the work, several senior managers, who had earlier committed to it, claimed other obligations, and the four managers who did participate could give little time to the investigations and subsequent discussion and analysis of the findings. Institutional mission statements and public pronouncements on quality are often quite 'boosterish'. The COL RIM simply actions this rhetoric by ensuring that senior managers give their real attention to the QA agenda.

The self-reviewers' first task is to scope and plan the review based on the survey results and thematic questions. Defensible scoping decisions are an essential pre-condition for verifiable self-review reports. Sound planning in regard to timelines and resource allocation are also important. Consequently, the COL RIM team members closely monitor the initial decisions of the self-review teams to help ensure that they embark on verifiable and sustainable courses of action.

In the more traditional approaches to self-review, the starting point is usually a full set of criteria against which to evaluate the organization. This is a daunting task, and there is a strong tendency to dwell at length on things that are going well and gloss over the rest. Also, as Greenwald (1980) and Kroll, Toombs and Wright (2000) indicate, strong, self-serving biases that ignore, suppress or disparage negative information may operate among the executive teams. COL RIM aims to counterbalance these tendencies through a preliminary narrowing of the scope to the issues raised in the staff survey which indicate potential strengths and weaknesses worthy of further investigation. The self-review process then involves assembling evidence to support or disconfirm the findings of the survey report, analyze the cause-and-effect relationships and provide honest and reflective answers based on the themes and evidence.

Verification

The verification team is made up of internal staff members under the supervision of an external lead verifier. The lead verifier is a QA professional, a COL RIM team member who trains the team in audit and evaluative principles and methods, and assures the quality of the verification. In order to avoid conflicts of interest, membership of the self-review and verification teams does not overlap. The verifiers are volunteers, selected for their enthusiasm rather than their status. They are the potential champions for quality in their respective departments who can diffuse new thinking throughout the institution.

In the first trial, the verification was the most positive part of the process. Working with the lead verifier, a team of eight volunteers worked intensively for 4 days. Vigorous debates ensued and as they gained confidence, team members challenged each others' findings, conducted further interviews, followed leads and obtained further evidence to support their conclusions. As the new data came in daily, the walls of the meeting room became covered with charts, plans, unresolved questions and to-do lists. The difficulty was in arriving at an overall judgement on whether the self-review could be verified. So the COL RIM team provided a three-level rubric of decision-making criteria: 'verified', 'threshold' and 'not verified'. The findings of the verification were considered in relation to the criteria for each level of performance. In the end, the findings clearly did not meet the criteria for 'verified' or 'threshold' and so the team unanimously concluded that the only justifiable conclusion was 'not verified'. The conclusion and findings were then presented to senior management. Even though the result was disappointing, the senior managers agreed that the findings truly reflected the issues they were grappling with.

Follow-up

After the verification report has been digested by senior management and decisions have been made on how to act upon the recommendations, the institution is required to share its action plan with COL. In regard to the initial trial, the institution's senior management is now monitoring its own action plan for implementing the COL RIM recommendations and is interested in repeating the COL RIM process again in 2011.

Some months later, as part of its periodic meta-review of the model, COL asks the institution to report on its experience of COL RIM implementation and account for what has changed as a result of the exercise. Time will tell if this level of follow-up is sufficient.

Conclusion

Self-review has been described as the most beneficial part of a QA process (Maseru, 2007). But, how often are the problems and issues arising really discussed openly and honestly? Our perception is that the overriding aim of many self-review reports is to make the institution look good so that the external auditors won't ask difficult questions or discover matters of concern. There appear to be at least three sets of problems here: the principal agent problem, information asymmetry and cultural power distance.

Principal–agent problems occur when a 'principal' commissions an 'agent' to perform tasks on his/her behalf but cannot ensure that the agent performs them in precisely the way the principal would like. The interests of the agent may be different from those of the principal. For instance, there may be territory and patch protection, which though inefficient organizationally, can be beneficial to the agent. This can result in disconnections, bottlenecks and failure to collaborate in achieving quality outcomes.

Information asymmetry occurs in transactions and decision-making where one party has more or better information than the other parties. External auditors inevitably have less information about the institution being audited than the managers and staff. They may therefore be vulnerable to misrepresentation, denied information, given incomplete or inaccurate information or provided with so much information that, lacking knowledge of the contexts, they cannot make informed judgments.

Cultural factors, such as high power distance and low tolerance of ambiguity, can also influence the willingness and ability of staff to find and report bad news in a self-evaluation process. Most of us who have worked in tertiary institutions, especially in developing countries, can attest to the fact that, even in internal documents, people prefer to tiptoe around areas of concern and 'a spade is rarely called a spade'.

Attempting to address these issues head on, COL RIM adopts approaches different from, and complementary to, other models of EQA. It uses pre-agreed principles of good practice, performance indicators and criteria indicators and makes use of surveys with a variety of informed stakeholders. It attempts to manage incentives within the institutions, provide resources for information gathering and review, and face some of the political and people factors that commonly inhibit honest self-assessment and change. It does this by verifying quality in terms of demonstrated ability to identify, analyze and plan to address issues of concern, which we take as a proxy for capacity to improve. What we have learnt to date is that real engagement and actual improvement are difficult to achieve and require a blend of hard external pressure and a soft internal development. The hard external approaches include the incentives and contractual arrangements in the MOU, the results of the survey analysis, and the involvement of the external verifier. The soft internal approaches include the training and provision of guidelines. Either approach without the other would be unrealistic.

COL RIM is still a work in progress. Its value seems to largely reside in its developmental orientation. By the end of the COL RIM process, the institutional staff members who were in the self-review and verification teams will have gained in-depth understanding of how quality can be managed and how EQA works. Most EQA agencies do not have the capacity or mandate to provide intensive training and support for the institutions to be evaluated, and few regulatory bodies are able to give developmental advice to the extent that COL RIM does. A feature of the 'QA industry' is that it is good at proliferating models but not so good at providing the soft skills, formative feedback, goals, training, knowledge and incentives needed to effect real change. We also believe that COL RIM develops systemic thinking and organizational communications, collaboration and learning, and helps to improve institutions without high stakes consequences for poor performance.

The weakness of COL RIM may lie in the current limited follow-up on the verification recommendations. A common feature of all the surveys so far analyzed is complaints by staff that decisions are not being followed up on. As with other survey tools, serious and challenging issues can be brought to light that institutional managers may wish to avoid facing up to. It remains to be seen in the further trials, and the first meta-review of the outcomes, if and how COL RIM makes a difference.

COL RIM aspires to be a democratic tool. Enabling staff to voice their views, transparency and multiple perspectives to cross traditional hierarchies are the core processes, not the audit or evaluation methods. It uses pluralism, rather than managerialism, to review and improve quality. COL RIM will continue to evolve in response to the needs of its stakeholders.

Notes

1 http://www.col.org/UnisaTrialAudit
2 http://www.col.org/ghanavisitation
3 http://www.col.org/SiteCollectionDocuments/COL%20RIM%20Handbook_Dec2009.pdf

References

Baser, H., & Morgan, P. (2008). *Capacity, change and performance: Study report.* Discussion paper No 59B, European Centre for Policy Management, Maastricht, The Netherlands. Retrieved from http://www.ecdpm.org/Web_ECDPM/Web/Content/Navigation.nsf/index2?readform&http://www.ecdpm.org/Web_ECDPM/Web/Content/Content.nsf/0/BD2B856F58D93E5FC12574730031FD6F?OpenDocument?

Commonwealth of Learning. (2010). *Handbook for the commonwealth of learning review and improvement model.* Vancouver: Author.

Greenwald, A. (1980). The totalitarian ego. *American Psychologist, 35*(7), 603–618.

Harvey, L., & Williams, J. (2010). Fifteen years of quality in higher education. *Quality in Higher Education, 16*(1), 3–36.

Huisman, J., & Westerheijden, D. (2010). Bologna and quality assurance: Progress made or pulling the wrong cart? *Quality in Higher Education, 16*(1), 63–66.

Kroll, M., Toombs, L., & Wright, P. (2000). Napoleon's tragic march home from Moscow: Lessons in hubris. *The Academy of Management Executive (1993–2005), 14*(1), 117–128.

Maseru, P. (2007). *Higher education quality assurance in Sub-Saharan Africa: Status, challenges, opportunities and promising practices.* World Bank Working Paper No. 124. Washington, DC: The World Bank.

16

QUALITY ASSURANCE IN OPEN SCHOOLING

National Institute of Open Schooling, India, and Open Junior Secondary School, Indonesia

Sanjaya Mishra*, Sitanshu S. Jena and Arief S. Sadiman

Introduction

Ten years have passed since the international community adopted the six Education for All goals in Dakar in 2000. The number of children out of school has dropped by 33 million worldwide and considerable progress has been made towards achieving universal primary education. However, there is a corresponding increase in demand for secondary schooling in the developing countries. Open and distance schools are increasingly recognized as a solution to this growing demand. Such schools are found in all parts of the world – the Commonwealth of Learning (COL) identifies 80 schools in the Commonwealth countries alone. Rumble and Koul (2007) find that while open schooling may have low status, be underfunded and sometimes yield poorer results than conventional schools, it certainly succeeds in providing education for remote and socially disadvantaged communities in ways never before possible. In this chapter, we examine the challenges of providing quality education in two of the world's largest open schooling systems – the National Institute of Open Schooling (NIOS) in India and the Open Junior Secondary School (OJSS) in Indonesia.

National Institute of Open Schooling

With over 1.18 billion people, India is the world's second-most populous country. Due to various social and economic problems, its conventional schools continue to underserve the population, particularly in disadvantaged and rural

*The ideas and opinions expressed in this article are those of the author and do not necessarily represent the view of UNESCO.

areas. Nearly 300 million people aged 7 years and above are illiterate and 42 million children in the age group 6–14 years do not attend school. There are problems of inadequate school infrastructure and resources, and there is a short-fall of over 1.2 million teachers. A concerned government continuously examines ways of overcoming these challenges and, looking at the alternatives, has opted for open learning.

The NIOS began as an Open Schooling Project under the auspices of the Central Board of Secondary Education in 1978, became the National Open School in 1989, was authorized by the Government of India to certify learners up to pre-degree level in 1990, and was re-mandated to act as the national apex body for open schooling and renamed the NIOS in 2002. NIOS functions under the aegis of the Ministry of Human Resource Development but is an autonomous institution which:

- Supports India's drive for universal education.
- Promotes national integration and integrated development of people.
- Is both a teaching and an examining body.
- Serves the educational needs of school dropouts and marginalized groups, including scheduled castes and tribes, rural youth, urban poor, girls, ex-servicemen and people with disabilities.
- Operates an open entry system that expects learners to have at least completed Grade 8 in a conventional school or the Open Basic Education (OBE) Level C of NIOS (learners can also self-certify their competency level at Grade 8).
- Imposes no maximum age limits, but expects learners to be 14 years and over.
- Sets its fees low and makes special concessions for girls, ex-servicemen and the disabled.
- Allows the learners freedom to choose subjects.
- Uses self-paced and self-directed learning.
- Uses multimedia study materials, including audio and video to supplement the printed self-learning modules.
- Provides continuous assessment through tutor-marked assignments.
- Provides learner support through study centres and a personal contact programme.
- Offers twice yearly exams – with credit accumulation.
- Offers on-demand examination throughout the year in selected centres.
- Allows nine opportunities in 5 years to complete a course and re-admission after 5 years.
- Allows re-evaluation of answer scripts, thereby making the evaluators careful in the first instance.
- Provides 24×7 call centre support and motivational and adolescent programme support.
- Is largely self-sufficient (only 10% of its operations are government funded).

In 2009–2010, NIOS had 419,000 enrolees and a cumulative student enrolment of 1.9 million in the 27 secondary subjects, 21 senior secondary subjects and over 80 certificate and diploma vocational programmes. Over 30% of the students enroled in the secondary and senior secondary courses and 55% of those in the vocational programmes were girls. The majority of students are aged 15–25 years.

The secondary and senior secondary programmes are equivalent to the Central Board of Secondary Education's Grade 10 and 12 programmes and have the same status for admission to higher studies and employment. Many students go on to study at conventional schools and colleges including the prestigious Indian Institutes of Technology. The students taking the vocational programmes go on to provide the skilled manpower that is so critical to India's economic growth. NIOS also offers elementary level courses through its OBE Programmes, provides access to resource persons in voluntary agencies and district literacy committees, and certification for school dropouts and neo-literates wishing to study at levels equivalent to Standards 3, 5 or 8 in the conventional system.

With its headquarters at Noida, Uttar Pradesh, NIOS operates through a network of 16 regional centres, two sub-regional centres and over 3,700 study centres across India, Nepal and the Middle East, and employs 251 full-time staff. It also operates a National Consortium for Open Schooling. The Government of India's Eleventh Five-Year Plan (2007–2012) charges NIOS with improving the quality of the existing State Open Schools in Andhra Pradesh, Assam, Chattisgarh, Delhi, Haryana, Jammu and Kashmir, Karnataka, Kerala, Madhya Pradesh, Punjab, Rajasthan, Tamil Nadu, Uttar Pradesh and West Bengal, and with establishing Open Schools in the remaining States. NIOS provides consultation and support to the Government on these matters and serves as the national resource centre for the State Open Schools.

The 2005 Central Advisory Board of Education's report on the universalization of secondary education[1] recommended that every State be enabled to provide open schooling in regional languages enhanced by a number of measures, including counselling and tutorial services. The Report of the Working Group on Secondary and Vocational Education for the Eleventh Five-Year Plan[2] expected the Open Schooling system to become responsible for educating 15% of the 92 million 14–18 years olds. Observing that only 2% of 15–29 years olds receives any formal vocational training and only 8% non-formal training, this plan also envisaged a rise in the annual participation rates in this sector from 3.1 million to 15 million and that the Open Schooling system would make provision for this. The *Saakshar Bharat Scheme 2012* (Ministry of Human Resource Development and Department of School Education and Literacy, 2009) aims to provide functional literacy for 70 million learners aged 15 and over by 2012, 60 million of whom are to be female, and envisages many of these neo-literates progressing to formal education. All of these expectations and projections clearly have massive implications for the NIOS, which is already the world's largest open schooling system.

While the conventional schools in India use textbooks that are developed by the National Council for Educational Research and Training and designed for teacher-based classrooms, NIOS develops its own course materials in forms appropriate to mainly self-study. The course needs are identified by the NIOS Academic Council or Government of India reports and recommendations. Concept papers are then drawn up, justifying the courses, reviewing similar courses and outlining the course frameworks. Subject committees then plan the course content, learning outcomes and learning activities. These plans are vetted by external subject experts before submission for approval by the NIOS Academic Council.

Once these proposals are agreed, NIOS faculty members undertake the materials development in accord with a style guide which ensures uniform standards and active learning. The materials must make clear the intended learning outcomes, aim to achieve meta-cognition and higher order learning, rather than mere knowledge and factual recall, be capable of being worked through with little or no support, and include tests, quizzes and feedback to help the learners assess their own progress. While most of the materials are print-based, supplementary audio and video materials are also produced and made available through the study centres and broadcast through the Indira Gandhi National Open University Gyan Darshan-I satellite transmission system. At each stage of development, the instructional design is formatively evaluated by NIOS faculty and external subject experts. The NIOS Evaluation Department takes responsibility for developing the assessment methods and examinations in accordance with the recommendations of the subject committees, employing a template that ensures that the question papers are of the required secondary, senior secondary or vocational education standards and levels. The courseware is then translated into the various languages and, once in use, is continually evaluated, revised and updated. Rumble and Koul (2007) questioned some of the English syntax but had no hesitation in commending the quality of the NIOS content and instructional design.

NIOS has established a Research and Development Cell. This supports the State Open Schools as well as NIOS. It operates a grant-in-aid scheme for research projects in open schooling, prepares guidelines for planning, monitoring and evaluating NIOS programmes, undertakes research for NIOS, contracts other organizations to engage in research projects and evaluates the quality of the learning materials, study centre and other student support systems and the cost-effectiveness of operations. It also conducts tracer studies on the learners.

The NIOS study centres provide administrative and academic support. Those supporting the secondary and senior secondary students are called Accredited Institutions and those supporting the vocational students are known as

Accredited Vocational Institutions. These centres are selected against strict criteria, and the teaching, assignment marking and other activities undertaken at these centres are monitored by academic facilitators in the regional centres. The teachers and facilitators at the various study centres provide practical guidance and support for the learners and facilitate group and collaborative learning. They are responsible for 30 contact hours for the theoretical components of courses and even more contact hours for the practical subjects. To be eligible for the final exams, the learners are expected to submit assignments for formative assessment by these teachers and facilitators. But because the grades for these do not count towards the final exam scores, many learners fail to take these assignments seriously. Moreover, students' results can be adversely affected by the failure of staff at these centres to submit records of the students' assignment work on time to the Evaluation Department, something which occurs all too often.

The overall NIOS pass rate in the secondary exams is around 32% and in the senior secondary exams 28%. By comparison, the overall pass rates in the conventional schools are about 90% at secondary level and 80% at senior secondary level. Rumble and Koul (2007) observe that dividing the pass rate in the NIOS system by that gained by students in traditional examinations, the relative effectiveness ratio is 35% but, if the best government-run secondary institutions are taken out of the formula, the subject pass percentages and overall NIOS results are comparable to those of an average school. This is no mean achievement, considering that NIOS serves a mix of dropouts, overworked adults, housewives and out-of-school children, many of whom start with more handicaps than do conventional students and are largely self-learners.

Issues and Challenges

NIOS works hard to achieve quality products and processes in accord with the clearly laid down standards and procedures. It is making increasing use of information and communications technology (ICT) in liaising with the regional and study centres, operating 24 × 7 admissions/enrolment, an interactive voice response system and a call centre, and providing question banks, on-demand exams and exam results and e-accreditation. However, NIOS still faces a number of challenges in ensuring quality:

- It is reliant upon the collaboration of thousands of study centres, schools, vocational institutions and voluntary and non-governmental organizations, so ultimately, it cannot be responsible for the 'last mile of service' to the learners.
- Its management system is highly centralized and top-heavy and needs to be more flexible, responsive and devolved.

- There needs to be better provision for online materials delivery and learner support and greater use of the mass media facilities available throughout India.
- NIOS has yet to make a major contribution to capacity building for the teachers and facilitators in the centres, both in its own operations and the State Open Schools.
- The role of the R&D Cell needs further clarifying and strengthening.
- Finding and retaining good course writers and courseware developers is very difficult. Organizing translators from English to Hindi, Urdu and regional languages and completing materials on time is also problematic.

OJSS (SMP Terbuka), Indonesia

Indonesia is an archipelago of more than 13,600 islands with a population of 237.56 million. It is a modern country with pockets of traditional and even ancient cultures. Education is the responsibility of the Ministry of National Education (MoNE) and Ministry of Religious Affairs (responsible for Islamic schools). There are 9 years of compulsory education, six of which are at elementary level (Grades 1–6) and three at junior high school level (Grades 7–9). There are two types of senior high school (Grades 10–12): one preparing students for university entry and the other, vocational education.

The government has long been concerned about educational quality and considers the development of the potential human resources to be very low. As a consequence of a 1974 Presidential mandate, there was first a massive growth in elementary schools and then in the number of graduates continuing on to junior secondary schools. However, geographic and socio-economic circumstances prevented many children from attending conventional junior secondary schools, so in 1979, the OJSS was piloted in five provinces to serve these disadvantaged children. Unlike the conventional junior secondary schools which charged tuition fees, OJSS schooling at this stage was free. In 1994, the OJSS system was extended to 27 provinces and the number of schools rose to 956. Four years later, there were 3,645 OJSS schools. However, the Ministry then began building many more junior secondary schools and abolishing the fees for attending these. As a consequence, the number of OJSS schools began to decrease, from 3,483 in 1999 to 2,111 in 2009. In 2007, the total number of students was 306,409. By 2010, it was down to 248,432.

OJSS is designed for 11–18 years olds who have completed elementary schooling or dropped out of conventional junior secondary schools. However, its priority is to enrol 13–15 years olds who, for whatever reason, are unable to enrol in a conventional school. The OJSS students follow the same curriculum as in the conventional schools, take the same national examinations, are graded in the same way and have

the same rights and opportunities for further study and employment as those graduating from the conventional schools. The only differences are in the learning environments and means by which the students learn. Rather than receiving full-time
face-to-face teaching, the OJSS learners must work independently or in groups
using print self-study modules, workbooks and less commonly, audiovisual aids.
They also have access to local facilitators (parents, primary school teachers or others
recruited within the local communities) in local learning centres 3–4 hours a day, 4
or 5 days a week. These facilitators are not expected to master the course content
or to be responsible for the learning outcomes, so the students are also required to
attend a local conventional junior secondary school ('mother school' or 'base
school') for up to 6 hours once or twice a week. Here they are helped by subject
teachers and access resources unavailable at the learning centres. The actual time
arrangements for this are a matter of negotiation between the learners and the
teachers. Where such regular attendance is not feasible, for example, because of the
distances involved or the learners having part-time jobs, face-to-face assistance may
be arranged in other centres closer to home or, as in North Sulawesi, OJSS may
provide boats for the teachers to visit their students.

The teachers assess the students' workbooks weekly, there are mid- and end-
of-semester tests and, as in the conventional schools, the students receive reports
on their performance at the end of each semester and school year, and are promoted to the next grade if their achievements justify this. Finally they sit the
MoNE exams.

During the pilot stage (1979–1984), the OJSS was managed by the Centre for
Communication Technology for Education and Culture. Since 1984, it has operated under the Directorate of General Secondary School, MoNE. At the district
and city level, responsibility for managing the OJSS system lies with the heads of
the local MoNE branches and at the school level, the headteachers. Irwanto,
Hendriati and Hestyanti (2001) observe that the success of OJSS depends very
much upon the quality of the headteachers and their commitment to enriching
the learning experiences, overcoming local difficulties and raising additional funds
and resources.

Internal evaluation of OJSS is carried out by the Directorate of Junior
Secondary Schooling. External evaluation is by units outside the Directorate.
Recent MoNE-backed initiatives to improve the quality of the work of the OJSS
include:

- Establishing two task groups at Directorate level; one responsible for quality
  and efficiency improvement, the other for expanding access. (Similar task
  groups have also been set up at the provincial, district and city levels.)
- Developing guidelines for managing the operations and operational costs of
  the subject teachers, local facilitators and learning centres and budgeting and
  implementing life skills education.

- Increasing training provision for principals and vice-principals to improve the quality of OJSS management and for subject teachers and facilitators to improve teaching and learning quality.
- Launching an annual OJSS Independent Learning Motivation Competition to motivate student learning in all Grade 7 and 8 subjects. (Grade 9 students are considered too busy preparing for the school and national examinations.)
- Introducing a similar competition for life skills education.
- Providing scholarships of Rp300,000 (US$33) per student for OJSS students from poor families. (However, because of the study costs and need for children to contribute to household incomes, only 6–7% of OJSS graduates then go on to a senior secondary school.)
- Strengthening life skills education by inviting schools to make proposals and apply for block grants and seed money for new initiatives. (In 2010, the Directorate of Junior Secondary Schooling allocated 900 life skills grant packages, each worth Rp30,000,000 or approximately US$3,300.)
- Developing study materials and associated teachers' manuals to prepare Grade 9 students for the school and MoNE examinations for science, mathematics, Indonesian and English.
- Increasing efficiency by merging learning centres that are too close to each other or attract only small numbers of students.
- Encouraging greater community and NGO participation in the creation and running of learning centres. (In 2010, there were 374 NGO-supported learning centres operating in 56 districts and cities in 15 provinces. These alone catered for 15,562 students.)

Issues and Challenges

Despite the fact that the OJSS has been operating in Indonesia since 1979, many people, even MoNE and other government officials, still look upon it as new and unconventional. So it is not only the students who must adjust to the OJSS; the large numbers of managers and teachers involved in the system must also adopt new attitudes and ways of doing things. Changing the mindsets of students, parents and the community at large also presents a major challenge. Changing decision-makers' and community perceptions of educational quality is also problematic. It is difficult to persuade them that the quality of the OJSS should not be just judged by the national examination pass rates, but by the full range of value-adding outcomes. None of this is easy and it all consumes time.

Until recently, it was not possible to supply every student with his or her own learning modules. This is now a target set by the OJSS Directorate.

Other challenges include:

- Improving the quality of the facilitators in order to make study at the learning centres more inviting, stimulating and conducive to serious study.
- The limited budget for operating the system in the mother schools and learning centres.
- The lack of coordination in management throughout the system.
- The late delivery of learning materials.
- The inappropriate siting of some learning centres.
- Finding and retaining sufficient numbers of capable and dedicated teachers and facilitators.
- The lack of ICT skills in teachers and facilitators.
- The low student attendance rates at the learning centres.
- The limited community participation and support (Sadiman & Rahardjo, 2005).

Conclusion

The two open schooling systems described in this chapter have much in common. Both provide access for those who are unable to attend conventional schools and operate open and flexible admissions and study systems. In neither system is the payment of fees a barrier. In the case of NIOS, the fees are very low and in the case of OJSS, no fees are involved. Both systems lead to nationally recognized qualifications. NIOS is a Government of India-recognized Examination Board, and its secondary and senior secondary examinations are equivalent to those of the States or the Central Board of Secondary Examination. In the case of the OJSS, the students sit the same exams as students in the conventional schools.

Both systems operate in environments where quantity tends to prevail over quality. However, in both countries, the public school systems are poorly equipped, so quality in NIOS and OJSS needs to be judged in this context. Both systems operate over great distances and in regions where communications, staffing and resource provision are problematic. Both operate as networks and depend upon the goodwill and capacities of many people in remote locations. The study centres in the Indian system are not owned by NIOS and only operate on a voluntary basis, so there is little direct control over their day-to-day operations, or in ensuring that the learners receive regular and appropriate support and feedback. In the case of OJSS, there is no guarantee that essential information is sent to head office in time.

Both NIOS and OJSS develop and provide print and audiovisual learning materials designed for self-study at a distance and arrange for some support from teachers and/or facilitators. In both systems, the learning materials production is by teams who ensure quality in content, language and instructional design. Both

NIOS and OJSS recognize the importance of learning through engagement and interaction and the importance of providing educational and social support for the learners. In the case of NIOS, the students are expected to attend at least 30 sessions at the study centres. However, attendance is not compulsory, so attendance can be quite irregular on the part of some students. It is compulsory for the OJSS students to attend the learning centres and the mother schools, learning from both facilitators and subject teachers.

The NIOS and OJSS are attempting to improve quality as well as access. However, neither system has a formal quality assurance (QA) framework of agreed standards and benchmarks for their products, services and support processes, as suggested by Kirkpatrick (2005). So any improvement in quality is bound to be variable. NIOS and OJSS also lack the documentation on the nature of the teaching–learning processes or needs for QA and improvement. For example, there are no data on student satisfaction levels with the courses, materials or student services. Anecdotal evidence in both organizations suggests that this aspect of quality leaves much to be desired, but in the absence of any quality benchmarks, there is no way of assessing or comparing whether the students are positive or negative towards their learning experiences. The immediate need for both open schooling systems is therefore to develop quality policies, standards, monitoring procedures and reporting systems for management, administration, teaching and learning, assessment and service delivery in order to ensure total quality care for their students. There is also need for transparent and accountable systems for judging the quality of management, assessment and examination operations. And it is important to assure that all of the staff involved in these open schooling systems are knowledgeable and passionate about distance education. So capacity building for assuring quality is highly important.

As COL (2010) observes, open schooling is becoming more and more prevalent in most developing countries and is enroling increasing numbers of learners, particularly at secondary school level, but QA is still very limited. At the time of writing, COL had just published a free online *Quality Assurance Toolkit for Open Schools*[3] for policymakers, managers and practitioners interested in helping their open schooling systems institute sound and explicit QA. Indirectly, it also seeks to alert policymakers to the importance of investing in quality open schooling. Open schooling must mean access to quality education, otherwise the millions who go through the system risk being unable to make meaningful contributions in the developing economies. The quality of the education is as important as the quantity offered.

Notes

1 http://www.education.nic.in/cabe/universalisation.pdf
2 http://planningcommission.nic.in/plans/planrel/11thf.htm
3 http://www.col.org/resources/publications/Pages/detail.aspx?PID=341

References

Commonwealth of Learning (COL). (2010). *Quality assurance toolkit for open schools*. Vancouver: Author. Retrieved from http://www.col.org/PublicationDocuments/pubQAOSToolkit.pdf

Irwanto, P., Hendriati, A., & Hestyanti, R. (2001). *Alternative education for disadvantaged youth in Indonesia*. Paris: UNESCO. Retrieved from http://unesdoc.unesco.org/images/0012/001261/126194e.pdf

Kirkpatrick, D. (2005). *Quality assurance in open distance learning*. Vancouver: Commonwealth of Learning.

Ministry of Human Resource Development and Department of School Education and Literacy. (2009). *Centrally sponsored scheme Saakshar Bharat*. New Delhi: Government of India. Retrieved from http://www.education.nic.in/Elementary/SaaksharBharat.pdf

Rumble, G., & Koul, B. N. (2007). *Open schooling for secondary and higher secondary education: Costs and effectiveness in India and Namibia*. Vancouver: Commonwealth of Learning. Retrieved from http://www.col.org/SiteCollectionDocuments/Open_Schooling_Secondary_Higher_Education_071707.pdf

Sadiman, A. S., & Rahardjo, R. (2005, October). *Institutional development to improve the Open Junior Secondary School access and quality*. Paper presented at *National Workshop on OJSS Institutional Development*, Yogyakarta, Indonesia.

17

ASSURING QUALITY IN SCHOOL DIGITAL ECOSYSTEMS

Michael Gaffney

Introduction

The increasing variety, reliability and use of digital technologies are changing how teachers and students learn and relate to one another. Emerging technologies and their application to teaching, learning, administrative and communication processes in schools challenge our ideas about student achievement, effective teaching practice and how schools are best organized and led. Together these changes call for a new way of thinking about the teaching and learning workspace for teachers and students and the approaches needed to monitor and assess the effectiveness of, and links between, the teaching and learning experiences.

Central to this thinking is the concept of the 'digital ecosystem', a concept explored in this chapter, and the criteria by which the performance of such systems can be evaluated. The distinguishing characteristic for assuring quality in school digital ecosystems is a focus on the systemic integration and alignment of the teaching and learning, administrative and communication functions and stakeholder awareness and consensus regarding the nature of such integration and alignment and the place of digital resources in achieving this.

The Concept of the School Digital Ecosystem

The term digital ecosystem is derived from the biological sciences which define an ecosystem as 'a localized group of interdependent organisms together with the environment that they inhabit and depend on' (*Encarta Dictionary*). A digital ecosystem refers to 'a distributed, adaptive, open, social and technical system, with properties of … scalability and sustainability, inspired by natural ecosystems'.[1] As in the world of nature, digital ecosystems have three distinctive characteristics: (i) the capacity to evolve and sustain themselves, (ii) vulnerability to external threats and undesirable mutations and (iii) interoperability to 'feed' and 'feed off' another (Ingvarson & Gaffney, 2008). Like natural ecosystems, digital ecosystems can be characterized in terms of their evolution and sustainability. The rate of evolution of digital technology has been extraordinarily rapid, deeply affecting the way we communicate, work, learn and play. And it seriously affects the sustainability of such previously regarded bastions as the music and newspaper industries, where, in many cases, the choice is now 'evolve rapidly or cease to exist'. Similarly, digital ecosystems are vulnerable to external threats and mutations. We see evidence of this in the problems caused by computer viruses and the concerns raised about privacy in an increasingly digitally-mediated information and communication space. We also see it in what have been referred to as 'disruptive innovations', that is to say, new ways of doing things (usually involving emerging digital technologies) that gain sufficient traction in difficult-to-manage 'fringe contexts' that the assumptions reflected in the mainstream practices begin to be questioned (Christensen, 1997; Christensen, Johnson, & Horn, 2008).

In school settings, the digital ecosystem concept applies to the need to keep student learning as the focus, to ensure that the technology supports the teaching and learning (rather than the other way round) and to achieve the necessary interoperability between the different digital information and communication systems to support the teaching and learning. The metaphor of a digital ecosystem raises the question of how everything in the school environment is connected in support of providing quality learning opportunities for young people: school leaders' and teachers' personal attributes, professional practices and capabilities; shared understandings with respect to teaching and learning with digital technologies; and the various elements that comprise the learning workspace, especially the digital technology infrastructure. The focus is on what each component of this infrastructure can provide and how each relates to other components in support of student learning (Ingvarson & Gaffney, 2008).

The digital ecosystem refers to the mixture of stakeholders (students, teachers, principals and school executive, parents, local community members, education authorities and governments) and digital resources in a context characterized by a significant degree of interdependency. Selected elements of school digital ecosystems are shown in Figure 17.1.

The nature of, and connections between, these various elements of the school digital ecosystem give rise to a series of questions about learning outcomes, teaching practices and uses of digital technologies. The numbers in Figure 17.1 refer to the following questions:

1. What does a teacher need to know about individual students and student cohorts in order to make good planning decisions?

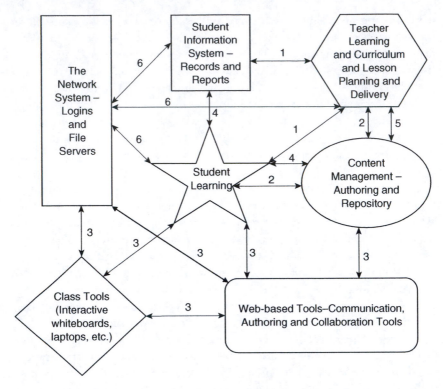

FIGURE 17.1   Selected sample elements of school digital ecosystems and questions
about connections

Sources: Ingvarson and Gaffney (2008); Vrasidas and Glass (2005).

2.   What content is being authored by and/or being accessed and made available
     to the students and teachers? How does this content link to the curriculum
     and how readily can it be accessed?
3.   What network tools are needed to support teacher and student collaboration
     and authoring? How reliable and accessible are these tools?
4.   How are the 'products' of the students' learning stored? Who owns them?
     How are they assessed and recorded?
5.   How are the resources developed by the teachers stored and shared? How are
     intellectual property and copyright issues managed?
6.   How open or closed is the network to the teachers, students, parents and
     others who are regarded as members of the school community?

These questions focus on how stakeholders in school communities learn and
work with each other and with the digital technology to achieve worthwhile
outcomes for themselves and others. In short, they relate to the emergence of a

new paradigm based on the concept of networked learning and the use of Web 2.0 technologies. As networked forms of provision and learning opportunities increase, dealing appropriately with these questions becomes ever more important.

Quality Assurance: Multiple Features and Stakeholders

From the perspective of school digital ecosystems, quality assurance (QA) is a multi-faceted, multi-level and multiple stakeholder endeavour. It is characterized by complexity not usually found in traditional, 'component by component' monitoring and evaluation processes associated with school use of information and communications technology (ICT). It may be considered a rational or technical process concerned with the use and interplay of online resources, technological infrastructure, curriculum programmes, assessment and reporting requirements, teaching practice, learning outcomes, school organization and education authority and government policies. At the same time, it is an essentially relationship–oriented undertaking involving teachers, students, the school executive and others with an interest in the quality of teaching and learning. These people are interested in what is going on, what is being achieved and why.

We are talking about important stakeholders here: students (with diverse needs, talents and interests); teachers (ditto) and specialists, including teacher librarians, ICT managers, technical support officers and bursars (each with their particular needs, talents and idiosyncrasies) and those in positions of authority at school, local education authority and government level. In regard to the school digital ecosystem, they want to know:

- What outcomes are being achieved and why – what are the important supporting and inhibiting factors?
- What is supporting what, and who is supporting whom – and for what purpose?
- Who makes the decisions and what criteria are used to make these decisions?
- Who is responsible for what and why?
- Who implements and how are the stages of implementation understood and integrated?
- Who is accountable and why?

A vibrant, sustainable school digital ecosystem is characterized by a central focus on student learning, technology that supports teaching and learning, and teaching, learning, administration and communication systems that 'talk' to each other. The integration of these various systems involves people as well as things; and the balance of attention between these two elements needs to be strategically and wisely managed. This is especially the case in circumstances where significant environmental factors in the form of government support and accompanying pressures and expectations begin to impinge on students, teachers and their interactions with each other and with the digital technology. A recent example of this is the Australian Federal Government's Digital Education Revolution (DER) initiative.[2] The aim of this is to 'contribute to sustainable and meaningful change to teaching and learning in Australian schools that will prepare students for further education, training and to live and work in a digital world'. The major thrusts of the DER are to:

- Provide ICT equipment for all secondary schools with students in years 9–12.
- Support the deployment of high-speed broadband connections.
- Support systemic change to increase the level of ICT proficiency for teachers and school leaders.
- Provide for online curriculum tools and resources.
- Enable parent participation in their child's education through online learning and access.

The Australian Government (2010) is aiming to bring about a 'DER' through a combination of hardware and software provision to schools and professional development and training support for teachers. If only it were that simple!

A national series of ICT Master Classes recently conducted by the author for the Australian Institute for Teaching and School Leadership revealed that Australian teachers and principals are not so much seeking 'a revolution', a radical change of order, but rather an informed and deliberate transformation of schooling and development of a new mindset among educators and policymakers (Gaffney, Cummings, Ennis, & Turner, 2010). They believe that leading teaching and learning in times of high-stakes testing and increasing demand for accountability calls for leveraging the pressure and capitalizing on the support available. While the investment in hardware, software and professional development is welcome, school transformation supported through emerging digital technologies cannot be realized by government announcements and funding alone. Informed, grounded professional insights and expertise from school-based practitioners is needed, along with education authority pressure and support, and well-designed government policies and targeted resource provision. Moreover, QA processes need to reflect the relational aspects of change at the technological, classroom, school and education system level. For all of these reasons, an 'ecosystem' perspective is warranted in encouraging, assuring and sustaining quality in the changes occurring in schools.

School transformation is a complex business as shown in the model of ICT implementation developed by Tearle (2003) which links the core practices of teaching and learning using ICT with the characteristics of the ICT implementation process and the whole-of-school characteristics. She argues that deeper consideration should be given to the mindsets, assumptions, beliefs and values of the stakeholders, and warns against 'piecemeal approaches which address discrete elements ... [which] will at best have limited outcomes' (p. 15). The concept of the school digital ecosystem is well suited to such considerations.

One means of managing the complexity and assuring the quality of school digital ecosystems is to identify and describe their constituent components. I will undertake this task by referring to two sets of components: (i) the digital resources (hardware and software) and (ii) the stakeholders (students, teachers, principals, parents and local community members, education authorities and governments).

Digital Resources

Digital resources fall into several categories: hardware (the technological tools and infrastructure that comprise a computer system), software (the programmes used on that computer system) and the Internet resources that reside in the 'cloud', requiring neither specific hardware nor software (beyond a browser) to be accessed.

A variety of criteria have been identified for assuring the quality of digital resources. For example, the availability, affordability and suitability of the resources to existing policy directions, infrastructure and teaching culture (Lee & Winzenried, 2009), the accessibility, usefulness and reliability of the hardware (Law, 2009), the accessibility and timely provision of technical support (Lee & Gaffney, 2008; Mumtaz, 2000) and the relevance of digital curriculum resources and appropriateness of digital content and their alignment with teachers' pedagogical practices (Cuban, 1986, 2001; Strijker & Collis, 2006).

Stakeholders

Student interest, motivation, access to and engagement with, digital technology and consequent learning achievement have been recurring themes in the research literature and provide important bases for assessing student and school outcomes and the impact of technology (Groff & Mouza, 2008; Mishra & Koehler, 2006; Moyle, 2010).

Teacher attitudes, knowledge and skills in using digital technologies have similarly been a consistent area of interest (Bingimlas, 2009; Mulkeen, 2003). Recent work by Mishra and Koehler (2006) has built on earlier formulations of pedagogical content knowledge by Shulman (1986, 1987), with the aim of identifying the essential qualities of teacher knowledge required for integrating technology into their teaching. They argue that effective teacher use of technology requires the development of a complex, situated form of knowledge that they call 'Technological Pedagogical Content Knowledge' (TPCK).[3] They characterize

TPCK as teacher knowledge of what concepts are easy or difficult to learn and how technology can help students overcome their learning problems. Assessing teachers' TPCK is an important feature of QA in school digital ecosystems.

Principals play a key role in the effective functioning of school digital ecosystems. Effective principals shape the culture of their schools in ways that foster an openness to change for the benefit of students. They recognize the range of human, educational, organizational and technological factors influencing change processes involved in the use of emerging digital technologies (Lee & Gaffney, 2008). They see themselves as involved in a process of school transformation and act to bring about change through the development and exercise of specific types of leadership capabilities – knowledge, skills and attitudes they use appropriately and effectively in new and changing circumstances (Duignan, 2006). Principals who help to achieve high-performing school digital ecosystems demonstrate five types of capabilities: personal, professional, relational, organizational and transformational (Gaffney et al., 2010). An important element of assuring quality is therefore monitoring the performance of principals with respect to these types of leadership capability.

The role and performance of ICT coordinators, administrators and inspectors are also critical. For example, when Özdemir and Kılıç (2007) and Akbaba-Altun (2006) evaluated the first stage of the US$11.3 billion World Bank/Turkish Ministry of National Education Basic Education Programme, which was designed to expand and improve the elementary school system and achieve ICT integration, they found that the ICT coordinators had been unable to fulfil their roles as developers and trainers because of inadequate training and time-release, and that the administrators and inspectors had received little or no training in the project's rationale, methods or intended outcomes and, as a consequence, were far from supportive.

The interest and participation of parents and local community members in schools is also an important factor in determining the quality of student and school performance. Hattie (2008), studying factors that impact on student learning, highlighted the importance of schools working with parents to develop a common language about teaching and student achievement. Assessing the quality of communications and home–school partnerships in developing shared language and expectations for student achievement is an important component in assuring the quality of school digital ecosystems.

Finally, we need to recognize that the performance of schools is significantly influenced by the political resources of governments and educational authorities. Research by Venezky and Davis (2002) conducted across 23 countries highlights the need for these central agencies to adopt comprehensive strategic planning approaches, develop and promote clear goals and policies, achieve targeted and equitable resource allocation and provide ongoing monitoring of programme delivery.

A School Digital Ecosystem QA Framework

The concept of the school digital ecosystem allows for the multiple features and stakeholder perspectives described in the previous section to be drawn together to form a QA framework comprised of two sets of school digital ecosystem components: digital resources and stakeholders, together with the performance criteria.

In keeping with the concept of a digital ecosystem, the QA framework needs to extend beyond listings of individual components and associated criteria to encompass a more holistic perspective. It needs to focus on links within and between the digital resources and stakeholder components, the degree of alignment and integration and the extent of stakeholder awareness and consensus evident in the system (Gaffney, 2010). For the purpose of this discussion, these terms are defined (from the *Encarta Dictionary*) as follows:

- Alignment. The correct position or positioning of different components with respect to each other or something else, so that they perform properly, that is, to achieve integration.
- Integration. A combination of parts or objects that work together well, the process of coordinating separate elements into a balanced whole or producing compatible behaviour.
- Awareness. Well-informed about what is going on in the world or about the latest developments in a sphere of activity.
- Consensus. General or widespread agreement among all the members of a group.

Performance criteria relating to alignment, integration and stakeholder awareness and consensus are central to QA processes in school digital ecosystems. This is because they focus on connections within and between the digital resources and stakeholder components. For example, these criteria might demonstrate the potential interplay between student learning achievement, the choice of digital technologies, the concerns and levels of teacher use of those technologies, the management of information, securing school information assets, networking with the home and other agencies, financing investment and managing risk. The QA framework shown in Figure 17.2 presents the digital resources and stakeholder components of the school digital ecosystem, and the criteria used to measure their individual performance and assure the quality of the system as whole.

Lessons Learned: Assuring Quality in Schools' Use of Digital Technologies

Recent Australian initiatives relating to ICT innovation in schools provide some valuable lessons about QA in the use of the digital technologies in schools.

School Digital Ecosystem

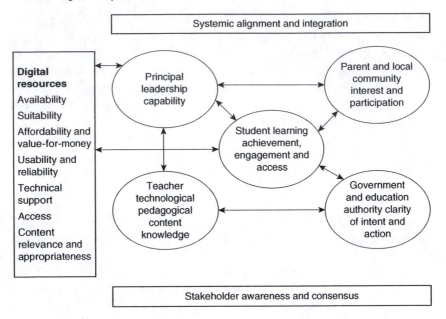

FIGURE 17.2 School digital ecosystem QA framework

Source: Gaffney (2010).

First, the experience of school communities across the country associated with the roll out of the DER has demonstrated a high degree of support for the government's initiative and willingness to make the most of the resourcing opportunities provided (Gaffney et al., 2010). However, it is also evident that unless the digital resources are strategically aligned and integrated by classroom, school and education system policy and practice, then much of the investment will be wasted.

Second, the successful transformation of schooling and effective use of emerging technologies relies on the mindsets and skills of school-based educators and policymakers. Moreover, it depends on the degree to which these stakeholders are able to develop awareness of the need and potential for school transformation and consensus on the means of achieving it (Gaffney, 2010).

These lessons underscore the need to take a systemic view in assessing changes in schooling supported by digital technologies. The metaphor of the school digital ecosystem used throughout this chapter is designed to capture the imagery required. Monitoring the evolution and sustainability of such systems, and guarding against their vulnerability to external threats and mutations, demands that careful thought to QA with respect to the digital resources, the stakeholders and to the relationships within and between these components of the system.

Conclusion

Robinson (2009, p. 238) observes:

> The fact is that given the challenges we face, education doesn't need to be reformed – it needs to be transformed. The key to this transformation is not to standardize education, but to personalize it, to build achievement on discovering the individual talents of each child, to put students in an environment where they want to learn and where they can naturally discover their true passions.

ICT gives the schools the tools and access to help achieve these ideals. This is why QA in school digital ecosystems is such an issue of significance for students, teachers, principals and educational policymakers. For students, a high-quality digital ecosystem can help to foster engagement and personalize their learning by recognizing their talents, needs and achievements within and beyond the school gates. For teachers, it highlights how different digital tools, teaching processes and curriculum content can be combined to best effect. For principals, the emergence of digital ecosystems underscores the need to engage in important decisions, to plan realistically and to match the technology to the kinds of aspirations for teaching and learning voiced above and for the school community as a whole. And for education policymakers, QA in schools' engagement with, and use of digital technologies not only serves as means of accounting to key stakeholders but also provides insight and direction about what works, what is needed and what is possible in schooling in an age of increasingly sophisticated and open learning.

In light of these observations, the importance of integrating and aligning practice with digital resources at classroom, school and system level and developing awareness and consensus among key stakeholders about the nature of school digital ecosystems and the criteria for assuring their quality is vital.

Notes

1 http://en.wikipedia.org/wiki/Digitalecosystem
2 http://www.deewr.gov.au/Schooling/DigitalEducationRevolution/Pages/default.aspx
3 http://www.tpck.org/tpck/index.php?title=Main_Page

References

Akbaba-Altun, S. (2006). Complexity of integrating computer technologies in education in Turkey. *Educational Technology and Society, 9*(1), 176–187.
Australian Government. (2010). *ICT innovation fund – guidelines 2010–2012.* Canberra: Department of Education, Employment and Workplace Relations.

Bingimlas, K. A. (2009). Barriers to the successful integration of ICT in teaching and learning environments: A review of the literature. *Eurasia Journal of Mathematics, Science & Technology Education, 5*(3), 235–245.

Christensen, C. M. (1997). *The innovator's dilemma: When new technologies cause great firms to fail.* Boston, MA: Harvard Business School Press.

Christensen, C. M., Johnson, C. W., & Horn, M. B. (2008). *Disrupting class: How disruptive innovation will change the way the world learns.* London: McGraw Hill.

Cuban, L. (1986). *Teachers and machines: The classroom use of technology since 1920.* New York: Teachers College Press.

Cuban, L. (2001). *Oversold and underused computers in the classroom.* London: Harvard University Press.

Duignan, P. (2006). *Educational leadership: Key challenges and ethical tensions.* Cambridge: Cambridge University Press.

Gaffney, M. (2010). *Enhancing teachers' take-up of digital content: Factors and design principles in technology adoption.* Melbourne: Education Services Australia.

Gaffney, M., Cummings, R., Ennis, M., & Turner, E. (2010). *Leading networked school communities: ICT master class series.* Melbourne and Brisbane: Australian Institute for Teaching and School Leadership.

Groff, J., & Mouza, C. (2008). A framework for addressing challenges to classroom technology use. *AACE Journal, 16*(1), 21–46.

Hattie, J. (2008). *Visible learning: A synthesis of meta-analyses relating to achievement.* New York: Routledge.

Ingvarson, D., & Gaffney, M. (2008). Developing and sustaining the digital education ecosystem: The value and possibilities of online environments for students. In M. Lee, & M. Gaffney (Eds.), *Leading a digital school* (pp. 146–167). Melbourne: ACER Press.

Law, N. (2009). Technology-supported pedagogical innovations: The challenge of sustainability and transferability in the information age. In C. Ng, & P. D. Renshaw (Eds.), *Reforming learning* (pp. 319–343). New York: Springer Science Business Media.

Lee, M., & Gaffney, M. (2008). *Leading a digital school.* Melbourne: ACER Press.

Lee, M., & Winzenried, A. (2009). *The use of instructional technology in schools.* Melbourne: ACER Press.

Mishra, P., & Koehler, M. J. (2006). Technological pedagogical content knowledge: A framework for teacher knowledge. *Teachers College Record, 108*(6), 1017–1054.

Moyle, K. (2010). Building innovation: Learning with technologies. *Australian Education Review Series Number 56.* Melbourne: Australian Council for Educational Research.

Mulkeen, A. (2003). What can policy makers do to encourage integration of information and communications technology? Evidence from the Irish school system. *Technology, Pedagogy and Education, 12*(2), 277–293.

Mumtaz, S. (2000). Factors affecting teachers' use of information and communications technology: A review of the literature. *Journal of Information Technology for Teacher Education, 9*(3), 319–342.

Özdemir, S., & Kılıç, E. (2007). Integrating information and communication technologies in the Turkish primary school system. *British Journal of Educational Technology, 38*(5), 907–916.

Robinson, K. (with Lou Aronica). (2009). *The element: How finding your passion changes everything.* New York, NY: Penguin Press.

Shulman, L. (1986). Those who understand: Knowledge and growth in teaching. *Educational Researcher, 15*(2), 4–14.

Shulman, L. (1987). Knowledge and teaching: Foundations of the new reform. *Harvard Educational Review, 57*(1), 1–22.

Strijker, A., & Collis, B. (2006). Strategies for reuse of learning objects: Context dimensions. *International Journal on e-Learning, 5*(1), 89–94.

Tearle, P. (2003). ICT implementation: What makes the difference? *British Journal of Educational Technology, 34*(3), 1–17.

Venezky, R. L., & Davis, C. (2002). *Que vademus? The transformation of schooling in a networked world.* Paris: OECD/CERI. Retrieved from http://www.oecd.org/findDocument/0,2350,en_2649_33723_1_119832_1_1_1,00.html

Vrasidas, C., & Glass, G. V. (2005). *Preparing teachers to teach with technology.* Charlotte, NC: Information Age Publishing.

18

SO FEW LESSONS LEARNED? QUALITY ASSURANCE IN THE GLOBAL TELECENTRE MOVEMENT

Richard Fuchs

Introduction

Sitting in on a workshop in rural Costa Rica with 45 or so information and communications technology (ICT) and telecentre activists, supporters and host organizations, was Yacine Kheladi, an Algerian by birth and a telecentre practitioner and consultant living and working in the Dominican Republic. The session was called 'Lessons Learned', and speaker after speaker recounted their experiences in starting telecentres and then, almost without exception, concluded their presentations with one or two PowerPoint slides headed 'Lessons Learned'. Kheladi was a veteran in this field. He had seen so many national governments, international development agencies and foreign donors announcing major new telecentre initiatives with a curious sense of hubris-fuelled self-discovery. No account was ever taken of what had gone before and had, or had not, worked in attempting to bring digital skills and tools to the developing world. Kheladi couldn't help but ask what was on his mind, 'why are so few lessons learned from the "Lessons Learned?"' The room went quiet.

This chapter examines the growth of the telecentre movement from its small beginnings into a worldwide networked system of knowledge sharing and skills transfer. Until recently, there was no credentialled training for telecentre managers. The movement's viral-like growth was almost entirely sustained by informal training and mentoring, an activist zeal for its mission, and the application of a simple idea reimagined and reinvented over and over again. Unfortunately, many of the telecentre start-ups did not benefit from the lessons learned or develop the capacity for sustainability, let alone continuous improvement. However, the global programme has now been created to support the establishment and sustainability of grassroots level telecentres. Founded by telecentre.org, the Telecentre Academy is beginning to provide systemic, formally accredited telecentre manager and operative training. But, as this chapter shows, there is still a need for more quality assurance (QA) in both the training and telecentre operations.

The Telecentre Movement

The telecentre movement began in a small Swedish farming community in 1985 (Oestmann & Dymond, 2001). Henning Albrechtson, a gifted linguist and translator of the writings of Alvin Toffler, decided to help the local farmers learn more about how well their small dairy enterprises were performing. He set up a few desktop computers in his house, loaded them with Lotus Notes, the dominant spreadsheet software at the time, and helped the farmers to learn how to produce profit and loss and cost/revenue statements for their dairy enterprises. He was soon not alone. The idea of the post-industrial economy, a society based on the provision of information, innovation, finance and services, was just taking root. In rural areas of Europe, Australia and Eastern Canada, development activists and computer aficionados saw that access to computers, and the skills that go with them, were fundamental to the future of their communities and livelihoods. The author of this chapter was one of these, establishing North America's first rural telecentre system in 1988 in Newfoundland, Canada. Northern Finland, Wales, the Scottish Isles, Queensland and Western Australia were among the other areas that soon began piloting telecentre systems. Oestmann and Dymond (2001) described the economic environment that animated the telecentre development:

> Even in advanced economies, there are rural and remote communities that have been left behind in terms of educational and technological equity and access. The technological revolution that is transforming our economies and societies into information economies and information societies meets with many obstacles in developing countries and is in danger of widening the now well-known 'digital divide'. Conversely, the technological advances provide the means for 'leapfrogging' – that is, the opportunity for developing countries to jump to a new paradigm before problems of delivery have been solved by traditional means, both in technical and economical terms.
>
> *(p. 2)*

It is important to note that all of this was happening well before the omnipresent Internet and the Web for information gathering and exchange, and in the absence of any regional or international forums or opportunities for online interaction. The idea that digital skills and tools could be important in local economic development was still missing from most conventional development policymaking. Additionally, the growth of these telecentres was not orchestrated by any central marketing or command centre. The early pioneers learned from each other by *ad hoc* means, swapping stories and achievements, sharing growing pains and encouraging others to become involved.

Almost a quarter of a century later, there are more than 100,000 telecentres across the world (O'Seachro, 2010). What began as a response to economic exclusion in peripheral regions of the post-industrial world has become a central mechanism by which development activists bring digital tools to marginal groups and regions across the world. These centres take various forms, operate according to different business or organizational models and, under various names, provide a range of functions and serve a range of community clientele. Some are government, non-government or local government supported; some are sponsored by international development agencies; some are purely commercial and some are university linked. What they all have in common is the provision of access to, and training in, ICT and other knowledge and skills for disadvantaged and community groups. Some telecentres also provide in-service training for public and business sector employees, while others help generate local employment and support local enterprise.

The fortunes of the telecentres have been mixed. The United Nations Conference on Trade and Development (UNCTAD, 2010) observes that many government or donor-sponsored telecentres in rural areas of low-income countries have proved unsustainable. It also notes that 'stand-alone' telecentres often fail to provide targeted enterprise support or integrate with other support systems that could provide complementary inputs. It suggests that they need to be designed and managed in response to the needs of the intended beneficiaries and based upon business models that enable them to operate beyond the donor-supported pilot stage and as components of broader development projects for the community at large. There is also the issue of adaptability. As UNCTAD observes, the role of public access points needs to be re-examined now that potential users have mobile Internet access and may prefer the privacy and convenience of mobile phones to using public facilities. So those who plan, manage and operate the telecentres need training in governance, managing community and operational issues and achieving sustainability as well as using technology to improve livelihoods and bring about other community benefits.

Until recently, telecentres had no systematic or institutional QA framework within which to 'learn the best and leave the rest.' Telecentres, and those who ran them, had to rely almost entirely upon non-formal workshops and informal mentoring to develop their organizational, operational and financial knowledge and skills. This approach to training telecentre personnel has certain advantages. It costs less (at least in the short run). It avoids the perils of the big system 'one-size-fits-all' approach and may be transferred from one context to another without cumbersome credentialist restrictions that may have more meaning for the trainers than the trainees. And it can be fast and 'just-in-time' in its design and delivery. This is why donors and others have used non-formal approaches to training telecentre operatives. There are, however, some major drawbacks. Non-formal learning programmes tend to have a short after-life and work best when the developers or designers are the ones delivering the training out in the field. They often lack follow-up or ongoing support, and they don't provide credentialling, something which the telecentre knowledge workers are keen for. More seriously, no-one knows if the non-formal approach actually results in improved management of telecentres because the long-term behavioural impact of the training has never been properly evaluated.

Recognizing the need for a formal training system to improve the quality of telecentre planning, management and operations, a new global initiative is now under way – the Telecentre Academy.

The Telecentre Academy

In 2005, at the World Summit on the Information Society in Tunis, a new multi-stakeholder initiative was announced – telecentre.org. Its purpose was to improve the impact and resilience of telecentres around the world by supporting the networks and organizations they work with and by helping to build a stronger, more durable telecentre ecosystem. It drew on a US$21 million funding pool created by telecentre.org's original social investors, Canada's International Development Research Centre, Microsoft Community Affairs and the Swiss Agency for International Development. More recently, the Philippines Commission for Information and Communications Technologies has joined this partnership. The telecentre.org programme provides grants and technical assistance to telecentre networks and organizations located throughout the world. It was originally organized around four pillars of development intervention:

*   Networks. Helping to create and support strong networks and organizations that make telecentres more effective, sustainable and valuable to communities.
*   Content and services for sustainability. Developing the high-value products and services that communities need and that telecentres can use to generate income for sustainability.
*   Knowledge sharing. Supporting the widespread sharing of ideas, learning, best practices and innovation.
*   Research. Investigating the impact of telecentres on social and economic development.

The organization now serves the 100,000 telecentres, more than 300 organizations and 200,000 individual stakeholders. Recognizing the need for telecentre manager capacity building, telecentre.org has launched the Telecentre Academy, designed to:

- Support the development of open curricula and promote the creation, coordination and improvement of common resources.
- Facilitate events, networking and knowledge-sharing activities, including encouraging the telecentre community to contribute to a shared, multi-lingual repository based on UNESCO's Open Training Platform, including curricula, certification standards, models, best practices, experts' list, etc.
- Provide a web-based learning management system with over 30 modules in four languages.
- Develop partnerships to secure additional resources and support.
- Reach out to governments and donors that support telecentres to help incorporate capacity building into their programme design.

The initial signatories to the Telecentre Academy were:

- University of Colombo School of Computing in Sri Lanka in partnership with the Information and Communication Technology Agency of Sri Lanka (the first of the national academies when the project was launched in 2008).
- Indira Gandhi National Open University in India (The Global Secretariat for the Telecentre Academy).
- University of Brasilia (where there are about 16,000 telecentres, although most of these offer only the most basic Internet access and services).
- University of La Frontera in Chile (working in collaboration with Biblioredes, a project of the Chilean Libraries, Archives, and Museums Bureau that helps libraries connect by the Internet with poor and isolated communities, the Department of Telecommunications, the Executive Secretariat of Digital Strategy and the National Women's Service).
- Universidade Eduardo Mondlane in Mozambique (which began piloting telecentres in 1999 in various settings to identify which services and technologies were appropriate to local development).
- Kyambogo University in Uganda (which collaborates with telecentre networks in East Uganda, Kenya, Rwanda, Burundi, Tanzania and various ICT development partners and projects).
- Sudan National Telecentre Academy (which is run by the non-governmental, non-profit Gedaref Digital City Organization).
- Sukhothai Thammathirat Open University in Thailand (working in collaboration with the Ministry Of Information and Communication Technology).
- University of the Philippines Open University (working in partnership with the Development Academy of the Philippines, Asian Institute of Journalism

and Communications, National Telehealth Centre, Open Academy for Philippine Agriculture, Intel Technology Philippines Incorporated and Microsoft Philippines Incorporated)
- Open University of Malaysia.

In August 2008, representatives of these institutions met at Indira Gandhi National Open University to launch the new Academy. Their target was to train and certify 10,000 people by 2010 and 1 million by 2015. They agreed to enter into revenue-sharing agreements with the Telecentre Academy to help further development at the national and global levels. These institutions then launched their own national telecentre management training programmes and others joined the network.

The providers must agree to work to a common curriculum for training telecentre managers which has been developed by content specialists in collaboration with the national academies. This curriculum comprises 12 core and five elective offerings. The core offerings are:

- Fundamentals of telecentres.
- Understanding communities.
- Community informatics.
- Telecentre planning.
- Fundamentals of telecentre management.
- Qualities of a telecentre manager.
- Introduction to computer and the Internet.
- Introduction to telecentre services.
- Community use of telecentres.
- Information management at a telecentre.
- Telecentre marketing and promotion.
- Assessing a telecentre's progress.

The electives are:

- National e-governance plan and common service centres.
- Community media.
- Government schemes and programmes through telecentres.
- Social entrepreneurship.
- Communications skills.

It is recognized that different telecentre systems and local experiences, circumstances and regulations need to be taken into account. So each national academy can establish its own version of the curriculum, translate the programmes into local languages and offer the programmes in the ways considered most appropriate. They may also develop and deliver other courses based upon local needs and opportunities. In 2010, for example, as well as providing training in telecentre management, marketing and promotion and e-government, the Chilean Academy offered a two-week course, Gender and Telecentres. The two training modules, one concerning Gender and Public Policy and the other Gender and Work, were run in conjunction with The National Women's Service, a government agency promoting gender equity, but were adapted to suit the contexts and circumstances of the local telecentres and their community-level 'knowledge workers'. Moreover, as Nassali (2009) observes in regard to experience of the East African Telecentre Academy, while these core and elective offerings provide the explicit learning that the managers and other operatives need, there are many other values and capacities that the participants can develop through incidental tacit learning such as motivational, mobilization and public relation skills.

There is certainly no shortage of online resources for the trainers or trainees to draw upon. The telecentre.org's online shelves are stocked with hundreds of free knowledge resources on all aspects of ICT and telecentres for development, and it is also possible to access the Telecentre Academy website, a customized version of the UNESCO's Open Training Platform mentioned earlier.[1]

Moving from an informal system of learning and mentoring to one linked to higher education institutions is not without its perils. Will the sense of mission, zeal and collegial sharing that has characterized learning within the telecentre movement to date be sacrificed to the vagaries of academic and administrative procedures? Will the managers and operatives gain real and long-lasting benefits from this formal training? Will the new commonly-agreed curricula and certification process result in more successful telecentre management and operations? And most importantly, in the context of this book, will the training itself have quality and will it help to improve the ways in which the telecentres are planned, managed, run and evaluated? These questions are still to be answered.

At the time of writing, the author was conducting an email-based survey with seven of the national academies: University of La Frontera in Chile, University of Colombo in Sri Lanka, Sukhothai Thammathirat Open University in Thailand, the University of the Philippines Open University, The Telecentre Academy in New Delhi, Open University of Malaysia and the non-government organization Colnodo in Columbia. The aim was to find out:

• Who were the participants in the training?
• How was the distance training being provided?
• What forms of QA, feedback and continuous improvement tools were being employed in the programmes?

The participants were telecentre managers and staff but it was shown that they came from diverse backgrounds. For example, the Academy of Chile reported that:

> ... the network Biblioredes are mostly professionals (librarians and teachers). However, in the Institute of Youth they are mainly young people who have only a secondary level, non-technical [training] ... It was complex work [to develop] a curriculum to serve all students as they all had different profiles.

There was clearly considerable interest in the training programmes. In some cases, it was the governments and national telecentre networks who were the main drivers of this agenda, in others, the telecentre operators themselves.

The models of delivery were shown to vary. The Academy of Chile's training modules are delivered online and asynchronously. It is found that this helps to prevent dropout due to trainees' problems with scheduled classes. It also makes use of videos and online forums involving students and tutors. In some other countries, the telecentres may experience poor telecommunications and unreliable Internet access, which inhibits their dependency on wholly online training. Some of the providers employ face-to-face or blended learning methods. One Filipino respondent reported:

> As the materials have been designed for distance learners, it will not be too difficult for self-study, which will take up about 80% of a student's study time. Another 10% will be allocated to face-to-face training which will be conducted at learning centres nearest the students.

There is some evidence that steps are being taken to check on the quality of the training. One respondent reported:

> [We] monitored the participation and quality of student participation and [the performance of] the Academic Tutors to verify that adequate care [had been provided] to students and to assess the quality of the pedagogical relationship.

In this particular instance, it transpired that not only had the participants in the training programme received grades from the university, but so had the Academic Tutors.

Some respondents reported on their use of pre-course quality assessment, post-completion interviews with students and analysis of course completion rates. One respondent observed:

> [This] starts with the development of materials through the quality circle approach. The materials are developed by a team composed of the subject

matter specialist as the writer, another subject matter specialist as reviewer [and an] instructional designer to ensure that the lesson is OK and the assessment is in perfect fit with the learning outcomes ... and the multimedia specialist for identification of appropriate medium to deliver the lesson and help learners achieve learning goals.

Another wrote:

[We] monitored the participation and quality of [the students] ... the academic tutors to verify that [they] delivered adequate care to students, and ... the quality of the pedagogical relationship. The student monitoring was essential, because it allowed control [of] the dropout of students and addressing their special needs.

Another observed:

[Feedback] is integral to the system ... [the] learners can communicate directly with the university faculty and officials and through the channels already in place ... at the end of each course, a formal evaluation of the course and the professor is conducted.

Yet another commented:

Students are the ultimate judges of an e-learning course. We conduct surveys and go through examination results to see whether the e-learning had any impact on their performance ... All of these tell the story of whether we have properly designed the course. Initially, we determine the number of hours an average student spends on a particular area of learning. [The] LMS tracks individuals or groups of students to evaluate whether the planning of the course has succeeded or not.

The preliminary findings of this survey suggest that the providers are well aware of the need for QA. Some of the systems employed derive from those already employed by the providing institutions or agencies. Others are custom-designed. However, as discussed below, none of the QA systems are systemic, organized or managed by the Telecentre Academy and there is clearly need for more development in this critically important area.

Conclusion

It will take time and effort to achieve their goals, but the Telecentre Academy and the national academies have the potential to improve the quality of telecentre management and operations through the provision of experience-based knowledge and skills training and long sought-after certification. However, there are many challenges for this fledgling initiative. For the telecentre managers and networks, the training is mission-critical and long overdue. For established institutions it could become just another course among many. Programmes and services could become mired in academic and administrative procedures, and the learning could become too removed from the learners and their particular needs and circumstances. There have already been instances of this occurring, so this is a matter that requires careful attention, both at the national and global levels.

Equally problematic is the fact that the entire set of associations among national training institutions and the Telecentre Academy are voluntary. There is nothing to prevent the institutions from changing the curriculum or deciding that they no longer wish to provide this training. Hopefully, the anticipated high demand and corresponding revenue stream from the course provision will serve as an incentive for the various partners in the consortium to remain true to what has been agreed.

Yet another problem experienced by the telecentres is retaining capable managers and staff once they have been trained and certified. This is especially an issue in the developing countries where, once individuals are found to be highly self-motivated and well trained in technology and organizational management, they are very likely to be recruited by private or public sector organizations. Hopefully, the continuous training provision will help to achieve continuity in providing qualified recruits to the telecentre movement.

Those who plan and manage telecentres have traditionally been primarily concerned with facilitating access to ICT infrastructure, online resources and most recently, wireless technology (Fuchs & Francisco, 2009). They have typically been less concerned with, and less skilled in, developing locally relevant content and services in forms that low-income users can readily access and absorb. As UNCTAD (2010) observes, the rapid growth of mobile access and micro-enterprises that can benefit from the new communications environment calls for new approaches. For example, there can be need for a combination of a business investor and a development partner. These changing circumstances, opportunities and needs call for a whole range of new capacities in the telecentre managers and staff. Along with the penetration of mobile phones within the 'back of the market' communities there is another growing trend which is affecting access to ICTs in development. 'Shared-use computing' is increasing at a faster rate than either Internet subscriptions or broadband access. This suggests that cyber-cafes and telecentres are playing an important role in how people, and particularly those who cannot afford their own technology, gain access to the Internet. As the users' familiarity and facility with computers and mobiles increases, they will be looking for new ways for these technologies to be used in accessing health, financial, educational and economic development services

(Fuchs & Francisco). This will again call for adaptability on the part of the tele-centre managers.

telecentre.org was based on the assumption that if telecentres could access quality support services their sustainability could be enhanced. In their external review of telecentre.org, Batchelor and Peña-López (2009) observed that better organization and management of knowledge should be a prerequisite for future interventions to assist telecentres. They also encouraged telecentre.org and its partners to develop improved systematic monitoring to assess the quality, replica-tion and impact of their operations. They found that while there was anecdotal evidence of how well activities were organized, there was little in the way of hard, longitudinal data on the efficiency and efficacy of the telecentre systems. As tele-centres move from providing ICT services to acting more as knowledge centres and providing what UNCTAD (2010, p. 90) describes as 'an ecosystem for ICTs, enterprise and poverty reduction', there is clearly need to continuously improve the quality of the telecentre management and capacity building.

Angelica Rojas Muñoz (2009), the General Coordinator of the Chilean Telecentre Academy, suggests that an important next step should be determining the quality standards and accreditation for the various Telecentre Academies, both to provide a seal of approval and to ensure continuing improvement. She proposes that these academies should be assessed on the basis of the quality of their course and instructional design, management of human and technological resources, effectiveness of teaching and learning and procedures for checking compliance with standards and continuous improvement. Such national approaches to QA need to be brought together globally so that the lessons learned can be under-stood, disseminated and implemented throughout the entire system. It remains to be seen if the Telecentre Academy at the global level can summon the resources and mandate to act on the lessons learned.

Most of this book's chapters concern QA and accreditation in open and dis-tance learning (ODL) in formal education. However, those who plan, manage and implement distance and online non-formal adult and community pro-grammes in developing countries also play a vital role in developing human capacity. They too need training and assistance in evaluating and assuring quality development initiatives to ensure that the expectations of the donors and the communities are met. This applies particularly to those who direct projects locally and work at the community level. Some formal recognition for such train-ing would also be extremely valuable. The work of the Telecentre Academy is a first step towards this objective.

Note

1   http://opentraining.unesco-ci.org/cgi-bin/page.cgi?d=1

References

Batchelor, B., & Peña-López, I. (2009). *Telecentre.org external program review.* Retrieved from http://idl-bnc.idrc.ca/dspace/bitstream/10625/45195/1/131636.pdf

Fuchs, R. P., & Francisco, K. L. A. (2009, November 9–12). *The new digital divergence.* Paper presented at the *6th International Conference on Information Technology and Applications (ICITA 2009).* Hanoi, Vietnam. Retrieved from http://www.icita.org/papers/33-sg-Fuchs-110.pdf

Muñoz, A. R. (2009). *Quality standards: Telecentre.org academies.* [PowerPoint presentation]. Retrieved from http://www.slideshare.net/arojas2010/quality-standards-1904059

Nassali, S. (2009, June 1). *Re: Principles and guidelines on curriculum development and implementation for the East African Telecentre Academy.* [telecentre.org blog]. Message posted to http://www.telecentre.org/profiles/blogs/principles-and-guidelines-on

Oestmann, S., & Dymond, A.C. (2001). Telecentres – Experiences, lessons and trends. In C. Latchem, & D. Walker (Eds.), *Telecentres: Case studies and key issues.* Vancouver: Commonwealth of Learning. Retrieved from http://www.col.org/SiteCollection Documents/prelims.pdf

O'Seachro, S. (2010, October). *A calculation of the number of telecentres.* Report for the International Development Research Centre. Retrieved from http://www.slideshare.net/arojas2010/quality-standards-1904059

UNCTAD. (2010). *Information Economy Report 2010: ICTs, enterprises and poverty alleviation.* New York & Geneva: Author. Retrieved from http://www.unctad.org/en/docs/ier2010_embargo2010_en.pdf

19

QUALITY ASSURANCE IN E-LEARNING FOR EUROPEAN SMALL-TO-MEDIUM ENTERPRISES

Torstein Rekkedal

Introduction

At the Lisbon Special European Council: Towards a Europe of Innovation and Knowledge of March 2000,[1] the European Union (EU) Heads of States and Governments agreed to make the EU 'the most competitive and dynamic knowledge-driven economy by 2010' (European Council, 2000). In 2010, it is generally agreed that the outcomes of the Lisbon Strategy are at best mixed. The European Commission (EC) report *Europe 2020: A Strategy for European Community Growth* observes that the EU was moving in the right direction before the global financial crisis but this event wiped out many of the gains, so that strong economic policy coordination and growth based on knowledge and innovation are now even more essential than before (European Commission, 2010). Achieving these goals will require continuing modernization and there is a common belief that this will entail the development and adoption of e-learning in business and industry, including small-to-medium enterprises (SMEs). This chapter outlines e-learning in European SMEs and discusses the quality assurance (QA) issues in this context.

e-Learning in European SMEs

Before the inclusion of new member states between 2003–2007, SMEs represented more than 99% of EU companies (European Commission, 2005). Now, with an EU of 27 countries, the number of SMEs has grown significantly, as has the requirement for training. The European Commission (2005) defines SMEs as enterprises employing fewer than 250 people with an annual turnover not exceeding €50 million or an annual balance sheet not exceeding €43 million.

This definition is important because it is mandatory for state aid schemes and community programmes within the EU. According to Eurostat (2009), of the 20 million active enterprises in the EU-27's non-financial business economy in 2006 (since which time Bulgaria and Romania have joined the EU), the overwhelming majority – 99.8% – were SMEs. Almost 92% of these were micro-enterprises employing fewer than 10 persons, 6.9% were small enterprises with 10–49 employees and 1.1% were medium-sized enterprises with 50–249 employees. Only 0.2% were large enterprises. The EC characterizes these SMEs as the backbone of the European economy. They provide two out of three private sector jobs, they make a major contribution to economic growth and they play a key role in innovation, research and development. The majority of SMEs are concerned with construction, hotels and restaurants, business services and distribution and retail. A smaller number are involved in manufacturing, mining, quarrying, transport, communications and utilities.

The quality of the training provided in or for SMEs is clearly of paramount importance. It can improve the employability and earnings of employees, raise productivity, increase profitability and provide the range of up-to-date skills needed to compete in the global marketplace. Training is needed both for new employees and to familiarize existing employees with new products, processes, services and commercial, legal and other requirements. SMEs are subject to high staff turnover, with many employees leaving for better paid work and better training opportunities in the larger companies, and training replacement employees adds further to the training costs. Many small businesses have limited finances, resources and time for employee training, so not surprisingly, SMEs have much lower participation rates in company-organized training than the larger enterprises. It is estimated that less than 25% of SME employees participate in vocational training courses and less than 60% of the companies provide training for their staff.

The EC identifies the challenges faced by SMEs in regard to training and proposes solutions in its *Guide for Training in SMEs*[2] and *Guide for Training in SMEs – 50 Cases of Good Practice*.[3] Encouraging the adoption of information and communications technology (ICT) in corporate training, the Commission argues that this must go beyond replacing, streamlining or accelerating current practices and should help create new and more effective ways of supporting educational and organizational innovation. The EC also manages the Leonardo da Vinci programme,[4] a scheme which promotes transnational vocational education and training for SMEs through networking or 'clustering'.[5] All of the EU countries have such informal networks for accessing, retrieving, applying and sharing knowledge and skills, in some cases linking with university and technical and vocational education providers (European Commission, 2006). One example of this is the Irish Skillnets, which supports 'learning networks' or 'communities of practice' among companies. Since 1999, this has facilitated over 18,000 Irish enterprises in over 200 networks and has enabled over 150,000 employees to upgrade their skills.

Farvaque, Voss, Lefebvre, and Schutze (2009) describe how SMEs in the tourism sector have formed online working groups and forums to exchange information and develop their competencies. Thus, if a particular issue arises in the Netherlands, it may be found that someone already has the answer in Estonia, Spain or elsewhere. Another Europe-wide initiative concerns rural tourism where the establishments are typically small, family-run businesses whose personnel lack training and have limited time for training. An online training module was collaboratively developed to check whether establishments meet the relevant standards, provide guidelines for improving standards and complement actual courses or visits (Farvaque et al., 2009).

Surveying e-learning initiatives in European enterprises, Paulsen (2006) concluded that SMEs can benefit from using:

- Generic courses offered on the open market by commercial e-learning providers.
- Sector courses developed by associations and/or cooperating partners.
- Internal courses developed with support from external providers.

Analyzing a number of case studies of e-training, he concludes that this form of provision has the following advantages:

- Flexibility in time and place. This is important because SMEs have small numbers of employees to take over the work of those who are absent on training.
- Cost reduction. e-Learning can reach and connect geographically dispersed groups and hence reduce the costs of travel and accommodation incurred in face-to-face training.
- Logistical advantages. e-Learning is swifter and easier to distribute than face-to-face or print-based training.
- Reduced time to market. e-Learning can increase competitive strength because of the accelerated time to market and because it can be accessed by a large number of employees as soon as it is available.
- Increased sales. e-Learning is a value-added service that customers appreciate.
- Improved ties between companies, companies and suppliers, and companies and customers. A well-trained workforce improves the image of the company, speeds up the delivery of its products and services and improves trust and communications.

From his findings, he also concluded that:

- Support from managers and supervisors is critical.
- e-Learning courses in which employees enrol at their own volition have rather higher completion rates than when they study as a result of

management's encouragement/direction. (However, he does acknowledge that some e-learning must be obligatory – for example in such areas as health and safety.)

- Motivation increases when courses are relevant to the trainees' work or personal interests.
- Motivation may be improved by the use of certification, the use of multimedia, face-to-face support and various incentive schemes.
- e-Learning results in better internal communications and a broader understanding of companies' products and services.
- e-Learning should build on practical, in-depth and up-to-date knowledge of the subject area and use appropriate methods and technology.
- Meeting face-to-face seems to have positive effects, but reduces flexibility and adds to the costs.

Quality in e-Learning

e-Learning quality is all about fitness for purpose. In e-learning for SMEs, the purposes are much clearer than in many educational contexts. It must serve the aims of the company by developing certain workforce competencies, and by helping to improve performance, productivity, processes, products, customer satisfaction and profits. It must also be cost-efficient relative to other forms of training and yield a greater return on investment. However, the owners and managers of SMEs will need evidence to convince them that e-learning can achieve their desired objectives.

Wirth (2006) observes that QA in e-learning can be undertaken for the purposes of international comparison, national accreditation, external and internal institutional review, information to users and consumer protection. It can take one of four forms:

1. QA. The three main organizations responsible for the QA agenda in the European corporate sector are the European Foundation for Quality Management (EFQM), whose Excellence Model has been adopted by over 30,000 organizations around the world, the International Organization for Standardization (ISO), which is responsible for thousands of standards concerned with quality, environmental friendliness, safety, reliability, efficiency, cost-efficiency and interchangeability in products and services, and Deutsche Institute für Normung e. V. whose standards cover almost every field of technology. All of these organizations have developed systems for QA in regard to e-learning products and services.
2. Best and good practice, examples/guidelines and benchmarking. These focus on the realization of e-learning solutions using continuous assessment against

examples of best and good practice. Examples include the *French Code of Practice in e-Learning* developed by Association Française de Normalisation and the *Quality Standards* of the Norwegian Association for Distance Education.

3.   Quality certification and accreditation. These are formal quality assessments executed by external accreditation or certification agencies using valid evaluation methods and clear quality criteria indicators. Examples include the European Foundation for Management Education (EFMD) CEL-Certification for e-learning-supported management courses and programmes and the European Foundation for Quality in e-Learning (EFQEL) with its UNIQUe quality label (see also Chapter 8), and eQCheck which accredits e-learning products using the Canadian Recommended eLearning Guidelines (Barker, 2002) (see also Chapter 22).

4.   Quality competitions and awards. Competitive ranking systems, quality competitions and awards are concerned with promoting high-level achievement rather than evaluating products and services against minimum criteria, as with certification and accreditation systems. A number of ICT and e-learning organizations award prizes for outstanding e-learning solutions. Examples of European awards are the European Award for Technology Supported Learning[6] and EFQEL Award[7] that has a specific category for adult and vocational training. An example of a national scheme is the UK National Training Awards[8] to businesses, organizations and individuals who achieve lasting excellence and success in training, including e-learning.

Another way of characterizing quality approaches is to regard them as *input oriented* (examining resources utilized for achieving desired outcomes), *output oriented* (examining ex-post-facto the extent to which outcomes have been met), *process oriented* (examining organizational processes) and *demand oriented* (examining the results of products or services in the marketplace) (Reglin, 2006). Whichever approach is adopted, for any SME planning to use e-learning to train its workforce, it is essential that the provider can vouch for its credibility through its QA system and is able to evidence that its e-learning provision has been evaluated and has achieved the required outcome(s) and provided a good return on investment.

Constraints on Achieving Quality in e-Learning for SMEs

Based on their survey of Austrian SMEs, Reich and Scheuermann (n.d.) list the following constraints on achieving quality in e-learning for SMEs:

*   e-Learning technologies, methods and strategies are mostly developed for the larger enterprises and are not necessarily transferable to the needs of SMEs.
*   SMEs operate in almost every sector of the economy. As a consequence, they vary widely in their training needs.

- Many SMEs are highly specialized, which makes the development of e-learning courses/programmes for their needs expensive and unattractive to commercial providers.
- SMEs have limited personnel, organizational and financial resources for training provision.
- There can be culture clashes with external training providers, especially in the public sector, who may be looked upon by SMEs as not understanding their business.
- Decisions regarding the introduction of e-learning are often not based on objective decision criteria, but reflect the attitudes of those responsible for the training.
- Learning needs are mostly identified through practical experience rather than the use of questionnaires or other formal means of identifying skills and information shortfalls.
- Most SMEs may be described as 'crisis-driven', that is to say, they respond to challenges and opportunities rather than engage in pro-active policymaking in regard to human resource development linked to strategic management goals.
- Where e-learning is introduced into SMEs, a lack of know-how often results in very narrow concepts of technology-based learning and a concern to keep costs low, neither of which is conducive to good applications.
- SMEs do not always have opportunities to select e-learning courses/programmes for themselves. Many depend on larger enterprises which already use these.
- SMEs that do have the option of selecting e-learning courses/programmes are often unable to scope and articulate their training needs and analyze the market before selecting products that may fail to meet the company-specific needs.
- If SMEs do find suitable learning materials, in many cases, they are didactically and methodically of poor quality.
- Some e-learning programmes are overly complex, lack user friendliness and are too costly and time-consuming.
- Much of the e-learning provided is 'isolated learning', when in fact the learning needs to be collaborative, concerned with finding solutions to real problems and linked to workplace realities.
- Tutors or facilitators involved in e-learning rarely have specific qualifications for their roles and their skills are typically those required for traditional training.
- Employees need immediate access to e-learning, but SMEs often lack the organizational and spatial requirements for 'just-in-time' e-learning on the job.
- SMEs rarely evaluate their e-learning provision.

They suggest that quality certification of products would probably foster development of higher quality materials.

e-Learning Quality as a Subjective Characteristic Related to the Learner's Needs

In the business world, products or services are delivered and then approved or rejected according to well-defined specifications. A high percentage of errors means that the production or service delivery is not cost-effective or does not meet the required standards. Learning is different from this; it is not a product that learners can buy, but a process in which they must engage. The learning outcomes and learners' subsequent workplace performance depend upon their attitudes, needs and learning styles, capabilities, willingness to work hard at their studies and capacity to apply the new learning to their work.

Ehlers (2004) argues the perspective of the learner is the most important dimension in e-learning quality. He categorizes e-learners into four types:

1. Individualist. Prefers individualized learning scenarios and self-directed learning, is content focused and is not so interested in interacting with tutors, fellow learners or others.
2. Pragmatic. Oriented towards personal needs, seeks information, advice and tutors' support as required.
3. Results oriented. Learning integrated with work, oriented towards instrumental purposes.
4. Avant-gardist. At the vanguard of media and technology and interested in interactive and rich didactic solutions to learning.

He concludes that e-learners' subjective quality requirements determine:

*   The amount of information about the training, outcomes and benefits they expect before embarking on the e-training.
*   The degree of structure and guidance they expect in their studies.
*   The form of instructional design they prefer.
*   Their dependency on the tutor/facilitator.
*   The extent to which they expect interaction and collaboration.
*   The kind(s) of technology they prefer.
*   Their attitudes to the costs, time and effort involved vis-a-vis the perceived benefits.

We also know that there are visual learners who learn primarily through the written word, auditory learners who learn primarily through listening, and kinesthetic learners who prefer learning by doing.

TABLE 19.1 Students' rating of the importance of support elements in e-learning

Support elements of e-learning quality	Relative importance
Feedback on assignments	1
Tutor access	2
Possibility of contacting tutors via, email, telephone, etc.	3
Information regarding course or module content	4
Information regarding course or module availability	5
Information regarding the programme to which the course or module belongs	6
Possibility of contacting the providing institutions by email, telephone, etc.	6
Online tutorials	8
Information on pricing	9
Access to real-time technical support services	10
Information regarding online learning techniques	11
Support regarding registration issues	12
Advice on accreditation, certification and further study	13
Information on the web regarding registration, access, etc.	14
Discussion forums/bulletins, etc.	15
Information relating to course costs, grants, etc.	16
Possibility of contacting other students via email, telephone, etc.	17

Source: Rekkedal and Qvist-Eriksen (2004).

Rekkedal and Qvist-Eriksen (2004) enquired into e-learners' views on the relative importance of the various quality aspects of e-learning (rated from 1 for most important to 17 for least important) (Table 19.1). The three most important quality dimensions were shown to be access to, contact with and feedback from the tutors, which indicates that many e-learners are dependent upon some form of human support. In e-learning in very small companies, the trainees may be studying on their own and feeling isolated. It is therefore important that there should be a tutor, facilitator, local supervisor or fellow employee to provide the all-important 'teacher presence' and 'social presence'. This can be provided face-to-face or online, synchronously or non-synchronously. For the same reasons, SME training may benefit from using 'blended learning', a mix of online, face-to-face and hands-on learning. The next two most important quality aspects related to the provision of information and guidance before starting study. Taken together, these findings indicate that the most important quality characteristics of e-learning programmes for SMEs are their appropriateness to the needs and circumstances of the trainees, balanced against those of the managers and the companies.

Conclusion

To help achieve a sustainable future, recover from the financial crisis and eventually achieve a competitive knowledge-based economy, a major transformation is needed in European workplace training. While the larger companies have the resources to develop or purchase e-learning solutions, these may be out of reach of many SMEs – and yet it is vital that they do not lag in competency development. They need to identify e-learning solutions appropriate to their needs and circumstances.

First, they need to determine the required outcomes. Then they need to think about who will provide the e-learning. They may be able to enrol their employees in commercial online courses or courses offered through associations, suppliers or chains. Or they may decide to co-purchase and share courses and programmes with companies with similar training needs. Or they may commission courses from vocational education and training institutions. Or they may turn to intermediaries to help them identify and meet their needs. Farvaque et al. (2009) reported on such a scenario in North-East France, a forested region with many small to medium-sized sawmills. These mills found it difficult to recruit qualified workers, so they had to hire workers who lacked the necessary skills and experience and then find ways of training them. As there was no nearby training centre serving this industry, it was not feasible to organize face-to-face training. The mills' first attempt to contract a training centre to provide online training was unsuccessful. The training was too 'bookish', too unrelated to the actual work conditions and involved asynchronous study. An intermediary then helped the companies enter into a new agreement with the training centre which specified the training modalities and commitments by the providers and the mill managers. The mill workers attended videoconferenced sessions at their work sites after working hours, and interacted via the Internet with the distant trainers, using computers, headphones and webcams lent by the training centre. This use of an informed intermediary enabled the training to be tailored to the firms' requirements and avoid any mismatch between the providers' perceptions and the companies' needs.

In deciding which provider and form of provision to use, the following questions need to be asked and answered:

- Does the provider have a good reputation? Are its e-learning courses/programmes accredited internationally/nationally or to business/industry standards?
- Does the provider have a QA system in place for its management, procedures and courses/programmes?
- Is the information about the e-learning course/programme sufficient to determine its quality according to the specific needs of the industry, SME and learners?

- Does the e-learning provision yield acceptable returns on investment?
- Does the course/programme include subject-related, social and/or technical support? Is this sufficient for the learners' needs?
- Do the format and mode of provision of the e-learning course/programme suit the prevalent working conditions?
- Does the e-learning allow for different learner preferences?
- Is the e-learning suited to cases where, for example, there is high staff turn-over, part-time working, a workforce which is very small, distributed over a number of locations or mobile, or shift working and weekend working?

Pauselli and D'Atri (2001) posit that for the effective application of e-learning in the workplace, it is necessary to learn with real data and real projects rather than theoretical issues and fictional case studies. Reich and Scheuermann (n.d.) observe that SMEs need to develop a 'learning culture' which values lifelong learning, both for self-development and strengthening the enterprises, and in which e-learning is systemically rather than spasmodically applied, concerned with long-term objectives and not simply immediate concerns, and above all, concerned with achieving quality outcomes. Attwell (2003) observes that there is currently a lack of generic, sustainable and easily transferable practices in regard to e-learning for SMEs. Rather, there is a pattern of isolated examples which indicate the potential of e-learning in this sector. He concludes that more research and development is needed regarding the structure of work and work organization in SMEs, the models and frameworks needed to support e-learning in these smaller companies, the infrastructure, resources, facilities and pedagogies that the SMEs can utilize, and the costs, cost-benefits and potential returns on investment with this mode of training.

Notes

1 http://europa.eu/legislation_summaries/education_training_youth/general_framework/c10241_en.htm
2 http://ec.europa.eu/social/BlobServlet?docId=4202&langId=en
3 http://ec.europa.eu/social/BlobServlet?docId=3075&langId=en
4 http://ec.europa.eu/education/leonardo-da-vinci/doc1021_en.htm
5 http://ec.europa.eu/enterprise/policies/sme/business-environment/training-mobility-smes/
6 http://eurelea.ice-karlsruhe.de/
7 http://www.qualityfoundation.org/index.php?option=com_content&view=section&layout=blog&id=25&Itemid=114&lang=en
8 http://www.nationaltrainingawards.com/databank/

References

Attwell, G. (2003). The challenge of e-learning in small enterprises: Issues for policy and practice in Europe. *Cedefop Panorama Series, 82.* Retrieved from http://www2.trainingvillage.gr/etv/publication/download/panorama/5144_en.pdf

Barker, K. C. (2002). *Consumer's guide to e-learning.* Vancouver, BC: FuturEd for the Canadian. Retrieved from http://www.futured.com/pdf/CanREGs%20Eng.pdf

Ehlers, U. D. (2004). Quality in e-learning from a learner's perspective. *European Journal for Distance and Open Learning.* Retrieved from http://www.eurodl.org/materials/contrib/2004/Online_Master_COPs.html

European Commission. (2005). *The new SME definition. User guide and model declaration.* Brussels: Enterprise and Industry Publications. Retrieved from http://ec.europa.eu/enterprise/policies/sme/files/sme_definition/sme_user_guide_en.pdf

European Commission. (2006). *50 Success stories: Leonardo da Vinci Community Programme innovative projects contributing to the Copenhagen Process – linking policy to practice.* Luxembourg: Office for Official Publications of the European Communities. Retrieved from http://ec.europa.eu/dgs/education_culture/publ/pdf/leonardo/success-stories_en.pdf

European Commission. (2010). *EUROPE 2020. A strategy for sustainable growth and jobs: Contribution from the President of the European Commission to the informal meeting of Heads of State and Government of 11 February 2010.* Retrieved from http://ec.europa.eu/commission_2010-2014/president/news/statements/pdf/20100210_en.pdf

European Council. (2000, May 23–24). *Presidency conclusions.* Lisbon: Author. Retrieved from http://www.europarl.europa.eu/summits/lis1_en.htm

Eurostat. (2009). *European business facts and figures.* Luxembourg: Office for Official Publications of the European Communities. Retrieved from http://epp.eurostat.ec.europa.eu/cache/ITY_OFFPUB/KS-BW-09-001/EN/KS-BW-09-001-EN.PDF

Farvaque, N., Voss, E., Lefebvre, M., & Schutze, K. (2009). *Guide for training in SMEs.* European Commission. Lille/Hamburg: Directorate-General for Employment, Social Affairs and Equal Opportunities. Retrieved from http://ec.europa.eu/social/main.jsp?langId=en&catId=89&newsId=544&furtherNews=yes

Paulsen, M. F. (2006). Conclusions: Success and quality in e-learning for SMEs. In M. F. Paulsen, & V. Vieire (Eds.), *State of the art report: e-Learning quality in SMEs – an analysis of e-learning experiences in European small and medium-sized enterprises* (pp. 151–154). Bekkestua, NKI. Retrieved from http://nettskolen.nki.no/in_english/elq-sme/Book_about_E-learning_Quality_in_SMEs.pdf

Pauselli, E., & D'Atri, A. (2001, April). Distance learning for SME managers. *Industry & HigherEducation Journal, 15*(2), 117–123.

Reglin, T. (2006). e-Learning quality and standards from a business perspective. In U. D. Ehlers, & J. Pawlowski (Eds.), *Handbook on quality and standardisation in e-learning* (pp. 433–442). Berlin: Springer.

Reich, K., & Scheuermann, F. (n.d.). *e-Learning challenges in Austrian SMEs.* Innsbruck: Institute for Future Studies. Retrieved from http://www.futurestudies.org/down/cooperation_collaboration_sme.pdf

Rekkedal, T., & Qvist-Eriksen, S. (2004). Support services in e-learning – an evaluation study of students' needs and satisfaction. *European Journal for Distance and Open Learning.* Retrieved from www.eurodl.org/materials/briefs/2004/Rekkedal_Qvist-Eriksen_EA.htm

Wirth, M. A. (2006). An analysis of international quality management approaches in e-learning. In U. D. Ehlers, & J. Pawlowski (Eds.), *Handbook on quality and standardisation in e-learning* (pp. 97–108). Berlin: Springer.

20

QUALITY ASSURANCE FOR E-LEARNING IN THE SOUTH KOREAN CORPORATE SECTOR

Cheolil Lim

Introduction

Urdan and Weggen (2000) observe that with technological change increasing the complexity and velocity of the work environment and growing demand for higher levels of knowledge, skills and employee retention, training and re-learning are essential in all of today's businesses and industries. In the challenging economic environment following the global financial crisis, it is even more important to ensure that employees are well skilled and knowledgeable, but time spent away from the workplace on training reduces employee productivity and company revenue. However, as increasing numbers of employees use computers in their workplaces, online learning enables them to access training at the time and place of their own choosing, and the Internet enables reusable and adaptable e-learning resources to be delivered to multiple locations easily and conveniently. This is why Lake (n.d.) observes that e-learning is expected to become the third most used application on the Internet after email and search. He reports that in 2004, corporate spending on e-learning was around US$5 billion globally and was expected to grow to around US$ 50 billion by 2010. Clark and Mayer (2008) report that between 2001–2006, computer-based instruction in the United States increased from 11% to 29% of all work-force training. Karen (2010) observes that in 2009, US companies delivered more workplace training with fewer training personnel and at lower cost by means of live online instruction and self-directed e-learning. A 2009 study in the United Kingdom showed that 64% of organizations were increasing their learning technology budgets to strengthen and improve training and develop a better qualified workforce (Little, 2009).

South Korea (Korea hereafter) has also witnessed rapid growth in corporate e-learning. Between 2004–2008, the revenue generated by the e-learning industry increased by almost 10% a year (Korea Education and Research Information Service, 2008). From the time that corporate e-learning began in 1999, a government-supported quality assurance (QA) framework has played a major role in establishing standards. This chapter describes the establishment and evolution of this QA framework over the past decade. It also provides a case study of a QA system adopted by a major company in accordance with these national standards. It concludes by discussing the lessons learned from these QA initiatives and offering suggestions for further work in this field.

Government Support for Corporate e-Learning in Korea

Korea is a high-tech industrialized economy and among the world's 20 largest economies. Much of its development has been due to close government and business ties. In line with this, the Korean government, and in particular the Ministry of Labor, has played a critical role in encouraging and supporting the development of corporate e-learning. The government's vision expressed in its Cyber Korea 21 Vision of 1997 was that Korea would be a creative, knowledge-based society whose competitiveness and living standards would be at the level of the advanced Organization for Economic Co-operation and Development (OECD) countries (OECD, 2000). It was recognized that technological innovation alone would not achieve this vision, that what was needed to build an information society by 2002 was market demand that pulled the technology. So goals were set for the establishment, not only of information and communications technology (ICT) infrastructure, but the promotion of new businesses, new jobs and increased productivity through the utilization of the new technologies. As a consequence of this government leadership and massive public investment, Korea's ICT industry emerged as the main pillar of the Korean economy, accounting for 13% of GDP and 30% of the total export volume (Yang, n.d.).

In line with this vision of a knowledge-based economy, the Ministry of Labor became the primary driving force in the adoption of corporate e-learning. In 1998, it selected seven Internet training providers to pilot 67 e-learning programmes for 7,167 trainees in order to determine whether e-learning should feature in government-supported training courses (Lee, 2005). Encouraged by the outcomes, the Ministry then incorporated e-learning in the Vocational Training Act of 1999. To be recognized as authorized e-learning, it had to be shown that a programme was designed to improve productivity or train job-seekers and workers wishing to change jobs and provided at least 20 hours of study. In that same year, the Ministry began providing financial support for corporate e-learning by including this form of provision under the Employment Insurance Reimbursement Policy. Under this scheme, which is still in operation, all Korean firms of any size must pay levies for their workers. If the firms then provide training for their workers, including e-learning, the training expenses are reimbursed. This scheme encouraged the large corporations to invest in e-learning. In 2000, there were about 2,696 online programmes on offer and, on average, each e-learning provider provided about 58 programmes. Most of these programmes were concerned with training in ICT. The remainder dealt with office administration and management, banking, insurance and other skills training. By 2008, the number of trainees participating in e-learning had risen from 20,000 to over 1.4 million, and the support fund for e-learning had grown from US$ 920,000 to almost US$ 65 million (Ministry of Commerce, Industry and Energy, Korea Institute for Electronic Commerce & Korea Association of Convergence Education, 2010). There was also a marked increase in carrying out research in corporate e-learning. For example, one-third of the articles in the 13 volumes of the Korean *Journal of Corporate Education* published since 1999 have addressed this topic (Lim, 2007).

The Australian Flexible Learning Advisory Group argues that agreed standards for e-learning systems, products and services are essential to ensure that e-learning environments are compatible, safe, efficient and dependable. It also suggests that they are important to supporting innovation, while at the same time, reducing unnecessary duplication of effort and complexity. The Ministry of Labor recognized this and identified the Korea Research Institute for Vocational Education and Training (KRIVET), a national policy research organization under the Prime Minister's Office, as the best location for an e-Learning Centre to encourage, support and monitor quality in corporate e-learning. A Corporate e-Learning Mid-period Development Plan (2004–2008) was developed by the Ministry of Labor and this e-Learning Centre which proposed measures for ensuring the necessary infrastructure, standardization and quality control for e-learning by commercial producers and in-house providers (Lim, 2007). More recently, regulations have been introduced to include blended learning, a scaled training fee structure based on the quality of the e-learning providers, and a tuition support system which allows individual workers to receive financial support when registering independently for e-learning.

In parallel with these developments, the Ministry of Commerce, Industry and Energy (later the Ministry of Knowledge Economy) released a report on the status of, and plans for, the e-learning industry – the content producers and suppliers of hardware and software. These plans concerned technology standardization, evaluation and assurance systems, vitalizing the e-learning market; improving legal frameworks and creating an e-learning network in industry, academia and government.

QA Issues

Since 2000, all corporate e-learning programmes receiving support under the Employment Insurance Reimbursement Policy have been required to be

TABLE 20.1 KRIVET's original criteria for evaluating Korean corporate e-learning
programmes

Evaluation dimensions	Criteria
Development and delivery	Appropriateness and quality of: • Content • Methods
Interactivity	Appropriateness and quality of: • Learner/instructor interaction • Learner/learner interaction • Learner/content interaction • Learner/programme manager interaction
Evaluation/assessment	Appropriateness and quality of: • Evaluation/assessment procedures • Feedback mechanisms
Learner support	Appropriateness and quality of: • Learner support • Technical support
Technology	Appropriateness and quality of: • Access • Technology • Interface/navigation

Source: Lee et al. (2009).

evaluated by the KRIVET e-Learning Centre. Table 20.1 shows the criteria by
which the quality of these programmes was originally judged.

Figure 20.1 shows the results of the corporate e-learning course evaluations
carried out between 2002–2005, during which period the percentage of
e-learning courses judged to be good (rated B) rose from 16.5% to 48.1%, while
the percentage of courses rating poorly (D and F) decreased from 27.5% to 5%.

However, these results failed to provide the complete picture of corporate
e-learning in Korea. Nearly 90% of all Korean corporate e-learning programmes
are in the form of tutorials, either in HyperText Markup Language (HTML) or
trainer-on-demand format (Lim, 2007). That is to say, they feature instruction followed by practice, multiple-choice questions or other assessment methods and
then some basic feedback. Various instructional design strategies are employed, for

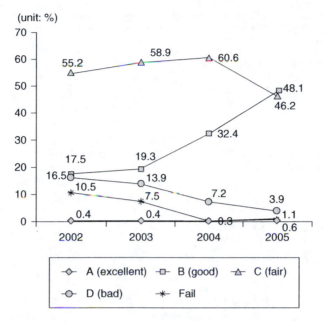

FIGURE 20.1 e-Learning course evaluation results (2002–2005)

Source: Ministry of Commerce, Industry and Energy, Korea Institute for Electronic Commerce & Korea Association of Convergence Education (2006).

example, Gagné's Nine Events of Instruction and Keller's Attention, Relevance, Confidence, Satisfaction model, using authoring tools such as Flash for animated presentations. The remaining 10% of e-learning programmes are simulations designed to hone technical skills. So ubiquitous are tutorials and simulations that the government's Employment Insurance Reimbursement Policy failed to take account of any other approaches that might be employed such as problem-solving or case-based learning, despite the fact that these can develop the very skills needed in today's workforce. Furthermore, the criteria laid down by KRIVET failed to be matched by specific guidelines, so the judgments on quality varied according to evaluators' perceptions and perspectives. It was seen that more specific guidelines were needed to ensure objectivity and consistency in this evaluation (Lee, 2008).

Lee, Byun, Kwon, and Kwak (2009) analyzed the outcomes of the Ministry of Labor's polices for e-learning, surveyed the opinions of e-learning providers and learners on the strengths and weaknesses of the current evaluation scheme, ran a series of e-learning forums and finally came up with a new set of evaluation criteria (see Table 20.2, overleaf). These emphasized quality of content as well as quality of training methods. A new evaluation system was then established,

TABLE 20.2 Revised evaluation criteria for e-learning programme design

Phase	Evaluator	Criteria
1	KRIVET e-Learning Centre	Relevance of training to job performance needs
		Suitability as an e-learning course
		Availability in the existing training market
		Future training demand
		Appropriateness of amount of learning
2	External experts in content and instructional design	Appropriateness of content and methods
		Appropriateness of evaluation
		Appropriateness of learner support
		Appropriateness of subject matter expert(s)

Source: Human Resources Development Service of Korea (2009).

involving both the e-Learning Centre and external experts in the field. The e-Learning Centre's role was to consider the eligibility of the e-courses – their relevance to the job performance needs, the extent of the training to be provided, the appropriateness of their delivery methods and whether such programmes were already in the market or would be in demand. The external experts' role was to judge the appropriateness and quality of the content and methods, learner support and evaluation/assessment.

The e-Learning Centre also enquired into how companies in the different fields were actually using e-learning. It was found that about 85% of the e-learning programmes were confined to office management, information and communication skills, finance and insurance (Lee, 2008). The new evaluation criteria favoured wider applications of e-learning needed to equip the workforce with the knowledge and skills that the future labour market needed – for example, in regard to clean energy and the environment, as recommended by the Ministry of Labor and Centre for the Evaluation of Skill Development Policy (2010a).

QA and e-Learning Providers

As stated earlier, to be eligible for financial support under the Employee Insurance Reimbursement Policy, e-learning providers are required to be evaluated by the KRIVET e-Learning Centre. This requirement applies both to e-learning vendors such as the Credu Corporation, a spin-off of the Cyber Training Team of the Samsung Human Resource Development Centre which is now an e-HRD company in its own right, and in-house providers of e-learning in companies such as LG Electronics. The prime purposes of this evaluation are to assure and improve

TABLE 20.3 e-Learning provider evaluation results

	2007	2008	2009
A (excellent)	11	17	15
B (average)	37	44	49
C (poor)	37	44	57
D (dropped out)	27	40	52
Total	112	145	173

Source: Ministry of Labor and Centre for the Evaluation of Skill Development Policy (2010b).

the quality of e-learning providers and provide impartial and reliable information on their standards and capabilities. Again, the evaluations are undertaken by the KRIVET e-Learning Centre and external experts.

The e-Learning Centre examines the eligibility of the providers in terms of the:

- Relevance of the e-learning courses provided/planned for.
- Market needs and provision.
- Appropriateness of the number and range of e-learning courses on offer/ planned for.

The external experts are responsible for determining the quality of the:

- Course/content development and delivery.
- Training methods.
- Assessment and feedback mechanisms.
- Technology and infrastructure provision.
- Learning management and support systems.
- Tutors and other support personnel.

In so doing, they take account of the trainees' evaluations of the courses and course provision, the participant/success rates and other outcomes.

Table 20.3 shows the outcomes of the 2007–2009 evaluation. Only a small number of providers rated A (excellent). Many of those rated B (average) or C (poor) were subsequently denied funding by the Ministry of Labor. This shows that the evaluation process is both rigorous and exacting.

A Case Study of e-Learning QA in a Major Corporation

AutoEverSystems is a member of Hyundai Kia Automotive Group. It is an ICT service company of this Group responsible for developing and providing almost

200 e-learning programmes in office practices, ICT and languages. The AutoEverSystems culture places a heavy emphasis on quality in products and services, just as in Hyundai Kia itself, and the company makes every effort to meet the government regulations, recommendations and expectations in regard to e-learning. In 2008–2009, AutoEverSystems was rated the Best e-Learning Company of the Year by the Minister of Labour. It has also received International Organization for Standardization (ISO) certification and sets a high benchmark for other corporate e-learning providers in the country. The AutoEverSystems QA system is concerned with providing guidelines for quality e-learning programme development and organizing teams and processes for quality control, as explained below.

Guidelines for e-Learning Programme Development

AutoEverSystems provides three sets of guidelines for e-programme development: instructional design guidelines, course development guidelines and evaluation guidelines.

The instructional design guidelines set out the standards and criteria for quality in the e-learning instructional strategies. These are expected to be adhered to both by AutoEverSystems and all external providers of e-learning programmes for Hyundai Kia. They concern the objectives, training methodologies, assessment and feedback and evaluation. They not only cover tutorial-type e-learning programmes but suggest a number of alternative instructional models such as problem-based learning and goal-based scenarios which allow learners to engage in solving authentic problems encountered in the workplace. Unlike many e-learning programmes in the Korean corporate sector, these guidelines place special emphasis on active participation in the learning process.

The course development guidelines concern e-learning project management. They set out the requirements for needs assessment, co-ordination and management in programme planning and development, the procedures for communications and collaboration between in-house developers and out-of-house developers, the analysis, design, development and testing of e-learning programmes and the management, improvement and updating of the resultant products and services.

The evaluation guidelines concern programme evaluation, process evaluation and production evaluation. The programme evaluation focuses not only on the quality of the content, instructional design, screen design, multimedia design, etc., but the validity of the learning objectives and testing strategies, the effectiveness of the user interface and navigation design and adherence to e-learning standards regulation. The process evaluation examines the validity and accuracy of the learning processes and outcomes and fitness for purpose of the programmes.

The production evaluation is concerned with the efficiency and effectiveness of all of the production processes.

Teams and Processes for Quality Control

Four groups are responsible for QA at AutoEverSystems: the QA team, the content development team, the content operation team and the external consultants. The QA team has overall responsibility for all of the quality procedures and criteria by which quality in the programmes is judged. It is also accountable for ensuring continuous improvement and providing training in QA. The content development team is responsible for applying the standards and criteria in developing or purchasing all e-learning courses and monitoring the programmes' quality from the trainees' and tutors' perspectives. The external consultants gauge the quality of selected e-learning programmes and report on how these compare with other providers' programmes and how they might be improved.

Thus e-learning production, management and operations by AutoEverSystems on behalf of Hyundai Kia Automotive Group is marked by systematic control over standards, strong internal teamwork and close collaboration with all external partners.

Conclusion

The events and issues described in this chapter lead to the following conclusions.

The clear vision and policy drive of the Ministry of Labor, centralized top–down approach and strong organizational support of KRIVET's e-Learning Centre have been key elements in encouraging corporate e-learning in support of a knowledge-based society. The development and application of a standardized QA framework has also played an important role in promoting quality in Korean corporate e-learning. This has encouraged the increased use of instructional design strategies such as attention gaining, motivating learners, providing feedback and exploiting multimedia (Lee, 2008). It has also helped the corporate e-learning providers to achieve at least the minimum required standards in web and desktop-based training provision.

Conversely, these QA standards may have prevented the corporations from exploring other, more innovative, forms of e-learning not covered in the standards. For example, the lack of interaction in many e-learning programmes may be partly due to KRIVET's over-emphasis on structured content and under-emphasis on dialogue, collaboration, communities of practice and knowledge management. This and the conventional approaches typically employed in face-to-face training, probably explain why so many corporate e-learning programmes simply deliver content by such easy and inexpensive methods as online versions of existing print material or streamed versions of existing training videos, with no provision for interaction or collaboration.

This suggests that new QA indicators and evaluation processes are called for. For example, more attention needs to be given to the potential of such tools as email, SMS, videoconferencing and chat to help employees share their tacit knowledge (personal 'know how' or 'know what' that has not yet been codified) as well as their explicit knowledge (knowledge that is articulated, codified, formalized, stored in various media and readily transmitted to others). Valuable human resources will be wasted if the managers fail to encourage and support their employees in sharing their thoughts and observations on their work experiences online as well as by face-to-face/hands-on means. Surveying employees in Korean Air offices worldwide who were studying online through the Korean Air Lines Cyber Campus, Handzic (2007) found that they preferred this to face-to-face training, but for acquiring explicit knowledge rather than sharing tacit knowledge. This again illustrates the reliance of Korean employees upon instruction, authoritative sources and what they regard as 'the right information'. Unfortunately, as Taifi (2006) observes, an overemphasis on explicit knowledge management leaves no room for tacit knowledge development, and senior and middle managers are often unaware of the importance of drawing on tacit as well as explicit knowledge in training. Nonaka (1991) identifies four ways of creating knowledge in organizations:

1. From tacit to tacit. Learning by observing, imitating, practicing and socializing.
2. From explicit to explicit. Combining separate pieces of explicit knowledge into a new whole.
3. From tacit to explicit. Recording employees' comments and discussions and then finding ways of converting this tacit knowledge into explicit knowledge.
4. From explicit to tacit. Reframing or interpreting explicit knowledge by using the employees' tacit knowledge so that the new knowledge can be understood, accepted and internalized by others.

Providing opportunities for these can help to achieve greater efficiency, flexibility and experimentation in work methods and attract and maintain a loyal and productive workforce (Smith, 2001). And the new information technology tools enable these to be achieved more conveniently, speedily and economically.

QA in corporate e-learning requires a greater emphasis on measuring improvements in workplace performance. As the Human Resources Development Service of Korea (2009) observes, QA in Korean corporate e-learning is currently mainly concerned with evidencing the attainment of instructional objectives, rather than how well the new knowledge and skills then translate into operations.

QA standards and criteria also need to promote the greater use of problem-solving, experimentation and other approaches that will help trainees apply their knowledge and skills to real-world situations. This cannot be achieved through one-way instruction. So there is need for a shift from trainer-led to trainee-centred approaches.

QA needs to take more account of the quality of the supervision and support provided for e-learning. Jurich (2001) observes the importance of line managers and immediate superiors being allies, rather than barriers, to the employees' training, encouraging and facilitating the trainees, especially those who lack the motivation or self-discipline to undertake the training on their own initiative.

There is need for more evidence of quality outcomes in e-learning for small and medium-sized enterprises (SMEs). In Korea, e-learning is mainly employed by the larger corporations such as Hyundai Kia, Samsung, LG, SK and Korean Air Lines. To encourage greater use of e-learning by SMEs, the Ministry of Labor's Bureau of Small and Mid-sized Companies is advocating sharing e-content and e-tutors, but the first task will be to convince the SMEs of the benefits and quality of such provision (see also Chapter 19).

The QA systems themselves need to be subject to periodic reviews to gauge their contribution to corporate e-learning. For example, KRIVET conducts formative evaluations annually with selected corporations and these in turn help KRIVET to continuously improve its QA system.

QA systems for corporate e-learning need to be responsive to changing training demands and opportunities, pedagogical paradigm shifts and technological advances. Employees can themselves now shoot YouTube-type videos demonstrating processes or procedures and make these available online for others to access. They can gain important up-to-date corporation information and training and discuss work-related issues by using smartphones and tablet computers. They can use social networking tools to identify others in their organizations with the specific expertise or skills they need and gain answers to problems via SMS and email. The use of MP3 players, notebooks and mobile phones mean that e-learning is no longer limited to fixed access points in the workplace. And on occasions, they may still opt for some mix of instructor-led and technology-based delivery.

As Urdan and Weggen (2000) observe, the e-learning revolution in the corporate world has only just begun.

References

Clark, R. C., & Mayer, R. E. (2008). *E-learning and the science of instruction: Proven guidelines for consumers and designers of multimedia learning* (2nd ed.). San Francisco, CA: Pfeiffer.

Handzic, M. (2007). E-learning portal: Enhancing user experience, In M. Handzic (Ed.), *Socio-technical knowledge management: Studies and initiatives* (pp. 107–118). Hershey, PA: IGI Publishing.

Human Resources Development Service of Korea. (2009). *Corporate e-learning manual.* Seoul: Author.

Jurich, S. (2001, May/June). Corporate e-learning: Three examples from across the world. *International Journal of Technologies for the Advancement of Knowledge and Learning, 3*(3), 29–30. Retrieved from http://www.techknowlogia.org/TKL_Articles/PDF/273.pdf

Karen, O. (2010). *The corporate learning factbook 2010: Benchmarks, trends and analysis of the U.S. training market*. Oakland, CA: Bersin & Associates. Retrieved from http://www.bersin.com/uploadedFiles/011110_ES_CLFactbook2010Overview_KOL_Final.pdf

Korea Education and Research Information Service. (2008). *Adapting education in the information age*. Seoul: Author.

Lake, S. (n.d.). *The case for e-learning*. *SkillCentric*. Retrieved from http://www.skillcentric.com/a_case_for_elearning.php

Lee, H. (2005). Promoting the knowledge-based economy through e-learning. In J. Kim (Ed.), *New paradigm of human resources development: Government initiatives for economic growth and social integration in Korea*. Seoul: KRIVET.

Lee, S. (2008). *Vocational competency development policy and corporate e-learning: Issue Paper, 2*. Seoul: KRIVET.

Lee, S., Byun, S., Kwon, S., & Kwak, D. (2009). *E-learning policy development strategies*. Seoul: KRIVET.

Lim, C. (2007). The current status and future prospects of corporate e-learning in Korea. *International Review of Research in Open and Distance Learning*, 8(1). Retrieved from http://www.irrodl.org/index.php/irrodl/article/download/376/779

Little, B. (2009, November). U.K. study finds "people problems" in e-learning. *eLearn Magazine*. Retrieved from http://www.elearnmag.org/subpage.cfm?section=opinion&article=126-1

Ministry of Commerce, Industry and Energy, Korea Institute for Electronic Commerce & Korea Association of Convergence Education. (2006). *e-Learning white paper 2005–2006*. Seoul: Korea Association of Conversions Education.

Ministry of Commerce, Industry and Energy, Korea Institute for Electronic Commerce & Korea Association of Convergence Education. (2010). *e-Learning white paper 2008–2009*. Seoul: Korea Association of Conversions Education.

Ministry of Labor and Centre for the Evaluation of Skill Development Policy. (2010a). *Training institutes evaluation for occupational competence development*. Seoul: KRIVET.

Ministry of Labor and Centre for the Evaluation of Skill Development Policy. (2010b). *Evaluation of corporate vocational education and training: Corporate e-learning briefing kit*. Seoul: KRIVET.

Nonaka, I. (1991). The knowledge–creating company. *Harvard Business Review*, 69, November–December, 96–104.

OECD. (2000). *Knowledge-based industries in Asia: Prospects and policies*. Paris: OECD.

Smith, E. A. (2001). The role of tacit and explicit knowledge in the workplace. *Journal of Knowledge Management*, 5(4), 311–321, Retrieved from http://www.uky.edu/~gmswan3/575/KM_roles.pdf

Taifi, N. (2006). Tacit knowledge and the knowledge management systems. *Knowledge Management Review*. Retrieved from http://knowledgemanagement-review.blogspot.com/2010/04/tacit-knowledge-management.html

Urdan, T. A., & Weggen, C. C. (2000). *Corporate e-learning: Exploring a new frontier*. Retrieved from http://www.astd.org/NR/rdonlyres/E2CF5659-B67B-4D96-9D85-BFAC308D0E28/0/hambrecht.pdf

Yang, S. T. (n.d.). *Digital divide & Cyber Korea 21 initiative*. Retrieved from http://unpan1.un.org/intradoc/groups/public/documents/APCITY/UNPAN007358.pdf

21

COMPETENCIES AND QUALITY ASSURANCE IN DISTANCE AND E-LEARNING

Insung Jung and Colin Latchem

Introduction

It is commonly held that 21st century educational providers need to be learner-centred and develop learning competencies in the learners that will equip them for continuing academic, vocational and personal growth. O'Banion (2000) suggests that such providers:

- Create substantive change in individual learners.
- Engage learners as full partners in the learning process.
- Create and offer as many options for learning as possible.
- Help learners form and participate in collaborative learning activities.
- Define the roles of learning facilitators by the needs of the learners.
- Succeed only when they can document improved and expanded learning for learners.
- Regard every member of the institution as a learner.

In regard to the competencies required in successful distance and online learners, Bates (2009) believes that the Conference Board of Canada's (1991) employability competencies have stood the test of time:

- Good communications skills (reading, writing, speaking and listening).
- Ability to learn independently.
- Social skills (ethics, positive attitude and responsibility).
- Teamwork skills, collaborative learning and networking.
- Ability to adapt to changing circumstances.

- Thinking skills (problem-solving; critical, logical and numerical skills).
- Knowledge navigation.
- Entrepreneurship (taking initiative and seeing opportunities).
- Digital literacy.

Some argue that it is a mistake to reduce education to mere vocational preparation and suggest adding to this list such attributes as self-realization, compassion and an obligation to society. Whatever the competencies to be developed, as Bates (2009) observes, they have implications for the curriculum (what is taught), the pedagogy (how it is taught or learned) and the assessment (what is examined).

These thoughts lead us to consider the competencies that are required in the leaders, managers, course and instructional designers, teachers and tutors in order to develop these competencies in the learners. This chapter explores the concept of a competency-based quality management system. In this, we use the terms capabilities, competencies and attributes interchangeably to signify the knowledge, skills, attitudes and behaviours required for achieving quality outcomes in open and distance learning (ODL).

Competencies in Leadership and Management

Daniel (2007) observes that success in distance and e-learning provision depends as much on open and effective leadership and management as technology and pedagogy. Leadership is concerned with envisioning and energizing. Management is essential for efficiency and obtaining results. Striking the right balance between these two important functions is critical for quality provision. Where there is no or poor leadership, there is a lack of direction, guidance and collaboration in organizations or programmes. Where there are visionary leaders but inefficient and incapable managers, visions will not translate into action. Birch and Burnett (2009) find that the major inhibitors to the adoption and integration of educational technology are a lack of academic leadership, clear vision, formal strategic planning and clear institutional policies, processes and standards. So let us consider the competencies required in leaders and managers and how they interrelate. Cartwright (2002), Sela and Sivan (2009) and others suggest a range of leadership competencies which may also be regarded as critical to quality in ODL and e-learning. These may be summarized as follows:

- Recognizes and responds to local, national, regional and international needs and opportunities.
- Challenges the status quo.
- Creates the vision and sets the directions.

- Creates an environment that encourages and cultivates the achievement of the vision and mission.
- Leads strategically and by best practice.
- Initiates and facilitates change.
- Fosters innovation and creativity.
- Inspires, influences and motivates others.
- Develops a competent and empowered organization.

Ciulla (1995) and Sendjaya (2005) suggest that moral capacity is another important attribute in leaders since their actions – and inactions – can have far-reaching effects on other people's values, thinking and behaviours. Miller and Hafner (2008) posit that leaders should also be capable of building significant partnerships with communities since these are vital sources of expertise and support.

Sometimes leadership in ODL is provided by governments. For example, Dhanarajan (2002) attributes the fast growing contribution of ODL in India to the far-sighted policies and commitment of that country's government. The Economist Intelligence Unit (2008) singles out Hong Kong, Singapore and South Korea as countries whose high level of e-learning readiness (the ability to produce, use and expand formal and informal e-learning in government, industry, education and the community) is largely due to government leadership. On the other hand, valuable initiatives in ODL can sometimes be due to individuals. For example, Daniel (2004) observes how fortunate the open universities were in their foundation and formative years. These all gained from having such vice chancellors or presidents as Walter Perry[1] at The Open University, Wichit Srisa-An[2] at Thailand's Sukhothai Thammatirat Open University, Ram Reddy[3] at India's Andhra Pradesh Open University (now Dr. B.R. Ambedkar Open University) and later, Indira Gandhi National Open University, Yilmaz Büyükerşen[4] at Turkey's Anadolu University and Gajaraj Dhanarajan[5] at the Open Learning Institute of Hong Kong (later Open University of Hong Kong). All of these were outstanding individuals who had the vision, commitment and tenacity to overcome indifference, criticism or hostility and break the insidious link between education and privilege. All were world-renowned idea generators who left an invaluable legacy of ideas and principles. The National Institute of Open Schooling in India and the Open Junior Secondary School in Indonesia (see Chapter 16) also owe everything to leaders who were convinced of the need for the provision of educational opportunities to underprivileged groups and the universalization of secondary education. In conventional schools, there is also need for inspired and well-informed principals, departmental heads and teachers to help to create a shared vision and an environment for authentic student learning (see Chapter 17).

When it comes to the managers of institutions and programmes, drawing on Drucker (1993), Handy (1993) and Bennis (1997), it can be said that they also need not only leadership capabilities, but also the capacity to:

- Help realize the leaders' visions and missions by incorporating them into daily practices.
- Maintain a customer focus.
- Keep abreast of the latest effective policies and procedures.
- Ensure that the critical organizational parts are designed and work together properly.
- Help other managers and staff to become more effective and efficient in their work.
- Develop teams and help them deliver results.
- Manage resources, people, processes – and themselves – to get the best possible results.
- Keep things on track and reduce the opportunities for distractions.
- Help overcome obstacles to change.
- Communicate and listen.
- Consult widely and take decisions wisely.
- Identify and proactively respond to risk.

These are all critical functions. As Belwati and her colleagues observe in regard to Universitas Terbuka in Chapter 11, quality assurance (QA) is not just a question of rhetoric by senior managers or grandiose mission statements or policy documents that are then never acted upon. Quality needs to be fully integrated into the planning, competencies and operations of every part of the institution. Only people make things happen and everyone's work in the institution should be assumed to have direct impact on stakeholder satisfaction. Working to achieve this should be the central mandate of all leaders and managers.

Competencies in Course and Instructional Design

QA in course and instructional design concerns the goals framework, the learners' entry behaviours and characteristics, the nature and quality of the teaching and learning, the test items and procedures, the pass and attrition rates and student and staff satisfaction with the processes and outcomes (progression to further study and/or employment and achievement of personal objectives). This not only calls for sound subject knowledge but the ability to plan and bring about professionally, vocationally and otherwise relevant learning which serves the learner, the provider, the discipline/field of study and the wider community. Nowadays, to develop quality course materials and learning environments that result in deep and relevant learning also requires competencies in exploiting the new tools of e-learning. We live in times of change, when social and technological forces are redefining what it means to learn, when learners come with new skill sets in mobile, digital, wireless technologies and when the wealth of information accessible to the learners makes the predetermination of content almost impossible.

The International Board of Standards for Training, Performance and Instruction (ibstpi)[6] has developed competencies and performance statements for instructors, instructional designers and training managers which accord with these needs. All of these competencies have been updated and globally validated and they have recently been expanded to include online teachers and trainers. The ibstpi competency statements are statements of behaviour, not personality traits or beliefs, but it is acknowledged that these often reflect attitudes. There is an implication that these competencies can be developed through training. The instructional design competencies deemed essential and advanced are as follows:

- Professional foundations

    - Communicate effectively in visual, oral and written form (Essential).
    - Apply current research and theory to the practice of instructional design (Advanced).
    - Update and improve one's knowledge, skills and attitudes pertaining to instructional design and related fields (Essential).
    - Apply fundamental research skills to instructional design projects (Advanced).
    - Identify and resolve ethical and legal implications of design in the work place (Advanced).

- Planning and analysis

    - Conduct a needs assessment (Essential).
    - Design a curriculum or programme (Essential).
    - Select and use a variety of techniques for determining instructional content (Essential).
    - Identify and describe target population characteristics (Essential).
    - Analyse the characteristics of the environment (Essential).
    - Analyse the characteristics of existing and emerging technologies and their use in an instructional environment (Essential).
    - Reflect upon the elements of a situation before finalizing design solutions and strategies (Essential).

- Design and development

    - Select, modify or create a design and development model appropriate for a given project (Advanced).
    - Select and use a variety of techniques to define and sequence the instructional content and strategies (Essential).
    - Select or modify existing instructional materials (Essential).
    - Develop instructional materials (Essential).

- Design instruction that reflects an understanding of the diversity of learners and groups of learners (Essential).
- Evaluate and assess instruction and its impact (Essential).

• Implementation and management

- Plan and manage instructional design projects (Advanced).
- Promote collaboration, partnerships and relationships among the participants in a design project (Advanced).
- Apply business skills to managing instructional design (Advanced).
- Design instructional management systems (Advanced).
- Provide for the effective implementation of instructional products and programmes (Essential).

Under implementation and management, it should be noted that there is mention of applying business skills. This term actually needs un-bundling because in distance and online education, there is often call for competencies in project, financial, logistical and human resource management, marketing and customer relations.

Competencies in Teaching and Tutoring

With the introduction of the new teaching and learning paradigms, many teachers and tutors are challenged to re-direct their role from transmitter of information to facilitator of learning and new knowledge creation (Collison, Elbaum, Haavind, & Tinker, 2000). Goodyear, Salmon, Spector, Steeples, and Tickner (2001) propose eight key roles for the distance or online instructor:

1. Content facilitator (facilitating the learners' understanding of the content).
2. Technologist (making technology choices to improve the online environment).
3. Designer (designing worthwhile learning tasks).
4. Manager/administrator (conducting administration and record keeping).
5. Process facilitator (welcoming, establishing ground rules, creating community, managing communication, modelling social behaviour and establishing own identity).
6. Adviser/counsellor (providing students with advice or counselling on a one-to-one or group basis).
7. Assessor (providing grades and feedback).
8. Researcher (creating new knowledge relevant to content and pedagogy).

This represents a considerably expanded role for teachers. They must learn to create and evaluate systems for solving new educational problems and discard any irrelevant structure and mechanisms that may have accrued around traditional practices. Unfortunately, distance and online learning sometimes suffers from hastily crafted courses and materials, inadequate preparation of teachers and tutors and a lack of educational support personnel. Schön (1983) argues that reflection should be central to professional practice. 'Reflection-in-action' and 'reflection-on-action' is required to build new understandings and inform actions in unfolding situations. All too often in distance and online education, there can be a divide between the thinking of the theorists, the findings of the researchers and the perceptions, procedures and practices of many of those involved with developing and delivering ODL and e-learning. It is important that the practitioners should be encouraged and enabled to give more thought to what is occurring, carry out experiments, test out new theories, generate new approaches and consider what further responses and moves are called for. There is also a great need for more situated learning by teachers who design and deliver the distance and online courses and programmes, that is to say, learning that is embedded within particular activities in specific institutional and social contexts and cultures and that develops competencies in communities of practice (Lave & Wenger, 1991).

Competencies in Using ICT in Teaching and Learning

It is clearly important to harness information and communications technology (ICT) competencies to educational management, curriculum and pedagogy. One set of competencies designed to address this issue is the *ICT Competency Standards for Teachers*,[7] a matrix of skill sets developed by UNESCO in collaboration with Cisco, Intel, Microsoft and the International Society for Technology in Education. These cover policy and vision, curriculum and assessment, pedagogy, use of ICT, organization and administration and teachers' professional development (Figure 21.1).

Each of the cells in this matrix is matched by lists of competencies with examples. For example, under professional development, it is stated that teachers should be able to:

- Use ICT to access and share resources to support their activities and their own professional development.
- Use ICT to access outside experts and learning communities to support their activities and their own professional development.
- Use ICT to search for, manage, analyse, integrate and evaluate information that can be used to support their professional development.

This matrix enables providers to assess their current educational policies in relation to their current and future goals, consider the possible impact of ICT on these policies and practices and choose approaches for harnessing ICT to their educational reforms.

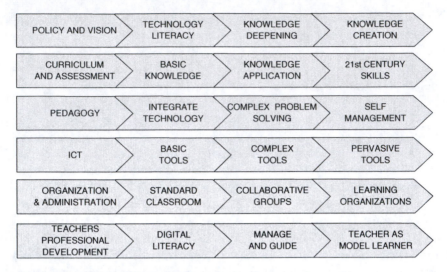

FIGURE 21.1 UNESCO ICT–CST competencies for teachers

Source: Redrawn from UNESCO (2008, p. 7).

Another set of competencies for online teaching staff in the university context is the Pennsylvania State University's World Campus Competencies for Online Teaching Success (COTS).[8] These derive from the personal experience of the faculty development director, an extensive literature review and video interviews with experts in the field on YouTube. The COTS competencies are concerned with understanding:

- Target population characteristics and how these influence learning.
- Students, their knowledge levels, diversity and cultural differences.
- The characteristics and challenges of online environments.
- Open-mindedness, confidence, enthusiasm and persistence.

They are categorized in six domains:

1. Attitude/philosophy.
2. Building community.
3. Class administration.
4. Faculty workload management.
5. Teaching and learning.
6. Technology abilities.

Within each domain, a set of competencies is listed. Competencies in building a learning community are considered particularly important. Included here are the capacities to:

- Create a warm and inviting atmosphere and sense of community among the participants.
- Exhibit effective written, verbal and visual communication skills.
- Enhance professor–student and student–student relationships and interaction in the online classroom.
- Contact students who are not participating and encourage them to participate.

Another detailed listing of competencies needed in teachers, tutors, trainers and trainers of trainers working in e-learning environments is the e-Learning Competency Framework for Teachers and Trainers,[9] created by the European Institute for e-Learning. Here the competencies are listed as:

- Preparing the learning event.
- Running the learning event.
- Supporting the learners.
- Assessing learner progress.
- Ensuring accessibility for learners.
- Evaluating the learning programmes.
- Managing the learning environment.
- Contributing to the learning organization.
- Managing professional development.
- Communications.

Some of the principal trends in the new teaching and learning paradigm summarized in this competency framework are:

- An increased emphasis on learner-centred and personalized learning.
- An accompanying responsibility on the part of learners for their own personal development and lifelong learning.
- Flexibility on the part of the teachers/trainers: being ready to respond to evolving situations rather than arriving with ready-made solutions.
- A change of role from 'expert' to facilitator, guide, coach and manager of the learning environment.
- A recognition that the learner may play the role of teacher and that content comes from the interaction of the participants as well as the educators.
- Collegiality, collaboration and creation of communities of practice among those with very different skills and backgrounds.
- Knowledge and learning seen as organic and connected to work and to other activities.
- An explicit responsibility on the part of teachers/trainers to promote equal opportunities, inclusiveness and the valuing of diversity.

- An increasing demand to encourage, recognize and validate non-formal learning.
- Access to learning resources and expertise throughout the world.

Competencies in Distance and e-Learners

As shown in Chapter 22 and elsewhere in this book, the quality of distance and e-learning not only depends on the providers but on the capabilities of the learners and the level and extent of their participation in the learning and creation of new ideas and knowledge. Distance and e-learner competencies are elaborated in several studies, for example, Dabbagh (2007) and Hong and Jung (2011). Those who are responsible for developing and delivering distance and e-learning programmes need the knowledge and skills to develop these capacities. However, important factors which ultimately only the learners can bring to their learning are self-motivation (Goodyear, 2002) and self-directive, meta-cognitive and collaborative competencies (Birch, 2002).

A Competency-based Quality Management System

Lawler (1994) suggests that the efficacy of designing organizations around job structures, which has dominated the fields of organizational behaviour and human resource management for decades, is being challenged. He argues that the global competitive environment and complexities that organizations now face require a competency-based approach, which in turn requires a fundamental change in virtually every management system within organizations.

Draganidis and Mentzas (2006) suggest that competency-based management entails four phases: competency mapping, competency diagnosis, competency development and competency monitoring. Competency mapping is needed to provide the organization with an overview of all the competencies needed to fulfil its vision, mission, strategic and business plans, project requirements and human resource management needs. The first phase involves defining the proficiency level for each job profile. The second phase is competency diagnosis, defining the gap between the type, number and level of competencies of the employees compared with what is required to meet the defined needs and targets. The third phase is organizing training and support to ensure that the proficiency levels match these needs and targets. The final phase is continuous monitoring to ensure that the competencies stay in line with changing needs and circumstances.

The competency-based quality management system for distance and online providers in Figure 21.2 follows this approach. Investing in such a process not only creates a large pool of highly experienced, knowledgeable, skilled and

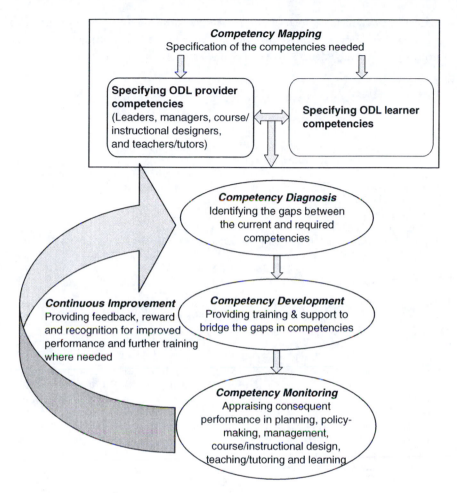

FIGURE 21.2   A competency-based quality management system for distance and online education

motivated people, but helps to build institutional and programme reputations and the all-important quality culture.

Conclusion

As in other knowledge-intensive undertakings, it is crucial to have the essential competencies in place for the provision of ODL and e-learning. But the knowledge and skills that provide the basis for gaining and sustaining quality and competitive advantage today will be different from those that will apply tomorrow. As Williams (1969) observed, like the constantly depreciating purchasing power of money, professional obsolescence is an unremitting, relentless, erosive process which demands astute, planned and continuing corrective action.

Notes

1 http://portal.unesco.org/education/en/ev.php-URL_ID=26277&URL_DO=DO_TOPIC&URL_SECTION=201.html
2 http://www.bic.moe.go.th/fileadmin/BIC_Document/highadmin-cv/wichiteng2.pdf
3 http://en.wikipedia.org/wiki/G._Ram_Reddy
4 http://en.wikipedia.org/wiki/Y%C4%B1lmaz_B%C3%BCy%C3%BCker%C5%9Fen
5 http://www.col.org/about/staff/sformer/Pages/gdhanarajan.aspx
6 http://www.ibstpi.org
7 http://unesdoc.unesco.org/images/0015/001562/156209e.pdf
8 http://psuwcfacdev.ning.com/page/attitudephilosophy-ap
9 http://www.eife-l.org/publications/competencies/ttframework

References

Bates, T. (2009, June 24). e-Learning and 21st century skills and competences. *e-Learning and distance education resources.* Retrieved from http://www.tonybates.ca/2009/06/24/e-learning-and-21st-century-skills-and-competences/

Bennis, W. (1997). *Managing people is like herding cats.* Provo, UT: Executive Excellence Publishing.

Birch, D., & Burnett, B. (2009). Bringing academics on board: Encouraging institution-wide diffusion of e-learning environments. *Australasian Journal of Educational Technology, 25*(1), 117–134.

Birch, P. D. (2002). *e-Learner competencies.* Alexandria, VA: American Society for Training & Development. Retrieved from http://www.astd.org/LC/2002/0702_birch.htm

Cartwright, C. A. (2002, January/February, 6–7). Today's CIO: Leader, manager, and member of the executive orchestra. *Educause Review.* Retrieved from http://net.educause.edu/ir/library/pdf/erm0205.pdf

Ciulla, J. B. (1995). Leadership ethics: Mapping the territory. *Business Ethics Quarterly, 5*(1), 5–25.

Collison, G., Elbaum, B., Haavind, S., & Tinker, R. (2000). *Facilitating online learning: Effective strategies for moderators.* Madison, WI: Atwood Publishing.

Conference Board of Canada. (1991). *Employability skill profile: The critical skills required of the Canadian workforce.* Ottawa: Conference Board of Canada.

Dabbagh, N. (2007). The online learner: Characteristics and pedagogical implications. *Contemporary Issues in Technology and Teacher Education, 7*(3), 217–226.

Daniel, J. (2004). *The sustainable development of open and distance learning for sustainable development.* Paper presented at *Commonwealth of Learning Institute Strategies for Sustainable Open and Distance Learning,* Canada. Retrieved from http://www.col.org/resources/speeches/2004presentations/Pages/2004-06-09.aspx

Daniel, J. (2007). Expanding open and distance education in an era of lifelong learning. *Journal of Lifelong Learning Society, 3*(1), 75–88.

Dhanarajan, G. (2002, December 6). *Open and distance learning in developing economies.* Paper presented at the *UNESCO Conference of Ministers of Education of African Member States (MINEDAF VIII),* Dar es Salaam, Tanzania.

Draganidis, F., & Mentzas, G. (2006). Competency-based management: A review of systems and approaches. *Information Management & Computer Security*, 14, 51–64. Retrieved from http://www.imu.iccs.gr/Papers/J53-IMCC-Draganidis%2BMentzas-2005.pdf

Drucker, P. (1993). *The practice of management*. London: Collins.

Economist Intelligence Unit. (2008). *E-readiness rankings 2008: Maintaining momentum*. New York, NY: EIU. Retrieved from http://www.eiuresources.com/mediadir/default. asp?PR=2008041001

Goodyear, P. (2002). Teaching online. In N. Hativa, & P. Goodyear (Eds.), *Teacher thinking, beliefs and knowledge in higher education* (pp. 77–101). Dordrecht: Kluwer.

Goodyear, P., Salmon, G., Spector, M., Steeples, C., & Tickner, S. (2001). Competencies for online teaching. *Educational Technology Research and Development*, *49*(1), 65–72.

Handy, C. (1993). *Understanding organizations* (4th ed.). London: Penguin Books.

Hong, S., & Jung, I. S. (2011). The distance learner competencies: A three-phased empirical approach. *Educational Technology Research and Development*, *59*(1), 21–42.

Lave, J., & Wenger, E. (1991). *Situated learning: Legitimate peripheral participation*. New York: Cambridge University Press.

Lawler, E. E. (1994). From job-based to competency-based organizations. *Journal of Organizational Behavior*, *15*(1), 3–15.

Miller, P. M., & Hafner, M. M. (2008). Moving toward dialogical collaboration: A critical examination of a university-school-community partnership. *Educational Administration Quarterly*, *44*, 66–110.

O'Banion, T. (2000). An inventory for learning-centered colleges. *Community College Journal*, *71*(1), 14–23.

Schön, D. (1983). *The reflective practitioner*. Basic Books: New York.

Sela, E., & Sivan, Y. Y. (2009). Enterprise e-learning success factors: An analysis of practitioners' perspective. *Journal of Information Technology Education*, *5*, 335–343. Retrieved from http://www.ijello.org/Volume5/IJELLOv5p335-343Sela674.pdf

Sendjaya, S. (2005). Morality and leadership: Examining the ethics of transformational leadership. *Journal of Academic Ethics*, *3*(1), 75–86.

UNESCO. (2008). *Implementation guidelines: ICT competency standards for teachers*. Paris: UNESCO. Retrieved from http://unesdoc.unesco.org/images/0015/001562/ 156209e.pdf

Williams, D. H. (1969, May 7). *Professional competence or obsolescence, which?* The Sir Thomas and Lady Dixon Lecture, Royal Victoria Hospital, Belfast, Northern Ireland. Retrieved from http://www.ncbi.nlm.nih.gov/pmc/articles/PMC2385003/pdf/ulster medj00127-0043.pdf

22

LEARNERS' PERCEPTIONS AND OPINIONS OF QUALITY ASSURANCE

Insung Jung

Introduction

It is a tenet of quality assurance (QA) that an organization that claims to have a 'customer focus' should take the time and trouble to understand and address its customers' needs. Harry Gordon Selfridge, who established the famous London store, and Marshall Field, whose store in Chicago was another shopping icon, are often credited with coining the phrase 'the customer is always right'. Both used it in their companies' advertising to make the customer feel special.

However, in the educational context, as Frydenberg (2002) observes, the providers of higher education are permanent fixtures in the teaching and learning landscape, while the learners are not organized into lasting groupings that can effectively influence the quality of the educational provision. Therefore, the standard-setters are the professional associations and accrediting agencies. There are few attempts to investigate the learners' perceptions and opinions in regard to QA. This is surprising in educational enterprises that claim to be 'learner-centred' and particularly in open and distance learning (ODL) contexts where learning quality does not merely derive from the products and services delivered to the learner, but the knowledge, understanding and relationships co-developed by the learners and the teachers in the teaching and learning processes, particularly in e-learning 2.0 environments (Ehlers, 2004). Clearly the learners' thoughts and views on the quality of ODL need be heeded, understood and incorporated with those of the providers in order to inform QA in ODL and e-learning.

This chapter examines learners' thoughts on quality in e-learning, considers the variables that can influence these perceptions and concludes by proposing a learner-centred QA framework for e-learning.

QA Guidelines for e-Learning

QA guidelines for e-learning have been developed by a number of national, regional and international agencies. These include the Commission of Institutions of Higher Education's Best Practices for Electronically Offered Degree and Certificate Programs,[1] the National Association of Distance Education Organizations of South Africa's Quality Criteria for Distance Education in South Africa (see Chapter 5), European University Quality in e-learning (UNIQUe) (see Chapter 8), the Asia Pacific Quality Network's recommendations for QA in e-learning (see Chapter 4) and the Australasian Council on Open, Distance and e-Learning benchmarks for e-learning in universities (see Chapter 9). All of these guidelines share common dimensions of e-learning quality such as institutional planning, infrastructure, course development, teaching and learning, student support, faculty support and evaluation. Some feature other dimensions such as financing, business results and returns on investment, reflecting the tendency to regard education as a business. But rarely are the learners' perspectives taken into account. In the corporate e-learning context, the trainees' needs and views on the quality of e-learning are similarly ignored. Here the QA guidelines commonly reflect the providers' concerns such as the relevance of the courses to the organizational needs and cost-benefits.

As Barker (2007) observes, QA claims from education providers alone are subjective and questionable at best. So let us examine two e-learning QA frameworks that do take students' needs and expectations into account: Canada's Open eQuality Learning Standards and the European Commission-funded Sustainable Environment for the Evaluation of Quality in e-Learning (SEEQUEL).

The *Open eQuality Learning Standards*,[2] first labelled the *Canadian Recommended e-Learning Guidelines* (Can REGS)[3] and endorsed by the e-learning community in that country were then launched in the global e-learning community as the Open eQuality Learning Standards. They were developed through a consensus-based process involving the various consumers of e-learning. It was found that the students' prime concerns regarding e-learning were the nature of the new knowledge and skills acquired; the value of the credits gained; the realization of personal goals and return on investment of money, time and energy. Only when these concerns of the learners had been identified were the processes and practices and inputs and resources needed in e-learning then defined. As Barker (2007) observes, these standards begin with what is most important to the learners: the assurance that they will study content and develop knowledge and skills that are relevant, recognized, transferable and applicable. Then they concern themselves with the teaching, learning, assessment and, when assured that these

are appropriate and effective, the nature and quality of the institution providing these.

The *SEEQUEL Core Quality Framework for e-Learning*[4] can also be applied
in all educational and training contexts. The most innovative aspect of this
framework is that it allows for the fact that not all managers, teachers or students have the same understandings of e-learning quality. It is argued that every
view of e-learning quality, and every approach adopted in e-learning, is legitimate because it is grounded on visions and values that cannot be homologated.
So this framework was built on the basis of the various users' perceptions of
quality according to the sectors to which they belonged, their roles in these
various sectors and their 'world visions'. These users, including students, shared
and debated their views, approaches and priorities regarding quality e-learning
in a web-based forum and were invited to rate the importance of each of the
proposed quality criteria. An *e-Learners Bill of Rights*[5] was subsequently developed to support the application of this QA framework. The objective of this
was to reflect on the rights, as well as the duties, of the e-learner within the
knowledge society. It was emphasized that while the traditional QA approach
concerns the quality of the relationship between the educational or training
provider and the 'knowledge consumer', a new approach is needed in which
the learners are active knowledge producers and the quality of a learning environment is measured against its ability to help the learners to produce, share
and value knowledge. There was also an accompanying *eLearners Quality
Guide*,[6] a collection of materials developed to guide novice as well as expert
e-learners in any decision process about e-learning and QA.

Let us now consider three empirical studies into learners' views on e-learning
quality.

Studies into Learners' Perceptions of e-Learning Quality

Employing a survey, focus groups, interviews and case studies, Cashion and
Palmieri (2002) identified a range of key features which Australian teachers
and students perceived as constituting quality online learning in vocational
education and training. While the learners and the educators agreed on most
of the main quality indicators in e-learning, important differences were
observed. The students rated 'flexibility' as the number one factor in quality
e-learning. This was rated far lower by the educators. Most of the educators
rated induction, communication with teachers and other students and a mix
of face-to-face and online learning as highly important, while the students
regarded these as less important. The educators believed that the students
would demand far more induction and support. This was not an expectation
of the students. Nor was the development of skills in using the technology
rated as very important by the students. This latter finding suggests that some

educators may be investing time and effort in planning and providing e-learning support that is not in fact needed by the learners and that it is essential to first ascertain the learners' e-readiness and e-learning readiness. It also transpired that the educators over-estimated the amount and quality of the communications expected by the students who considered that basic email contact with their teachers was quite sufficient. It should, however, be noted that in this particular study, most of the e-learning courses were lecture based with minimal requirement for interaction with other students. Further studies are needed into the extent and nature of the online interaction needed by students. Like the educators, they may well have many pressing demands on their time and may judge their requirements to be at a purely functional level. Another key point emerging from this study was that the students identified such personal attributes as self-motivation, good time management, organizational skills and commitment as factors contributing to e-learning quality. They admitted that their own laziness, lack of motivation and self-discipline and boredom with their studies could work against quality outcomes. This observation echoes the findings of Golladay, Prybutok, and Huff (2000) and others that learning in online environments requires a significant amount of discipline and self-motivation, and a significant investment of time, particularly where the requirement is self-study, as opposed to interacting within a community of online learners. These are behaviours that some students are more willing to commit to than others. This study certainly showed that educators and learners may not always be looking for the same qualities in e-learning.

As Ehlers (2004) observes, Web 2.0 allows learners to interact and collaborate with each other and create and discuss knowledge in a virtual community, rather than viewing and learning from content created and controlled by others. This is made possible by the growing number of applications such as chat, conferencing and social networking sites, blogs, wikis and so on. It is this that really differentiates distance and online education from the customer-market paradigm of the corporate and business world. Knowledge is not something to be traded in courseware and used by the learner, but generated through interaction between the learners, their tutors, fellow learners, the learning resources and other sources of ideas and information in the real or virtual world.

Certainly a customer focus is needed, but if every care has been taken to ensure quality in the instructional design, learning environment and support and encouragement for the learner, and if the learner fails to contribute, is abrasive and spoils everything for the other learners and the teachers, then in that case, the customer is wrong. In fact, even in the corporate world, it is accepted that customers are not always right in their expectations. For example, if had been up to the customers, Sony would never have produced the Walkman, because they told the market researchers that they did not need a small radio to listen to while walking around.

In a second study, interviewing European learners with extensive experience of e-learning, Ehlers (2004) identified seven key factors by which they judged quality in e-learning:

1. Tutor support (especially important in this dimension is bidirectional interaction).
2. Cooperation and communication (online discussions, group activities, face-to-face communication, etc.).
3. Technology (where technical requirements are fulfilled they are taken for granted and do not contribute much to the perception of quality, but where the expected standards are not met, the learners will certainly react against this).
4. Costs–expectations–benefits (the cost and effort that learners give to the learning has to be seen as having a positive relation to the benefits and the outcomes).
5. Information transparency (in the course or institution/organization offering the course as well as individualized counselling on course content, learning methodology or technical advice).
6. Course structure (a personal and individualized support structure including 'teaching presence' and 'social presence').
7. Didactics (background material on course topics, use of multimedia, provision of feedback and individualized tasks).

Just as Cashion and Palmieri (2002) found in Australia, these European learners clearly valued individualized e-learning arrangements which addressed their special learning needs and regarded the cost-benefits of e-learning as important. Again, providers often disregard these two factors.

In a third study, Jung (2010) invited South Korean e-learners to rate seven factors in evaluating e-learning quality: interaction, staff support, institutional QA mechanism, institutional credibility, learner support, information and publicity and learning tasks. Of these, it was found that staff support was perceived as the most important indicator, followed by institutional QA mechanism and learning tasks. These findings clearly differ from those in the two western studies cited above and may reflect the tendency for ODL learners in Asia to be more teacher dependent, a reminder that, as mentioned elsewhere in this book, cultural factors need to be taken into account in considering learning and perceptions of quality in e-learning.

In contrast to studies in Australia by McNaught (2001), and in Japan by Saito (2009) in which learners rated technological support as a critical factor in judging the quality of online or blended learning, this did not emerge as an important issue with these Korean learners. This may be attributable to the fact that over the years the South Korean government and governmental agencies have worked hard to promote and support the advancement of e-learning in schools and tertiary institutions, with the result that many students are in now a high state of e-readiness. Around 30% of the respondents in this study had previously studied on more than 10 e-learning courses, 21% had taken 4–6 courses and 34% had taken 1–3 courses. Forty-five percent of the students described their experience with the Internet as 'extensive' and only 4% described it as 'very limited'. However, had this study been conducted with less experienced e-learners, the results might well have been different.

These three studies serve to show that there can be a number of variables leading to significant differences in students' perceptions of quality in e-learning. It may be useful to examine this issue more closely.

Variables Affecting Learners' Perceptions of e-Learning Quality

Learning Style

The learner's preferred learning style is one of the most important variables affecting his/her perceptions of the quality of the distance and/or e-learning experience. Ehlers (2004) identifies four preferred learning styles in European e-learners: content oriented, goal oriented, needs oriented and interaction oriented. Within each of these sets, e-learners had different needs. For example, content-oriented learners were found to pay closer attention to the course material and less to course presence or collaboration, whereas interaction-oriented learners placed more value on the discussions and communications. Lu, Jia, Gong, and Clark (2007) explored the relationship between online learning behaviours and Kolb's (1984) learning styles: diverging (feeling and watching), assimilating (thinking and watching), converging (thinking and doing) and accommodating (feeling and doing). They found that convergers and assimilators spent more time on online reading while divergers and accommodators spent more time in online discussion. Applying Galotti, Reimer, and Drebus's (2001) concept of separate and connected knowing, Miyazoe (2010) explored the relationship between learning style, gender and adaptability to online study in Japanese college students. She found that 'connected learners' of both genders – those who empathize and like to share experiences, avoid confrontation and only ask questions when they feel that they understand things from the others' points of view – had high adaptability to online discussions. On the other hand, 'separate learners', those who like to remain objective, use logic and draw on reliable sources such as textbooks, respected teachers or their own direct experience, and had low adaptability to interactive online learning.

Other differences in learning styles have been identified by Beaudoin (2002) who found that there could be 'overactive' online learners who are continually contributing to the work and ideas and the more reflective and less visible 'lurkers' who may nevertheless still be fully engaged, and Ford and Chen (2000), who found that cognitive style, levels of prior experience, motivation, age and gender were linked to strategic differences in navigation by students using a hypermedia-based tutorial.

These individual learning styles and preferences play an important role in the way students feel, interact and learn in online learning and will clearly influence their assessment of the quality of such experiences.

Technological Proficiency

While most providers regard technology support as a critical quality factor in online learning, learners in countries where social uses of technology are widespread or whose prior experience with the technology is extensive do not seem to rate this factor highly. However, as Muilenburga and Berge (2005) observe, online learners with lower comfort and confidence levels in using technology will perceive technology problems and access as serious barriers to online learning, and learners who have never before taken an online course will rate technical problems, cost, Internet access and lack of technical skill as significant barriers to their learning. Selim (2007) found that next to teacher characteristics, Arab college students perceived technology support as a critical factor in quality e-learning. There is clearly need for more studies into the variations in, and links between, e-readiness and e-learning readiness.

Motivation

Dabbagh (2007) found learners' interest in study and academic self-concept to be important variables in successful e-learning. Muilenburga and Berge (2005) found that students who are highly motivated and enjoy online learning are more readily embrace social interaction as a means of online learning. Those learners who have low motivation and expect to engage in e-learning with minimal effort are clearly bound to differ in their judgements on the quality of the e-learning provision from those who are interested in acquiring new skills and knowledge through all means possible in e-learning.

Other Personal Factors

There may be differences in the perceptions of quality in males and females, humanities and natural science majors, older and younger learners and those with special learning needs (Jung, 2010). More studies are needed to investigate the influence of these personal variables in learners' assessment of e-learning quality.

Instructional Design and Content Variables

The design of the e-learning environments can also affect learners' perceptions of e-learning quality. Redmond and Lock (2008) and others found that learners' perceptions of quality in e-learning correlated with the extent to which they valued peer interaction online, the provision of plentiful information and challenging workloads. The extent to which teachers intervene and take the lead is another factor where views may vary on the quality of the instructional design. Barker (2002) found that the transferability of learning into work situations is an important determinant of quality for Canadian e-learners. Cashion and Palmieri (2002) found that flexibility in content and study was highly important for Australian e-learners. Espinoza, Dove, Zucker, and Kozma (1999) found that American high school students studying online placed more value on highly structured curriculum content. Jung (2010) found that in judging the quality of e-learning, Korean adult learners place less value on the content and more on the learning tasks.

Cultural Variables

Culture also plays an important role in learners' perceptions of quality e-learning. In the high-context Asian cultures, words are less important than contexts, things are inferred through tone of voice, use of silence, facial expression, body language and the status of speakers, and communication is more indirect and formal (Latchem & Jung, 2009). Here telelecturing of on-campus presentations and blended learning, both of which retain elements of face-to-face communication, are often preferred over the more impersonal totally online text-based study via the Internet. By contrast, in the low-context Western societies, where communications are of shorter duration, more task-centred, less concerned with context and more dependent upon words than non-verbal means, the majority of e-learning programmes are text-based and use asynchronous online discussion.

Figure 22.1 presents a learner-centred QA framework for e-learning that takes these variables into account. There is clearly need for further studies into all of these variables in order to determine the differences in learners' perceptions of e-learning quality.

Conclusion

In Europe, the Bologna Process has put increasing emphasis on involvement of students in the QA of higher education and, as the European Association for Quality Assurance in Higher Education reports (Alaniska et al., 2006), students are increasingly involved in providing feedback on courses they have taken, contributing to the development of learning and teaching, participating in university decision-making, and otherwise representing their views and exercising their

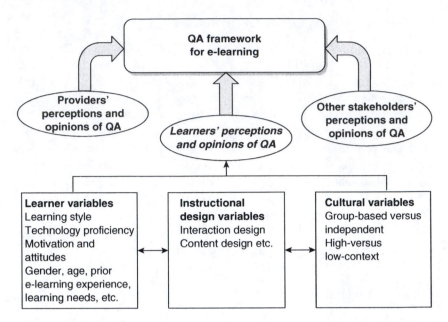

FIGURE 22.1   A conceptual framework for learner-oriented QA for e-learning

rights. Their voices are being heard, their views are being taken seriously and they are increasingly involved in the improvement and enhancement of their own learning experiences.

In developing QA frameworks for e-learning at the institutional, departmental and programme/course level, and in devising the instructional design and techno-logical means by which such quality provision will be pursued, it is important to consult with the students and undertake more research into their preferences and learning patterns in order to determine:

- To what extent do students with different learning styles, motivation and technological competencies differ in their perceptions of quality in e-learning?
- To what extent do learners with different prior learning experiences perceive the quality of e-learning differently?
- To what extent are learners' perspectives of e-learning quality culturally determined?
- To what extent are providers' and learners' perceptions of e-learning quality coinciding, complementary or in conflict?
- How can findings on learners' perceptions on e-learning quality be applied to improve the quality of QA frameworks for e-learning and help to develop the culture of learning?

Notes

1 http://www.ncahlc.org/download/Best_Pract_DEd.pdf
2 http://www.eife-l.org/publications/quality/oeqls/intro
3 http://www.futured.com/pdf/CanREGs%20Eng.pdf
4 http://thor.lrf.gr/seequel/SEEQUEL_core_quality_Framework.pdf
5 http://www.eife-l.org/publications/competencies/billofrights
6 http://thor.lrf.gr/seequel/SEEQUEL_eLearners_user_guide.pdf

References

Alaniska, H., Codina, E. A., Bohrer, J., Dearlove, R., Eriksson, S., Helle, E., & Wiberg, L. K. (2006). *Student involvement in the processes of quality assurance agencies*. Helsinki: European Association for Quality Assurance in Higher Education. Retrieved from http://www.enqa.eu/files/Student%20involvement.pdf

Barker, K. C. (2002). *Consumer's guide to e-learning*. Vancouver, BC: FuturEd for the Canadian. Retrieved from http://www.futured.com/pdf/CanREGs%20Eng.pdf

Barker, K. C. (2007). e-Learning quality standards for consumer protection and consumer confidence: A Canadian case study in e-learning quality assurance. *Educational Technology & Society, 10*(2), 109–119.

Beaudoin, M. F. (2002). Learning or lurking? Tracking the 'invisible' online student. *The Internet and Higher Education, 5*, 147–155.

Cashion, J., & Palmieri, P. (2002). *The secret is the teacher: The learners' view of online learning*. Leabrook, Australia: National Centre for Vocational Education Research. Retrieved from http://www.ncver.edu.au/research/proj/nr0F03a.pdf

Dabbagh, N. (2007). The online learner: Characteristics and pedagogical implications. *Contemporary Issues in Technology and Teacher Education, 7*(3), 217–226. Retrieved from http://www.citejournal.org/vol7/iss3/general/article1.cfm

Ehlers, U. (2004). Quality in e-learning from a learner's perspective. *European Journal of Open and Distance Learning*. Retrieved from http://www.eurodl.org/materials/contrib/2004/Online_Master_COPs.html

Espinoza, C., Dove, T., Zucker, A., & Kozma, R. (1999). *An evaluation of the Virtual High School after two years of operation*. Menlo Park, CA: SRI. Retrieved from http://ctl.sri.com/publications/downloads/evalvhs2yrs.pdf

Ford, N., & Chen, S. (2000). Individual differences, hypermedia navigation and learning: An empirical study. *Journal of Educational Multimedia and Hypermedia, 9*, 281–312.

Frydenberg, J. (2002). Quality standards in e-learning: A matrix of analysis. *International Review of Research in Open and Distance Learning, 3*(2). Retrieved from http://www.irrodl.org/index.php/irrodl/article/viewArticle/109/189

Galotti, K. M., Reimer, R. L., & Drebus, D. W. (2001). Ways of knowing as learning styles: Learning MAGIC with a partner. *Sex Roles, 44*(7/8), 419–436.

Golladay, R., Prybutok, V., & Huff, R. (2000). Critical success factors for the online learner. *Journal of Computer Information Systems, 40*(4), 69–71.

Jung, I. S. (2010). The dimensions of e-learning quality: From the learner's perspective. *Educational Technology Research and Development*. Advance online publication. doi:10.1007/s11423-010-9171-4.

Kolb, D. A. (1984). *Experiential learning experience as a source of learning and development*. New Jersey: Prentice Hall.

Latchem, C., & Jung, I. S. (2009). *Distance and blended learning in Asia*. New York: Routledge.

Lu, H., Jia, L., Gong, S. H., & Clark, B. (2007). The relationship of Kolb learning styles, online learning behaviors and learning outcomes. *Educational Technology & Society, 10*(4), 187–196.

McNaught, C. (2001). Quality assurance for online courses: From policy to process to improvement? In G. Kennedy, M. Keppell, C. McNaught, & T. Petrovic (Eds.), *Meeting at the crossroads: Proceedings of the 18th annual Australian Society for Computers in Learning in Tertiary Education 2001 Conference* (pp. 435–442). Melbourne: University of Melbourne. Retrieved from http://www.ascilite.org.au/conferences/melbourne01/pdf/papers/ mcnaughtc.pdf

Miyazoe, T. (2010). Learning styles and gender online: The attitudes towards thinking and learning scale and the classroom community scale. *Proceedings of World Conference on Educational Multimedia, Hypermedia and Telecommunications* (pp. 3413–3422). Chesapeake, VA: AACE. Retrieved from http://members3.jcom.home.ne.jp/t.miyazoe/ED-MEDIA_2010_with%20page.pdf

Muilenburga, L. Y., & Berge, Z. L. (2005). Student barriers to online learning: A factor analytic study. *Distance Education, 26*(1), 29–48.

Redmond, P., & Lock, J. V. (2008, March 3–7). *Investigating deep and surface learning in online collaboration.* Paper presented at the *International Conference of the Society for Information Technology & Teacher Education.* Las Vegas, NV. Retrieved from http://www.editlib.org/ d/27931/proceeding_27931.pdf

Saito, T. (2009). Quality assurance of distance education/e-learning. *Report of Project Group 3: Asia Pacific Quality Network.* Retrieved from http://www.apqn.org/files/virtual_ library/project_reports/pg3_project_report_february_2009.pdf

Selim, H. M. (2007). e-Learning critical success factors: An exploratory investigation of student perceptions. *International Journal of Technology Marketing, 2*(2), 157–182.

23

CONCLUDING REMARKS

Quality Matters

Insung Jung and Colin Latchem

Introduction

The aim of this book has been to initiate dialogue on and work towards common understandings of the need for quality and quality assurance (QA) in open and distance learning (ODL) and what is entailed in the process. It has provided examples of policies, frameworks, guidelines and best practice in QA and accreditation in ODL across the globe. It has identified the challenges in ensuring quality at national, regional and international levels and in the Information Age. It has also recorded lessons learned by policymakers, managers and practitioners. It has shown that, as in all other forms of education, QA in ODL needs to be performance- or outcomes-based, concerned with systemic change and aimed at continuous improvement and achieving a culture of quality and self-accountability. It can also be shown that there are costs in not applying QA. In this final chapter, we consider these issues further.

Outcomes-based QA in ODL

Addressing the 2009 UNESCO World Conference on Higher Education, OECD Secretary-General Angel Gurría (2009) observed: 'The first [priority] is access and equity ... the second priority area is efficiency and effectiveness [and] the third key area is quality and relevance' (pp. 3–5). In regard to the first priority, Gurría observes that while substantial advances have been made, there are still many challenges in ensuring equity between different social groups and between males and females in the developing world and there is still enormous under-utilization of human potential. In regard to efficiency and effectiveness, Gurría argues that institutions need to work smarter to achieve good governance and greater accountability. In regard to quality and relevance, Gurría describes the

UNESCO/OECD *Guidelines for Quality Provision in Cross-border Higher Education*[1] as a great example of collaborative effort to ensure consumer protection in a fast-growing but hard to regulate area. In terms of relevance, he refers to OECD's *Education at a Glance*[2] which illustrates a wide range of educational outcomes, comparing, for example, student performance in key subject areas and the impact of education on earnings and employment.

The Higher Education Funding Council of England (HEFCE, 2005) argues that the most powerful quality indicator for any institution or programme is whether the students have actually developed the pre-specified competencies and that QA should therefore place an emphasis on this over any other variables. However, the OECD admits that for all its expertise and gathering of data, it has no reliable international data on such learning outcomes. OECD has therefore decided to involve around 150 universities in 15 OECD member countries in a 2011–2012 feasibility study to see whether an Assessment of Higher Education Learning Outcomes (AHELO) can be developed to test what students in higher education know and can do upon graduation. It is envisaged that AHELO could be a tool for testing:

- Generic skills common to all students, such as critical thinking, analytical reasoning, problem-solving and written communication.
- Discipline-specific skills.
- Contextual information to link the data to student background and learning environment.
- The value-added measurement. What each university brings to the learning process.

The aim is to assess both the inputs (what the students bring to their degree studies) and the outputs (what they graduate with). It is recognized that students' education is greatly influenced by the quality and support of the teachers, the available resources and whether or not the environment is conducive to learning. Value-added or learning gain will not be measured during the pilot, but the methodologies and tools for evaluating this will be explored in subsequent work if the initial study yields positive results. Fully implemented, AHELO is intended to be a tool for universities to assess and improve their teaching, students to make better choices in selecting institutions, policy-makers to ensure that the considerable amounts spent on higher education are well spent and employers to know if the skills of the graduates entering the job market match their needs.

Such an outcomes- or performance-based approach to QA is yet to be explored by ODL providers. But it needs to be applied not only in higher education. If it proves viable, it could be applied for testing the quality of outcomes in all forms of distance and technology-based learning including applications of ICT in conventional classrooms, open schooling, workplace-based training and formal and adult and community education. Many claims are made that the various ODL methods and technologies can improve teaching and provide learning environments that enable problem-solving, creativity, flexible thinking, collaboration and lifelong learning. The outside world now demands more evidence in support of these claims. As shown elsewhere in this book, it can never be taken for granted that all governments, institutions or the general public hold ODL in high regard. There is always need to evidence:

- The learners' competencies, capacities and depth of learning, retention and graduation rates and subsequent employability and engagement in lifelong learning.
- Students' satisfaction with their learning experiences and learning outcomes both during their studies and after graduation.
- Employer and community satisfaction with the learning processes and outcomes.
- The contribution to achieving educational and economic competitive advantage.
- The value and reputation of the ODL institutions, programmes and courses.

In an age of cross-border education, QA is not only needed at national, but regional and international levels.

A Systemic Approach to QA in ODL

QA requires a systemic approach. It needs to begin by establishing the needs of students, employers and society at large. The outcomes required determine the policies, management procedures, resources and systems that are needed and how these must interact and work with each other. Failure in one element can affect the others and ultimately the outcomes. For example, if an e-learning course fails to improve learning outcomes, this may be attributable, not only to poor instructional design or learner support, but to the failure by government or institutional managers to provide the necessary professional development, time release, resources or other measures essential for achieving quality outcomes. The next stage involves determining the qualitative or quantitative performance indicators (PIs) and/or critical success factors (CSFs) by which to judge the quality of the processes and outcomes. PIs apply to the inputs and processes critical to achieving quality outcomes. CSFs apply to strategic gains such as:

- Increased external funding, revenue or profit margins.
- Attracting new partnerships, markets or students.
- Improving what the staff know and can do.
- Capacity to appoint and retain the very best staff.
- Capacity to survive or advance in the face of change and challenges.

Some institutions employ benchmarks. For example, Merisotis and Phipps (2000) identify 24 benchmarks organized into seven categories that distil the best strategies currently used by US colleges and universities engaged in online learning:

1.   Institutional support benchmarks. These concern activities by institutions that help to ensure an environment conducive to maintaining quality Internet-based teaching and learning. They address technological infrastructure issues, a technology plan and professional incentives for faculty.
2.   Course development benchmarks. These concern the development of courseware by faculty and/or commercial enterprises.
3.   Teaching and learning benchmarks. These concern instruction, interactivity, collaboration and feedback.
4.   Course structure benchmarks. These concern advice on the course objectives, concepts and ideas; the resources and materials provided to students and the agreed-to response times and expectations of the students.
5.   Student support benchmarks. These concern information about admissions, financial aid, etc. and the technical and other training and support provided for the students.
6.   Faculty support benchmarks. These concern the training and support provided for faculty in the transition from classroom to online teaching and learning.
7.   Evaluation and assessment. These concern the effectiveness of online learning in terms of educational outcomes, costs, enrolments, etc.

Other systems for assessing distance and online learning outcomes are referred to elsewhere in this book.

In a typical institutional or programme audit, the auditor (who may be external or internal and an individual or a team) starts by formulating an audit plan; setting out the objectives; quality requirements; groups to be audited and the scope, processes, timeline and location(s) of the audit. She/he then examines the institutional/programme strategic plan and/or QA plan and the policies and procedures for assuring quality, and creates a checklist of the quality requirements, measures to be used and data sources to be accessed in regard to each of the specified outcomes (Table 23.1 on page 259). The auditor then apprises the auditees of the quality requirements and tasks them with helping to provide the information required in these regards.

The data can be gained through a variety of means, all of which have advantages and disadvantages (Table 23.2 on pages 260–1). Audits typically employ a mix of these.

The auditor then studies the various findings, and surveys or meets with the designated groups to verify whether or not the operations and practices align with the strategic or QA plan and are consistent across the institution or programme.

TABLE 23.1 Planning for gathering data for QA audits and self-reviews

Outcome	Performance indicator 1	Source(s) of data	Method(s) of collecting data	Who is to be responsible for collecting the data	When and where the data are to be collected
	Performance indicator 2	Source(s) of data	Method(s) of collecting data	Who is to be responsible for collecting the data	When and where the data are to be collected
	Performance indicator 3	Source(s) of data	Method(s) of collecting data	Who is to be responsible for collecting the data	When and where the data are to be collected

Compliance or non-compliance is recorded and in the case of non-compliance, the auditor conducts further investigations into the extent and causes of this. An analytic rubric may be used for evaluating the key performance indicators (KPIs) or CSFs quantitatively or qualitatively (Table 23.3 on page 262).

A similar approach may be adopted in judging the effectiveness of the institutional/programme QA system and what actions still need to be taken to assure and improve the quality of policies, procedures and performance (Table 23.4 on page 263).

After analyzing all of the findings, the auditor draws up a report, detailing the review process, findings, ratings of the quality of the policies, procedures and practices, the overall conclusions and ways in which quality might be improved. The auditor then discusses the report with the auditees to ensure that nothing has been overlooked or misunderstood and then produces and submits the final report.

QA as Continuous Improvement

Quality is a moving target. Acceptance criteria and quality expectations are always changing and there are always new quality challenges, as the following stories show.

In the 1950s and 1960s, Japanese goods were associated with cheapness, ubiquity and poor quality. Japanese industry then invented some highly successful quality approaches such as *kaizen* (change for continuous improvement), Taguchi methods (working to produce outcomes on target, recognizing that failure to do this not only results in loss to the customer but to the producer) and *kansei kougaku* (measuring customers' emotional feedback about products to drive improvement). As the Japanese companies embraced these approaches, their brand image improved as did the motivation and commitment of their employees.

TABLE 23.2 Means of gathering data for QA audits and self-reviews

Methods	Purposes	Advantages	Disadvantages
Documentation review	Reviewing strategic plans, QA and other policy documents, finances, etc.	Ensures that documented policies and procedures comply with the required standards, etc.	Takes considerable time. Information may not be well organized or complete. Information may be inaccurate or misleading
Case studies	Understanding how plans, policies and procedures translate into action in critical areas	Reveals at the micro-level whether or not plans, policies and procedures are reflected in the day-to-day work of selected areas. Identifies discrepancies or non-compliance	The in-depth information and intimate details about particular cases may be insufficient to be generalizable
Observation	Seeing at first hand how policies and programmes actually operate	Reviewing a small sample of the operations confirms whether managers, staff and students know and follow the procedures they are meant to be following	It can be difficult to interpret and categorize the processes, interactions and behaviours
Questionnaires	Gaining and analyzing staff and students' views on policies, procedures, practices and outcomes	Can be administered to many people. Anonymous and relatively inexpensive to administer. Yields quantitative and qualitative findings	May take a long time to create and administer. Response rates may be low. Wording can bias responses. People may not be willing to answer questions or only answer them superficially. Open-ended questions yield interesting answers but generate large amounts of data for processing and analyzing

(Continued)

TABLE 23.2 (Continued)

Methods	Purposes	Advantages	Disadvantages
Interviews	Learning about managers', staffs' and students' experiences, thoughts and feelings and how these compare with each other and the other findings	Interviewing of a cross-section of individuals reveals the degree of consistency in following policies and procedures and the culture and morale of the institution	Inconsistency in questions can affect the data. Time-consuming. Can only be conducted with relatively few people
Focus groups	Exploring managers', staffs' and students' views on specific experiences or suggestions	Sampling the views of different groups in various contexts can give rise to unexpected issues that are illuminating and have high apparent validity	Can be difficult to convene. Participants' responses may be different from those of non-participants. Non-responses can be problematic

TABLE 23.3 An analytic rubric for judging the achievement of KPIs or critical success factors

KPIs/CSFs	Exemplary (4 points)	Good (3 points)	Developing (2 points)	Unsatisfactory (1 point)	Unmet (0 point)	Total score
KPI/CSF 1	Statement on why the outcome is considered exemplary	Statement on what is good about the outcome	Statement on the progress being made towards achieving the outcome	Statement on why the outcome is considered unsatisfactory	Statement on how and why the outcome is not being met	0, 1, 2, 3, 4
KPI/CSF 2	Statement on why the outcome is considered exemplary	Statement on what is good about the outcome	Statement on the progress being made towards achieving the outcome	Statement on why the outcome is considered unsatisfactory	Statement on how and why the outcome is not being met	0, 1, 2, 3, 4
KPI/CSF 3	Statement on why the outcome is considered exemplary	Statement on what is good about the outcome	Statement on the progress being made towards achieving the outcome	Statement on why the outcome is considered unsatisfactory	Statement on how and why the outcome is not being met	0, 1, 2, 3, 4

TABLE 23.4 An analytic rubric for judging the quality of a QA system

Stated outcomes	Policies and procedures	Monitoring systems	Performance standards	Response to problems and shortcomings	Action needed	Total score
Outcome 1	Statement on quality of policies and procedures	Statement on quality of monitoring procedures	Statement on quality of performance standards	Statement on steps taken to rectify problems and shortcomings	Statement on action needed	0, 1, 2, 3, 4
Outcome 2	Statement on quality of policies and procedures	Statement on quality of monitoring procedures	Statement on quality of performance standards	Statement on steps taken to rectify problems and shortcomings	Statement on action needed	0, 1, 2, 3, 4
Outcome 3	Statement on quality of policies and procedures	Statement on quality of monitoring procedures	Statement on quality of performance standards	Statement on steps taken to rectify problems and shortcomings	Statement on action needed	0, 1, 2, 3, 4

In the 1960s, engineers at Datsun (the forerunner of Nissan) began working on the 240Z. They aimed to create a small car that offered performance, comfort and a competitive price against the European and American cars and would improve their company's image in the minds of consumers. Once they managed to get this little car to go from 0 to 60 miles per hour in less than 9 seconds, demand was overwhelming.[3] But Japanese manufacturers did not stop at benchmarking. They then started aiming for continuous quality improvement – producing what Sony called 'next generation products'[4] which came at half the price but offered the same performance, or in the case of the Japanese motor industry, provided features that were either unavailable in European or US cars or optional extras incurring additional costs.

We may draw parallels here between the evolution of QA in Japanese manufacturing and in ODL. First, there is need to demonstrate that ODL can be a more economical but legitimate mode of education and dispel any distrust of education delivered outside the classroom and supposedly lacking in interaction. Once these concerns have been addressed, there is need to prove that this form of education is of a higher quality and provides many additional services and benefits to the learners. This is essential if ODL is to attract the quality of staff and students, resources and government support needed for continuous improvement. As shown in Chapter 2, The Open University's (OU) founding Vice-Chancellor, Walter Perry, determined from the very outset that this would be a university that taught better than any other university in the UK. And this was not just rhetoric. It became self-evident in the radical open admissions policy – requiring students to take two foundation courses before moving onto higher levels of study – the new areas of study and new forms of courseware pioneered by the OU and subsequently adopted by the conventional universities, the new pedagogical methods for mixed ability students (a third of whom have entry qualifications lower than those normally required by UK universities), the use of home experiment science kits, radio and TV broadcasts, residential schools and most recently, the sharing of OU learning resources with a global audience through iTunes U and OpenLearn. The outcome of all this? The OU ranks among the United Kingdom's top universities for its teaching quality and attention to students' needs.

Quality can never be taken for granted. It has to be continually worked for. In recent years, Toyota and Honda have had to make massive vehicle recalls. Japan Airlines, the once proud flag carrier, has had to file for bankruptcy. Sony has lost its lead to the likes of Apple Inc. and has suffered quality mishaps. China and South Korea are overtaking Japan economically. According to MSN (2010), the causes of this are global expansion and competition, a tendency to embrace the status quo and self-complacency bred from success or a 'too-big-to-fail' attitude. In the US, Boeing's production of the long-range Dreamliner aircraft has been dogged by problems, forcing the company to write off billions of dollars in production costs and compensation claims for undelivered aircraft. According to Productivity Press (2008), the reasons for this have been a lack of close working relationships and trusting partnerships in the production chain, low-wage, trained-on-the-job workers with no previous aerospace experience, a QA cycle time that was out of sync with the production rate and a lack of qualified inspection/QA personnel. All of which problems can be found in some ODL systems.

The lessons from these examples are clear. Quality can be assured only where policies, regulations and quality controls intersect with all practices, QA is pursued at every stage, and everyone in the process is properly trained and committed to high quality. Achieving quality outcomes can be particularly challenging for ODL institutions that fail to prepare their staff or give them the time and support they need for course/courseware development and teaching, and that are heavily dependent upon casual and part-time teachers and tutors who have only limited career paths and job security. Furthermore, it would be argued that ODL providers should no longer simply be concerned with trying to prove that their products and services measure up to the standards of conventional education. They should have the confidence – and the evidence – to show that their systems and methods are superior to many of those in conventional education and are particularly well suited to the new needs of the knowledge society and Information Age.

From External Control to Culture of Quality

As suggested in other chapters, there is a need to progress from QA as external control to a culture of quality. External control of QA typically involves auditing and imposing standards and measures on educational providers or ensuring that they adopt these by means of rewards and/or sanctions. Bradley (2005) argues that external QA encourages accountability and conformity rather than enterprise and diversity and that the direct transfer of QA methods from the corporate into the university sector and emphasis on targets and 'bottom lines' leads to simplistic conclusions about success or failure. Liston (1999) observes that the purpose of QA is not simply to evidence mistakes and shortcomings but to learn from and rectify these. Kis (2005) remarks that ownership of the system, let alone its intended outcomes, is unlikely to be achieved by interventions from a distance and will at best result in compliance to the requirements of the system, rather than a genuine concern for quality and improvement. Harvey (2002) expresses concerns that continuous monitoring by a controlling agency requiring overly bureaucratic procedures results in detailed paper trails and a loss of academic autonomy – and entirely stifles development and innovation.

A culture of quality begins with the leaders and managers and is characterized by shared beliefs, values, attitudes and behaviour patterns, a positive internal environment, links between internal and external accountability, continually improved outcomes and satisfied customers and stakeholders. Biggs (2001) refers to the 'reflective institution', which continually improves its practices by removing any impediments to quality teaching and learning caused by distorted priorities in institutional policies and procedures. In a quality culture, QA is no longer an adjunct, but central to long-term policy formulation and the deployment of human and other resources. The leading US quality guru, W. Edwards Deming (1986), posited that to ensure that the entire system works well, it is necessary to:

- Create constancy of purpose for improvement of products and services.
- Adopt and institute leadership for change.
- Cease dependence on inspection to achieve quality. Build quality into the product in the first place.
- Constantly improve every process of planning, production and service, and thus constantly decrease costs.
- Institute a vigorous programme of education and self-improvement for everyone.
- Drive out fear, break down barriers between staff and departments, encourage teamwork and eliminate slogans, exhortations and targets that are beyond the power of the workforce and create adversarial relationships.
- Put everybody to work to accomplish the transformation.

Quality Costs

Many educational institutions find the bureaucratic procedures, paperwork, time and additional costs of external and/or internal QA are untenable. So evidence is needed to confirm that hiring external QA consultants, commissioning external QA reviews, establishing QA offices, guidelines and reporting systems, training staff, collecting extensive data and so on do bring financial and other material benefits and add value to ODL provision. There is always need for cost containment or cost reduction in education, so in conducting QA, it is important to consider the *total quality costs* of preventing, finding, and correcting faults and failures in systems, products and services (Feigenbaum, 1956). The total quality costs comprise prevention costs, appraisal costs and internal and external failure costs.

Prevention costs are those costs incurred in avoiding defects in ODL systems, programmes and services at the very outset – which is arguably the prime role of QA. These are the costs of consulting students and other stakeholders on their needs and expectations, QA policymaking, conducting QA meetings, providing QA training and implementing QA procedures for monitoring and ensuring quality in the management, organization, curriculum, pedagogy, instructional design, course delivery, technical services, learner support and the QA system itself.

Appraisal costs are those costs involved in the in-process and final inspection/testing of systems, products and services to assure that these conform to the required standards, and preventing failure costs before these products and services enter the public domain.

Failure costs result from systems, products or services not conforming to requirements or user needs. They can be internal or external. Internal failure costs occur before the final creation or implementation of systems, products and services for the end-users. The later these are detected, the more costly their remediation. The costs incurred at this stage are those of re-working or abandoning systems, products and services and then replacing them and once again reviewing them, and the opportunity costs (the costs of not implementing alternative systems, products and processes). External failure costs arise with failure in the actual delivery of systems, products and services. They are incurred in receiving, investigating and responding to students' problems and complaints, installing unplanned-for support systems, cancelling products and services, supporting multiple versions of products and services, developing, implementing and marketing new systems, products and services, loss of income from students' fees, grants, government incentives, partnerships, etc., refunding, public relations activities to counter bad publicity, loss of reputation and again, the opportunity costs. External failure costs can be much higher than internal failure costs. Where ranking, performance-based funding or resource allocation apply, these can have major financial implications. There are costs in losing reputation and goodwill and failing to attract the very best staff and students.

It is important to determine these various costs in order to differentiate between the actual cost of a system, product or service and what the reduced cost would have been had there been no failure. It is also important in order to see what savings might have been achieved through better quality management.

Pirozzi (n.d.) argues that all of the above costs can be reduced through the adoption of smarter QA systems. He argues that higher-quality products and services can be more quickly and efficiently delivered, require less support and remediation and result in greater user satisfaction and confidence in the systems, products and services – all of which raise the morale of all those involved. He points out that where systems are defective, the prevention and appraisal costs are very low but the failure costs are very high, yielding a high total quality cost. On the other hand, with zero defect systems, the failure costs are very low but the prevention and appraisal costs are very high. To optimize the total quality costs, it is important to achieve a balance between these extremes. Pirozzi admits that capturing the data needed for QA is difficult and expensive, so it is also important to determine whether the benefits of tracking the total quality cost will provide sufficient return on investment to make paying for the implementation of the QA system worthwhile.

Kaner (1996) observes that without persuasive evidence and arguments, complaints about quality will often be rejected as subjective. So he suggests consulting those directly involved to garner their complaints about the time and costs of

particular defective systems, products and services. The evidence of these stakeholders can then be used to show that not only has there been a failure to achieve
quality, but that this failure has costs attached to it, that there is an agreed best
way of remedying the situation, and that the cost of this can be traded against
certain other savings and cost benefits.

W. Edwards Deming (1986), who played a key role in training top Japanese
management in improving quality in their production systems, argued that by
adopting appropriate principles of management, organizations can increase quality and reduce costs by reducing waste, staff attrition and litigation and increasing
customer loyalty. One of his Japanese proponents has posited that when organizations focus primarily on *quality*, quality tends to increase and costs fall over time
but when people and organizations focus primarily on *costs*, these tend to rise and
quality declines over time.

Conclusion

Bates (2010) tells of a lecturer in one of the universities he visited saying, 'I have
the same feeling about QA processes as Goebbels had for culture: whenever
I hear the words I reach for my gun'. At another institution, he was told, 'We
put in place a QA process for online learning that was so hideously bureaucratic,
none of the faculty wanted to do it'. Asking whether there was a similar process
for classroom courses, he was told, 'Of course not'. These observations lead Bates
to suggest that because e-learning is still often under a cloud of suspicion, this
can give rise to more demanding forms of QA than are applied to conventional
teaching and learning. He also observes that QA can act as a brake on innovation
by being predicated on past best practices using older technology. So QA needs
to be approached with due care. Overly costly and bureaucratic QA procedures
must be avoided at all cost. But, as argued throughout this book, quality matters.
Where there are no independent QA agencies in operation, these need to be
established. Where institutions have not yet implemented QA systems, they need
to develop the frameworks, criteria and ways of judging the quality of their ODL
provision or on-campus applications of e-learning. And where there are errors
and problems and user complaints that waste time and resources, providers need
to identify and implement the policies, systems and processes necessary for
reviewing and improving the ways things are done.

As currently conducted, QA is typically concerned with assuring that minimum standards are met. In ODL, minimum standards are not good enough.
Rigorous and critical self, peer and external reviews are required to identify the
new standards needed as education and training face the realities of globalization
and the digital age. Currently, the methods and uses of the new technologies tend
to be governed by the conventions, rules and protocols of those they aim to
replace or compete with. QA should not simply be mandatory, external and

concerned with accountability, but voluntary, internal and concerned with developing a quality culture and commitment to quality improvement.

This book has raised many questions and, hopefully, supplied some useful answers. We hope that the case studies and ideas in this book will inform further debate, and lead to improvement in the management and provision of, and community regard for, ODL in all of its forms and applications.

Notes

1 http://www.unesco.org/education/guidelines_E.indd.pdf
2 http://www.oecd.org/document/52/0,3343,en_2649_39263238_45897844_1_1_1_1,00.html
3 http://www.conceptcarz.com/view/makehistory/185,0/Datsun_History.aspx
4 http://www.wtec.org/loyola/ep/c6s1.htm

References

Bates, T. (2010, June 22). *In search of quality in e-learning.* Retrieved from http://www.tonybates.ca/2010/06/22/in-search-of-quality-in-e-learning

Bradley, D. (2005, March 30). *Quality assurance and diversity.* Paper presented at the *INQAAHE Biennial Conference,* Wellington, New Zealand.

Biggs, J. (2001). The reflective institution: Assuring and enhancing the quality of teaching. *Higher Education, 41,* 221–238.

Deming, W. E. (1986). *Out of the crisis.* Cambridge, MA: MIT Press.

Feigenbaum, A. V. (1956). Total quality control. *Harvard Business Review, 34*(6), 93–101.

Gurría, A. (2009, July 5). *Introductory remarks: The new dynamics of higher education and research for societal change and development.* UNESCO World Conference on Higher Education, Paris. Retrieved from http://www.unesco.org/education/wche/speeches/Angel-Gurria-OECD-2009WCHE.pdf

Harvey, L. (2002). The end of quality? *Quality in Higher Education, 8*(1), 5–22.

HEFCE (Higher Education Funding Council of England). (2005). *HEFCE strategy for e-learning.* Retrieved from http://www.hefce.ac.uk/pubs/hefce/2005/05_12/

Kaner, C. (1996). Quality cost analysis: Benefits and risks. *Software QA, 3*(1), 23. Retrieved from http://www.badsoftware.com/qualcost.htm

Kis, V. (2005). *Quality assurance in tertiary education: Current practices in OECD countries and a literature review on potential effects.* Paris: OECD. Retrieved at http://www.oecd.org/dataoecd/55/30/38006910.pdf

Liston, C. (1999). *Managing quality and standards.* Buckingham: Open University Press.

Merisotis, J. P., & Phipps, R. A. (2000). *Quality on the line: Benchmarks for success in Internet-based distance education.* Washington, DC: The Institute for Higher Education Policy. Retrieved from http://www.ihep.org/Publications/publications-detail.cfm?id=69

MSN (2010, January 31). *Toyota is part of a list of issues for Japan Inc.* Retrieved from http://www.msnbc.msn.com/id/35169972/ns/business-world_business/

Pirozzi, R. (n.d.). *Understanding quality cost.* LogiGear Corporation. Retrieved from http://www.logigear.com/newsletter/understanding_quality_cost.asp

Productivity Press. (2008). *What went wrong with Boeing's Dreamliner?* New York: Taylor & Francis Group. Retrieved from http://leaninsider.productivitypress.com/2008/12/what-went-wrong-with-boeings-dreamliner.html

CONTRIBUTORS

Editors

Insung Jung is Professor of Education, Media and Society at the International Christian University in Tokyo, Japan, and a board member of the International Board of Standards for Training, Performance and Instruction (ibstpi) and the International Development Research Centre-sponsored Openness and Quality in Distance Education in Asia project.

Colin Latchem was formerly the Head of the Teaching Learning Group at Curtin University, Perth, Western Australia and a former National President of the Open and Distance Learning Association of Australia. He now consults, researches, writes, edits journals and speaks at conferences on distance education.

Chapter Authors

Professor Emeritus Anuwar Ali is the Vice-Chancellor and President of Open University Malaysia in Kuala Lumpur. He was formerly the Vice-Chancellor of the National University of Malaysia, Director of Higher Education at the Ministry of Education and Chairman of the Malaysian Examinations Council.

Tian Belawati is the Rector of Universitas Terbuka in Jakarta, Indonesia, a former President of the Asian Association of Open Universities and an Executive Committee member of the International Council for Open and Distance Education.

Mark Brown is the Director of Teaching, Learning and Distance Education at Massey University, New Zealand's leading university for distance learning.

Neil Butcher is the Director of Neil Butcher & Associates in Johannesburg, South Africa, providing policy and technical advice on distance education and educational technology to African and international clients.

Denise Chalmers is the Winthrop Professor and Director of the Centre for the Advancement of Teaching and Learning at the University of Western Australia in Perth, Australia and a former Director of the Carrick Institute (the Australian Learning and Teaching Council).

Rajesh Chandra is the Vice-Chancellor and President of the University of the South Pacific. He was the Foundation Vice-Chancellor of the University of Fiji.

Kate Clarke is the Director of the UK Open University Validation Services which validates higher education programmes in the UK and worldwide.

Willie Clarke-Okah is the former Higher Education Specialist at the Commonwealth of Learning and project leader for COL RIM. He is now President and Principal of New Century New Compacts in Ottawa, Canada, providing services including the management of open and distance learning systems.

Michael Crock is the Executive Director Academic Products and Services at Open Universities Australia in Melbourne.

Sir John Daniel is President and CEO of The Commonwealth of Learning in Vancouver, Canada, and the former Assistant Director-General for Education, UNESCO and Vice-Chancellor of The Open University.

Teresa De Fazio is the Assistant Director, Study and Learning at RMIT University in Melbourne and the former Manager of the Student Experience Unit at Open Universities Australia.

Caroline Donovan is a manager with the New Zealand Qualifications Authority in Wellington, New Zealand and she was instrumental in developing and trialing COL RIM.

Ulf-Daniel Ehlers is an Assistant Professor in Information Sciences for Production and Operations Management at the University of Duisburg-Essen, Germany and the Vice-President of the European Foundation for Quality in e-Learning (EFQEL).

Richard Fuchs is the CEO of Futureworks Consulting Inc., Nova Scotia, Canada, and the Vice-Chair and Member of the Board of Trustees of the Telecentre.Org Foundation.

Michael Gaffney is the Chair of Educational Leadership at the Australian Catholic University and a researcher, consultant and policy adviser to Australian governments on twenty-first century schooling.

Sarah Hoosen is a project manager and researcher with Neil Butcher & Associates in Johannesburg, South Africa.

Sitanshu S. Jena is the Chairman of the National Institute of Open Schooling, Noida, Uttar Pradesh, India.

Shannon Johnston is Assistant Professor, Higher Education Development at The Centre for the Advancement of Teaching and Learning (CATL) at The University of Western Australia, Perth, Australia.

Asha Kanwar is the Vice-President of the Commonwealth of Learning in Vancouver, Canada. Before joining COL, she was consultant in open and distance learning at UNESCO's Regional Office for Education in Africa and Pro Vice-Chancellor of Indira Gandhi National Open University in India.

John Ketonen is a quality assurance manager responsible for developing and implementing QA policies and processes at Open Universities Australia in Melbourne.

Denise Kirkpatrick is the Pro Vice-Chancellor for Learning, Teaching and Quality at The Open University, Milton Keynes, Buckinghamshire, England.

Cheolil Lim is a Professor in the College of Education and Director of the Academic Leadership Institute for Competence-based Education, Seoul National University, Korea.

Stewart Marshall is the (Barbados-based) Director of Special Initiatives in the Office of the Principal at The University of the West Indies Open Campus and UNESCO Chair in Educational Technologies.

Kathleen Matheos is the Associate Dean, Extended Education, at University of Manitoba, Canada.

Sanjaya Mishra is the Programme Specialist, Section for ICT in Education, Science and Culture in the Knowledge Societies Division of UNESCO, Paris, France.

Nancy K. Parker is the Director of Institutional Studies at Athabasca University, Alberta, Canada.

Geoff Plimmer is a Senior Lecturer in the School of Management at the Victoria University of Wellington, New Zealand and was instrumental in developing the COL RIM.

Torstein Rekkedal is a Professor in the Norwegian School of Information Technology and Director of Research NKI Distance Education, Norway.

Winsome Russell is the Associate Vice-President, Academic Management and Quality Assurance at the University of Technology, Jamaica.

Yoni Ryan is Professor of Higher Education at the Australian Catholic University. She has extensive experience in staff development and the use of innovative educational technologies.

Arief S. Sadiman is the founding member of the Indonesian Open Junior Secondary School and a former Director of Southeast Asian Ministers of Education Organization (SEAMEO) Secretariat.

Dianne Thurab–Nkhosi is a Teacher Training Facilitator/Senior Lecturer in the Instructional Development Unit of The University of West Indies, St Augustine, Trinidad and Tobago.

I.G.A.K. Wardani is a Professor of Education (Curriculum and Instruction) in the Faculty of Teacher Training and Educational Sciences at Universitas Terbuka, Jakarta, Indonesia.

Aminudin Zuhairi is a Senior Lecturer and the Head of the Institute of Learning Materials Development, Examination, and Information Systems at Universitas Terbuka, Jakarta, Indonesia.

INDEX

Note: page numbers in **bold** refer to illustrations.

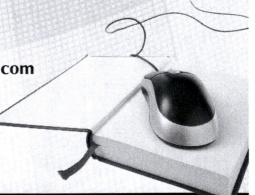